WA 1281548 9

D1756379

ONE WEEK LOAN
UNIVERSITY OF GLAMORGAN
TREFOREST LEARNING RESOURCES CENTRE
Pontypridd, CF37 1DL
Telephone: (01443) 482626

Books are to be returned on or before the last date below

Writers on Writing

Recent Titles in
Contributions to the Study of World Literature

Writers on Writing

THE ART OF THE SHORT STORY

Edited by Maurice A. Lee

Contributions to the Study of World Literature, Number 128

Westport, Connecticut
London

Library of Congress Cataloging-in-Publication Data

Writers on writing : the art of the short story / edited by Maurice A. Lee.
        p.   cm. — (Contributions to the study of world literature,
    ISSN 0738–9345 ; no. 128)
    Includes bibliographical references and index.
    ISBN 0–313–31592–2 (alk. paper)
        1. Short story—Authorship. 2. Authors—20th century—Biography.
    I. Lee, Maurice Angus, 1938–   II. Series.

    PN3373.W77 2005
    808.3′1—dc22   2005001874

British Library Cataloguing in Publication Data is available.

Library of Congress Catalog Card Number: 2005001874
ISBN: 0–313–31592–2
ISSN: 0738–9345

First published in 2005

Praeger Publishers, 88 Post Road West, Westport, CT 06881
An imprint of Greenwood Publishing Group, Inc.
www.praeger.com

Printed in the United States of America

The paper used in this book complies with the
Permanent Paper Standard issued by the National
Information Standards Organization (Z39.48-1984).

10 9 8 7 6 5 4 3 2 1

For Hermine—a wife of long distance with a bold spirit and great heart that shortens it daily.

Contents

Acknowledgments

I would like to thank, first of all, Dr. Mary Rohrberger, the brilliant short-story scholar, who taught me as both an undergraduate student and graduate student, and who enlightened the texts with her insightful and thoughtful criticism; who introduced me to a much broader world of short fiction; and who inspired me to become a teacher myself. It is further dedicated to the short-story writers included in this volume, as well as those who wanted to be involved but for various reasons were unable to, for their patience with me in my determination to have a text that reflected their honest thoughts— thoughts not couched in public relations, ego, or status, but thoughts of their beliefs, concerns, attitudes, and passion for short fiction. I would be remiss if I did not also dedicate this text to the participants in the short-story conferences I have directed these past 10 years. Among the participants are friends, colleagues, and both established and emerging scholars who have shared their vision and expertise about the short story with me in many languages and reflecting many cultures. I am pleased to note that many of them are now life-long friends. A special dedication is to the noted critics Charles May, Susan Lohafer, Austin Wright, and Suzanne Ferguson, who allowed me to "grow" among them in my amateurish beginnings of short-story criticism, especially Susan, whose professionalism and compassion were at times overwhelming in her generosity to ensure that the conferences went well, that I had all the support I needed year after year, and that I was on panels with them to test my short-story theories. Finally, my dedication is to my parents, Willie R. and

Bertie Mae Lee. Were they living, they would be proud of a son whom they taught to read, who was given short stories by his mother during the summer to keep him quiet, and who was taught the quiet dignity of self in the face of adversity by his father. It is a lesson I am still trying to learn. Short stories are great, but they are not enough.

Preface

Short stories have always been more than fiction to me. When I was a freshman student at Oklahoma A&M University (now Oklahoma State University) in Stillwater, Oklahoma, I encountered a form of racism with which I was unfamiliar and which I did not expect. Growing up in the town of Muskogee, Oklahoma, with its segregated school system, prejudice and racism were things that happened in the streets, or among ignorant folks, and the respect for education was so prevalent in Muskogee that anyone striving for it received a certain amount of respect. Families that kept their children in school and later sent their children on to college were admired, regardless of race or income. So when I hit the campus and found racism and prejudice among students, I was in shock.

It was not unusual to be walking to class and hear the word *nigger* being yelled out. Of course, you could never tell who said it, because when you looked in the direction of the voice, no one was looking. Occasionally, someone would be staring at you, but you had no way of knowing if this person had yelled or if he was simply daring you to say something. Or you could be walking and two or three girls behind you would be speaking of your body parts, in particular what you had between your legs, and they would be saying, "Now, I bet he has a big one, and black—look how black he is." Or they might say, "Hey boy, do you like white pussy?" And when you looked around, they all would be giggling; once in a while, one would have a very red face.

I did not know how to respond to such ugliness and meanness. By the time you got to class, you were so angry and embarrassed that you just sat there, holding back the tears, trying to listen to the lecture. You could eventually gather yourself, because there was no fear of being called on by the instructor. For the professors, you did not exist.

One professor did call on me once; it was the first day of class. He called my name and said, "You know, no Negro has ever graduated from this class." I thought he was somewhat ahead of himself and replied, "Well, no Negro has ever been in this class; so if you will just teach, I will try to learn." I had a lot of mouth even then, but in reality, I was scared to death, and could feel my knees betraying my false sense of confidence by shaking uncontrollably. I left before the class was over to giggles and laughter. I cried silently all the way to the dormitory. I worked my butt off in that class, but could get no better than a C, no matter how hard I tried. I think it was a class in physics, but to this day, I cannot be certain. I must have gone through that first year in a daze.

To survive, I wrote. I would write poetry, short stories, or simply thoughts about what had happened. Two yells of *nigger* would become a poem; the girls' rude comments would become thoughts of reverie or some essay about my family. Once I had urine thrown on me from a passing car, and that was enough for a short story. I had plenty of material for my evening pastime, and I probably wrote every day, and from new material.

I only lived about 100 or so miles from Stillwater, yet I did not go home until the scheduled holidays: Thanksgiving, Christmas, Easter, and spring break. I did not have enough money to call home regularly, so I wrote. I would write and tell Mom how I was doing and that I was fine and that school was good. I was too tired and angry one evening to write these usual edited comments and sent her one of my poems instead. She would write back and say some encouraging words, sometimes with a five-dollar bill inside, and then sign, "Your loving mom." So, I then started sending everything that I wrote each day. I would save them up and send them once a week, or every other week, but she received many types of correspondence from me that semester.

Daddy, who depended on Mom to keep him informed about me, asked her once how I was doing. Mom replied, I am told, "Well, he is doing fine." Then when Daddy asked what she meant, was he writing letters often, Mom said, "Well, he is writing, but he is writing poems and such." Daddy was somewhat puzzled and frustrated, and said, "What do you mean? Why is he wasting his time writing poetry and such nonsense?" In answer, Mom showed him what I had been sending her.

Daddy worked harder than any man I ever knew, and he was about to go out to work; it was six in the morning. He sat down, read the poems and the short stories without stopping, got up, said nothing to Mom, gave her the poems and things, and left. Mom told me later that she had never seen such a look on his face. Well, maybe once.

It was a Friday morning, and I had the luxury of a late class—11 a.m.—and I was enjoying the time to sleep. I didn't have breakfast that morning, which was a big thing, because the next meal would not be until lunch and I didn't have money for any snacks. But the morning was sunny and bright and I simply wanted to rest; the luxury of staying in bed late is something that all freshmen enjoy, it being so rare at home.

I got a call from the front desk that I had a visitor. I was shocked and scared; this could not be good. I was not expecting anyone, and everyone I knew was at home or somewhere else. Who could it be; what could it be? I got dressed and went downstairs. To my utter amazement, there was my father sitting on a sofa in the lounge room, waiting for me. He got up when he saw me, and he had the strangest look.

"Daddy," I said, still completely in shock, so glad to see him but expecting the worst. Clearly, something was the matter at home; or, even worse, something had happened to Momma. "What are you doing here? Are you okay? Is mom okay? Is something wrong?" I was already close to tears, because my daddy never did anything like this, ever; this could not be good news. "I'm fine," he said, smiling, also close to tears, I could see, "and your mother's fine." He paused. "Nothing's the matter." "Really?" I said. "You promise?" "Yes," he said, "everything is okay, I just came out to see how you are doing, and if you need anything." The tears were about to come for sure. "Well, yeah, everything is fine."

I said, "You came out here just to ask me that, to see about me. You could have written, you know." (My daddy seldom wrote; he relied on Mom to do that.)

"Well, I wanted to see for myself," he said. There was a long pause and then he said, "I read your poetry and stories." Another long pause. "You sure you're all right?" We started walking.

I hugged him close, the tears now streaming down my face, but with much love, joy, fear, sorrow, sadness, and all that occurs between father and son at such moments. He said, "You know, you write good." I still could not say anything more. We walked outside and started walking around campus. "How did you get here?" I asked. "Well," he said, "I borrowed your uncle's car." Now, my daddy could not drive a lick; he rode bicycles all the time, and the one time he got behind the wheel, he almost crashed. "How in the world … " I started, and he stopped me before I could finish. "I never even thought about it," he said. We walked for about an hour and then went back to the dormitory. I was going to miss class today, and I didn't care. It wasn't until we were back to the dorm that I realized I had not had one yell of *nigger,* no under-the-breath comments about my manhood, no urine in the face. When he got ready to leave, Daddy gave me a hug so hard I thought he would crush me, but I did not complain one bit. "Keep on writing," he said. "I love you too, daddy," I said. He waved, and I could tell that he was crying.

So, for me, short stories have always been more about real life, and it is no surprise that the life is often my own.

Maurice A. Lee

Introduction

The idea for this text began in 1994, when I was asked to be the next director of an international short-story conference, with a commitment to the stories being written in English. I was at the University of Northern Iowa, and Dr. Mary Rohrberger, the cosponsor of the previous conference, which had been held jointly at the University of Northern Iowa and the University of Iowa in 1992, asked me to consider taking on the task of directing the conference. By directing, she meant gathering a list of writers and scholars to invite to the conference, getting external and internal funding, and developing a program. I was convinced over a glass of scotch and Godiva chocolates.

We settled on a theme, "Voices of Diversity," and put together a stellar list of writers, which included Isabel Allende, Amiri Baraka, Richard Bausch, Clark Blaise, Richard Ford, Wilson Harris, Bharati Mukherjee, Judith Ortiz-Cofer, Sonia Sanchez, Leslie Marmon Silko, and Amy Tan. Noted critics invited and attended included Selwyn Cudjoe, Daryl Dance, Suzanne Ferguson, Morton Levitt, Susan Lohafer, Charles May, Annis Pratt, Kenneth Ramchand, Austin Wright, and of course, Mary Rohrberger, who is known as the most prominent critic of the short story since her book *Story to Anti-Story* appeared in the 1960s. What impressed me about the conference was the intellectual exchange between writers and critics and the fact that they were often in disagreement about the genre as it related to both creativity and meaning, but were often in agreement about its importance in the classroom or in the field of American letters. I did detect a bit of frustration among the writers, because they were the creators of the literature, but others (i.e., the critics) seemed to have the authority to state exactly what these writers had created, or more specifically, to define the strengths and weaknesses of the stories. At that moment, I decided that a text that gave the writers a voice to speak on the short-story genre was in order.

My field of study, however, was primarily American, African American, and Caribbean literature, and I had not studied the short-story genre in depth, as had the critics, although in many ways it seems as though I have been studying the short story for much of my academic career, and it—that is, the essence of it—still seems as elusive as ever. So for the next six years I studied the genre in depth; continued as the director of the conference, which is held every two years; and in 2000 put a proposal to Greenwood Publishing Group about a text in which writers were given the opportunity to speak about the short-story genre in any way they deemed appropriate. I was of the opinion that it was time for writers to be given their due and have their say about what they themselves were writing. I am pleased to state that the publishers at Greenwood agreed with me. The text that follows, therefore, represents my efforts over the past four years to collect essays from writers of the short-story genre.

I was amazed at the response I received from writers. It was clear, upon talking with them, that they longed to speak about the genre. I was pleased as well that many of the writers who attended that first conference were now willing to contribute their voice to this text and to encourage others to contribute as well. These essays represent one of the most extensive and exhaustive compilations of critical perspectives by writers to date on the short-story genre.

My approach to the text mirrored my approach as director of the conference—namely, to get a broad representation of writers, from the noted and well-established ones to those just emerging; to solicit essays globally in order to have a broad spectrum of views outside of the United States, which is so noted for mastering the short-story form; and finally, to treat them all equally. So in this text, there are Pulitzer Prize–winners; writers who have won several and various awards, both academic and creative; and writers who have just written and published their first set of stories. There are writers from all over the world. What impressed me as I began to read and edit the essays was the incredible commonality of the respect, awe, angst, and wonder that all writers seem to have for the short story. I am reminded of a statement made by Isabel Allende at the Third International Conference on the Short Story in English, the first one I directed, that she did not like to write short stories anymore and would not do it. "It's too hard, too much work," she said, "much more difficult than writing a novel." This statement is significant, not only for the respect that Allende has for the genre, but for the fact that many writers just beginning their careers often choose the short story as a starting point because they think the genre to be easier. According to Allende and many authors in this text, that is not the case.

In this volume, there are 33 essays ranging in length from 12 pages to 1 1/2 pages, and covering the spectrum of issues on the genre: length, definition, publishing problems, gender and cultural issues, verisimilitude, problems with stereotyping or categorizing, disputes with critics and critical theories, the relationship of art to artist and of artist to critic (with some writers being both), pedagogy, form and structure (separate from definition), and autobiography, including issues of honesty and dishonesty. A preview of some of the essays is worth noting.

Amiri Baraka, a poet not known for his short stories, but who wrote *Tales,* a series of stories, early in his career, when asked to comment on the short story form, or the relationship between words and the genre says, "This writer has been studying and experimenting to introduce an un-new scale relating specifically to WordMusic. Wherein the words relate directly to the music as NOTES. So that to write a poem is to write a piece of music.... Speech is Educated Space." For Baraka, everything (words, music, form, meaning) is TIED (Time, Infinity, Emotion, and Drums—the African beat and heart). When Baraka writes a poem, he writes music and he tells a story, with the poem and the beat being the carrier as story.

Alfred Birney, a well-known author in the Netherlands but little known elsewhere, starts his thoughts on short fiction by talking about how long it takes him to write. "If someone were to ask me about setting records," he says, "I'd look at how long it took me to write a short story or a novel. My speed record for the sprint lies at three days, for the distance run nine months." Birney is about much more than time of writing, however, and provides some of the more interesting aspects about the impact of culture on the short story. In effect, he uses what he perceives as historical and multicultural short-story characters to populate his novels. His approach is not only novel, but opens up questions about the relationship between the two genres and the role of the writer in negotiating that space when dealing with social and political issues.

Clark Blaise, one of my favorite authors, takes an approach to his definition that I did not expect. Even though he writes more novels than short stories, he feels that short stories are the "expansive literary form of our age; novels the condensed." "Stories," he continues, "say the most about a very few moments. The novel says the least about a great many more." For Blaise, the short story must be the defining "curtain-dropping note" that the writer must recognize. Blaise feels that every character in great short stories has an Achilles' heel, and if the writer does not realize this, then there is no worthwhile story.

Lucy Ferriss, a writer teaching in the East, feels that the short story is in danger, not of being forgotten or slowly dwindling away, but because of its usefulness. It is used in high schools, in college writing classes, as a jump start for new writers, in advertisement, and finally in M.F.A. programs. From her point of view, it has become so user-friendly that it is "almost impossible to retain the value of the short story as a unique, solitary, and irreplaceable reading experience." At the same time, she feels that "this is what we must do if we are to prevent the literary story from going the way of the verse epic or the public epistle."

What is clear from Baraka, Blaise, and Ferriss is their sense of a relationship among the writer, reader, and story unlike any in the novel. Clearly the term *epiphany* comes to mind when hearing such phrases as "holding our breath" or "never being the same after reading a story." These words are embedded in the essays by the authors mentioned above. Yet I feel that they are saying something more. I think they are saying that the short story has a life of its own, and that when it shows us glimpses of what words are capable of saying and conveying, it also shows us our own capabilities and limitations. Thus, the reader lives and grows as the story does, and the experience is immediate.

Richard Ford's approach is more pragmatic. "Here's how you write one," he says. "First, enough of all this hoo-ey (as my father used to say) about the short-story form. The form is this: I write it; I call it a short story; it is one. End of argument.... I just have to want to call it a short story. There's no police involved in this business." Ford's article deserves close reading, because as he continues in his writing and seeks to qualify his pragmatic approach to the genre, he becomes more and more uncomfortable with the process of definition, not only because of how this may be perceived, but because there is never enough time and space to do justice to a topic of this historic dimension, and Ford is clearly cognizant of the importance of history in the defining moments of the short-story genre. The sense and importance of history is clearly evident in the Ford essay.

Janette Turner Hospital, a wonderful writer from Australia, includes in her essay a comment from painter Georges Braque. Paraphrasing Braque, Hospital states that he feels that art cannot be explained, that the more one tries to explain it, the more mysterious it becomes. For Hospital, "if there is no mystery ... there is no short story." Hospital is one of the most ardent believers in the integrity of both the short story and the novel forms. In other words, she firmly believes that the two genres have different forms, structures, functions, and beginnings and endings. Note her poignant comments about the role of the concept of "loss" in the short-story genre.

I started this introduction with Baraka and his bond between the word and music. This collection of essays in some respects is the relationship between the short story and itself. I asked students in class one day "the short story—what is it?" One student in the back of the classroom, seemingly not paying attention said "what it is." Students laughed. I didn't know if he was responding to my question or correcting my sentence structure, but I liked the response. Using the phrasing "what it is," instead of the normal "what is it" utilizes a reverse speech pattern which changes a question to a declaration. And at times, when reading short stories by the writers included in this text, I feel that the stories have that declaration of "what I am," rather than "what am I." With this in mind, I propose the point of view, therefore, that the short story is an active and not a passive form; that is screams its definition as it writes its own story. In this way, the genre is both the painting and the painter, as Hospital would maintain, or the story and the teller, as Blaise and Ford would maintain.

Allow me to address this issue from a different perspective, one that may seem irrelevant but is critical and useful in understanding the many thoughts and ideas about the short-story genre inherent in this text. When I first visited my in-laws in Jamaica, I noted that when someone left the house, he or she said, "I'm not here" as they were leaving. Now, this saying is completely different from the normal "I'm leaving" that I would expect. The "I'm not here" expresses a fact not yet in evidence; at the same time, there is the reality of the person still standing in the room. I believe that the mystery that Hospital speaks of; the mobility that Baraka sees, mutability in effect, constantly changing; the pragmatism and uncertainty that overwhelms Ford; and the cultural history of Blaise represents this phenomenon—the evidence of a short story in our presence, in particular in our creative minds, and the certainty that before long, it will not be there. That is why I personify the short story in my brief definition that "the short story is 'what it is' just before it becomes a novel," because I believe the short story knows it is one long before the writer does. It sits idly by—waiting for him or her to try different approaches, change symbolisms and metaphors, try new sentence patterns, even shorten its length—and just waits until the writer realizes that what is done is enough. Ford spoke of "less is more," because the more difficult thing to do is end a short story. Hopefully, if the author is attentive enough, he or she will end it before he messes it up. I think that the short story assists the writer in the knowing. I can state without reservations that the writers included here know when to write and when to stop. The stories they tell about what, why, and how they write are a joy to read, and I am pleased that I am able to present them to you.

Maurice A. Lee

1

The Short Story: Definition

Short Story and Poetry

Amiri Baraka

The short story should be a sacred form—since it's the most common way we tell our lives and everybody else's. That's why, in my opinion, the most effective kind of story is short indeed, very short and pointed. Short enough and pointed enough to make your teeth curl.

Sembene Ousman, Isaac Babel, Franz Kafka, Maupassant, Henry Dumas, Richard Wright's first book *Uncle Tom's Children.*

Check Ousman's *Tribal Scars.* The flat, acrid mystery of them. A world appears, it turns a few times, these turns are called revolutions, and then it disappears.

It does not *cease to exist.* It goes somewhere else. Another dimension is a good explanation. Someone borrowed my book, but even disappeared the mysterious unwinding remains.

In fact you hear me passing some of this on to you. So it reappears inside your head, making revolutions.

One short story I wrote insisted itself into review years after a friend laid it on me. And when it returned, it was as some kind of self-defining legitimization of my self for my most constant audience. That group behind the eyes.

It was like this, and dig the dimensions of this whole retelling as another reappearance.

I was riding in an airplane going somewhere—logically enough. But in that enforced reverie, perhaps to read poetry or speak—somehow I began to formulate an idea that I could do something different. I guess that was it. Something like that.

I was telling myself, "If I wanted to make money writing I could do it." My (nonexistent) God what a sad idea to be stuck with. "If" is very Dantesque.

Something like a religious concentration camp. I was concentrating on a very campy idea.

I thought Hey (there was perhaps no Hey!) If I wanted to make money writing I could do it. For instance (there was no for instance) For instance, if I . . . no I thought *if* (again?) If I wanted to . . . I bet.

I thought I could write a commercial story. (What an idea! What would that be?) I knew in that frame of mind that—I wanted—I thought I said to myself—I could get a story in *Playboy!!*

And that is when I made a kind of bet with myself. My lips might have moved. Sometimes my lips move when I read my self silently.

So this story an old friend told me many years ago at the Cedar Bar jumped out of the Black Hole as needed. I sat there in the plane and wrote the story exactly as I remembered it. Because I felt such a story was just the kind of "thing" that *Boy* would like to play with.

It had everything, mystery, reminiscence, sex (Marona Mia!). A guy walks in a bar tells me a murderous, he said, true tale and I wrote it out finally, years later, in an airplane going wherever. You see how the tale was carried, in many levels and dimensions.

And it proved out. Barely 10 days after I passed it to the agent, he sold it—you bet—to *Playboy*. It was called "Norman's Date."

What was it about? Well the punch line was this guy wakes up with this new love in the middle of the night after frantic lovemaking and the woman is sitting over him with a pair of scissors in her hand!

So? I know there's a level of that alright. But it was a story. A short story. My first book of short stories I called *Tales* in the grand literary tradition, but also because that's what my mother and grandmother called my excursions away from the truth. They meant *reality*, which has more troops. But they called such digressions Tales. Like Maupassant.

The dedication to my sister Kimako in *Tales* read "To Lanie Poo who's heard boo coos" (our black "French" for "a bunch").

And that is the sense of it for me—tales, or even tails, the last part of the fact, its rear, my grandfather said, the last part of the chicken to go over the fence!

At this point is the connection with poetry. Verse is a turn, simply. Like a wheel has regular changes. Because they are regular, it is evolution, in a sense. It, that wheel, will disappear eventually, but it is turning in the same place. (But even so it moves! something.)

That verse is literally, a *turning*. Except what we *want* is *vers libre*, free verse. Never having been that, *free*, we want it badly.

For black people, Freedom is our aesthetic and our ideology. *Free Jazz. Freedom Suite. Tell Freedom. Oh, Freedom!* And on!

So that verse is the same changes. Running changes, just running them, over and over.

Free verse they say. To mean going through changes and making changes. Syncopation, like they say. Pick up the rhythm. Because, for me, even the real mystery of the story, which is deep too—I go on—because a story is a place some thing is stored. Usually seeds—what you seed is stored. In the story.

In the verse it will come around regularly. It is the wheel. The Human Will. To go into the future. To go forward. Beyond what you see. From see to see. Seven Sees, but watch out for the eight ball, a double wheel. Wheel over wheel, infinity turned upright!

But poetry is the *what*. Like the change—going forward, or electrically speaking. (You see this is funny because I've already gone ahead and put you in it, some of you know it.)

Not Watts but the What. What is it flowing? Because it does flow. We all are pallets on (or in or as) the *flow*.

Tears, for instance, are made of water. Salt water. They flow. From the eyes. What see. Ripped, the drops, like waves. You see?

So poetry is cries. The poet or griot pours it out, cries out, like in Europe they had a town crier. They thought the griot carried olds as news for, old news, old knews, all knews.

In Africa we called ourselves Diali. (Perhaps the vibe that Yeats recalled in "Lapis Lazuli" … "Their ancient glittering eyes are gay.") Djali. Not crying, as griot, to cry out. But Djali, laughed so hard tears came to my eyes or laughed to keep from cryin! Ancient glittering eyes. Every one. The eggs. The egos. The for instances. Instant after instant turning, changing, free, the possibility in God's eyes. Possibility is God with two left eyes.

And when we do our thing, make it, we say Djeli Ya—like Mr. B. (who some confuse w/ me) saying Djeli Ya, Djeli Ya. Djeli Ya! Like That!

The short story is a breath of life. Both dimension and basic function. Like the lungs expanding retracting. The circle of transbluesent spirit in and out connected like a wheel, a circle, how we go, our role.

The poet is a basic storyteller and these are the shortest stories. (Hey, not necessarily. People like Browning and Dante and Tolson, God Knows, could run that telling on and on—but perhaps that is why it was verse, so it could roll on and on).

What is one difference is the dependence on rhythm. The great short-story writers use rhythm, of course. I don't think you can make the most penetrating use of language—as content or form—without it being rhythm sprung.

It is the splitting of the one into two. What follows the one going on. Forward The eye and the being The ego and the entity The woman (All is womb sent everything issues from the womb the black hole).

But the dialectic, the opposites, from woman comes man into woman man comes.

The manifestation (see?) of the eye that sees. The are that bees. The proof. The conclusion. There is Be and At. Two things or one thing and one not thing is the whole.

The heart, for instance, it thumps and the silence is past of the not silence. That is what a hole is.

So the splitting of the endless which is endless because it does not stop except its go is only possible because of its not go.

Like speed on the sea is measured in knots.

I'm saying that the short story always exists as water dipped for drinking from an unlimited water. A big sea (A Langston Huge sea) see (how are I spelled this?).

To get it out. The water to drink requires we be at that place to dip it.

The rhythm is the dialectic that creates description. Everything is a story. Rhythm is the most basic, the shortest of all stories the Be and the At.

To separate these, together, looking, is the open story. The tale. Time and place. Together as flow is the rhythm, the endless story.

So the story wants to make sense. The poetry is what sense is made out of.

Like Pres sd his solos. The greatest of the players did all. Tell a story. They were a story. Pres was the Djali. And Djeli Ya. Djeli Ya. Djeli Ya!

Poetry *wants*. Short story wants something. Something is what poetry is. Short story gives it a name.

The Joys of the Brief Encounter

Alecia McKenzie

Sustained narrative. That was the term the judge of the literary competition kept using as he tried to explain why my thick collection of short stories had lost to a slim novel. Sustained narrative. The words evoke something magical, phallical, macho. Isn't this what everyone dreams of: the long foreword, the twists and turns, the drawn-out climax, and the sustained satisfaction, all leading to prizes for prowess? Meanwhile I, as a short-story writer, would like to see people fantasizing instead about the joys of the brief encounter—passion compressed and then exploding in 10 to 15 minutes. This form of engagement never goes on and on, with blah here and blah there, when specific, pointed action can be so much more satisfying. Of course, I may never be able to persuade old-fashioned judges and profit-minded publishers that the brief encounter, literature-wise, is worth exploring, savoring even, but I can still try. In this essay, I have identified a few pleasures particular to the genre.

1. When it's over, you long for more. Compare this feeling with that of the "sustained" experience, where you often find yourself thinking, "Well, that was nice, but way too long. It took all my time." I have frequently heard fans of the brief encounter saying: "I really wanted it to continue, to see what would happen next." Such yearning for continuation adds spice to the interaction.

2. Since there are only a few true experts at this "un-mainstream" activity, being a connoisseur or an artisan is like belonging to a highly selective secret society. After your initiation and a few trials, you never again wish to get caught up in the sustained-narrative craze. Where's the fun in doing something that every Jill or Jack is doing?

3. Masters and mistresses of the genre are always willing to try something novel and exciting, as opposed to those mired in the tradition of sustainment. In fact, as a

certain Mr. Walcott has said, practitioners of the sustained narrative still seem to live in the century before last. With a few exceptions, there is little that's novel in their style.

4. The brief encounter nearly always involves quirky, original characters, full of passion and individuality. You remember them for a long time. Sometimes they can change your way of seeing and feeling, all in the space of a few minutes.

5. Finally, if the brief encounter is bad, and on rare occasions it can be, then the joy is that it's brief.

Let Me Tell You a Story

András Nagy

When a question is posed, maybe a serious or a paradoxical one, the answer could be as in the title: Let me tell you a story! It is a common response in our cultural context, in which stories of different forms and of different traditions seem to communicate very fluently and eloquently—sometimes even with some aesthetic value "added."

"How is that everyone has a story and each story is sad in some way?" asks the protagonist of Péter Nádas's novel *The Book of Memories*, the autobiographical hero of the great Hungarian story writer and novelist, just when these stories to tell are to share a past the lovers lived separately, and now they would get to know each other: both in the biblical sense and by these stories that fulfill the wish of lovers of being united.

"Let me explain it to you with a story" is a very common form of joke (the traditional urban folklore of Central Europe), and quite often with Jewish figures, when the wise rabbi is asked a question his answer starts with the above-mentioned reference to the story.

"What is your story?" is the first question to a newcomer in a prison cell, and his/her future may be very much depending not only on the story he/she has and the one that probably brought him/her here, but also on the way the story is told.

Story seems to be a common language, traditional and articulated, complex and yet deeply personal, included in the "greater narrative" of time, fate, history—and to be used for communication whenever other communicative forms seem to be unfit or unsatisfying. Or just boring.

These were at least my conclusions as a story writer and a story reader, and, when a short story is in the focus, my only concern is whether a story could be short. Of course the text can (and must) be limited, but even the most determined length refers to a larger cultural context the story is being built upon (or into), without including any of it into the text.

What *short* is, is very hard to define: the whole *War and Peace* of Tolstoy must be very brief for God, but the shortest summary of the story of a soap-opera episode is unbearably long for me. However, the reference to the length probably is a synonym for a literary genre in which composition and limitation play a determinative role.

To "recycle" is a very common metaphor once invented to explain this form: the iceberg seemingly has similar features—the bigger part is unseen (untold) as it is floating under water, and meanwhile the tiny top that is in our sight refers to the parts hidden. Not being really familiar with these products of Nordic seas, I just imagine that the part above the water is the result of a process of great importance.

In case of icebergs and stories, this process should be also referred to. Quoting the famous aphorism of the German philosopher Hegel, the object equals the history of the object. This may conclude in a paradoxical definition: the story is the (hi)story of the story.

This is why the above-mentioned request—"let me tell you a story"—could help to define what *story* may mean in a larger cultural and historical context. But when describing it, I would just refer to small parts of the iceberg, maybe just to three segments of the whole entity, being very aware of the fact that the larger part remains untouched. And I shall talk about icebergs in the European sense, but I do know that Latin American or Russian icebergs are very different.

Thinking about the history of this literary genre—the novella as short story is translated into Hungarian (actually the word was borrowed from the Italian)—it immediately reveals the secret of its birth, which was connected to the great catastrophes of Europe: the Black Death. The first European author of stories as literary forms (at least following some historical interpretation) was Giovanni Boccaccio in his *Decameron,* inspired by the deadly epidemic in Florence of the Middle Ages, when a selected group of youngsters decided to withdraw from the sick city and keep each other amused and, maybe, alive by telling stories. This form of communication—the story telling—is of extreme importance in the dark context, and, at the same time, by this form are revealed the greatly sensual episodes of love, passion, and many other determinant adventures of everyday life. The opposing (darker) tones are very determinant and masterfully composed into the chain of stories, referring to the limits of the genre in one sense and at the same time to the unlimited craving for happiness. The flow of stories is of the same intensity as the joy of life, expressed unconditionally in the *Decameron,* by using any "epical excuse" at hand. This form of communication seems to be the basic condition for survival—that proves to be successful by the end of the narration.

For the birth of the modern story another—maybe more abstract—catastrophe was needed to provide the necessary contrasts and contradictions the genre needs. When referring to the golden age of short stories, to the French nineteenth-century story writing and to its classic, Guy de Maupassant, his inspiring Black Death was probably the painfully revealed nature of a society that they were not only living in but they were fighting for and not so long ago they were ready to give their life for: the modern world of bourgeois democracy. It meant also fresh capitalism, struggle for everyday life, and the contradictory process of the birth of individuality. The stories Maupassant shares with us are equally shaped both by the hopes and by the disappointments of the same process, as reflected by the protagonist—the individuality—that has already lost all illusions in the modern world, and yet there is no different future, no alternative, and even the pure existence is the product of this very same progress. Each of his stories are the epical reflections of this new universe, once so full of hopes and now more and more emptied out by each step the narration takes. Again: The stories are to communicate both the expectations and the disappointments in the very same form.

The late modern story, the twentieth-century novella, was probably influenced in its greatest authors, like Kafka, Babel, or the Hungarian István Örkény, by a literary form, inspired by an ongoing "catastrophe," as the state of the world. "The Hasidic tales of the Judaic tradition" used the often-enigmatic epical form as a key to open up the secrets of the world we are not able to change but we may be able to understand by decoding its hidden messages—but definitely not on a theoretical or abstract level. These episodes, seemingly fragmented, deeply enigmatic, often very brief and with no traditionally composed story "to tell," were at the same time a religious, artistic, and intellectual summary of the experience of generations, living for ages in an epical distance from the society of the majority, and being very familiar with the magical knowledge of the kabbalah. In the context of persecution, sufferance, and hopeless wandering these stories were to keep alive the tradition of the greater narrative of redemption, of messianic hope, and that an overall meaning for our existence may be provided.

We may understand from the (hi)story of the story, at least as this genre is being created by some of its greatest masters, that this form is to communicate something complex and often controversial, in which no necessary conclusion, moral, or message are included but the described episode(s) itself. We could probably paraphrase Gertrude Stein and her famous reference to the rose the following way: A story is a story is a story. Even common readers may often experience that the text itself is "wiser" than the author himself/herself, as the literary genre seems to provide the knowledge for those using it.

Talking about communication by stories, it is important to emphasize that everything we talk about is expressed in and determined by the language—all the facts and features are coming to life by the use of words, grammar, syntax, and so forth. The universe of the language is the very same of story writing. However, when it comes to the "actualization" of the language to tell a story, it is important to notice that this is also determined by the episodes that are included in the text. It may well conclude in unusual use of the language (Boccaccio in his time with the Italian) or to use some seemingly inapplicable "official" language (that of the bureaucracy of the Austro-Hungarian monarchy by Kafka) to express the absurdity of existence, with all the monsters and paradoxes included.

But when it comes to the tradition of the great artists of this literary genre, the function of storytelling becomes similarly communicative as language itself. The words, the grammar, the syntax, and so forth of the language can be easily compared to the "ingredients" of this kind of communication— where we may well find the smaller meaningful units (like words), the ways and rules for connecting them (grammar), and the strategies for composition (syntax). All these are necessarily personal (for the author) and changed or modified by each actualization (depending on the cultural context), but in the theory of literature analysts could and did experiment with such concepts, often successfully. This form of communication can be compared to (and influenced by) other forms of forwarding messages, not necessarily on an intellectual or theoretical level. For example, shortly before Boccaccio's time, pictures played the lead in religious communication and/or music in churches as well as in archaic forms of community. A somewhat similar process is present in our contemporary civilization, where visual information (particularly in motion) became extremely dominant, with its pace often challenging our receptive capacity. Stories are basically modified by this new and overwhelming flow of information; even the concept of the story is changing, as it can be experienced in modern forms of writing, answering with the sensitivity of the storytellers to the need of the audience.

All these modifications also change the language of the stories—however, it doesn't really modify the stories as language, the form of communication that answers the challenges of the contemporary world. On the contrary: literature seems to be again in the avant-garde to experiment with new forms of communication. The language of the stories is changing, the new "grammar" is breaking the rules of the old one, and literary taboos do not exist anymore. Language itself is permanently bombarded by new experiences, facts, ways of expression, and so forth—the same way stories are to answer the needs of this changing universe, which includes new social, historical, even transcendental/metaphysical experiences to deal with.

If we were to pose the question "What is your story?" to the whole literary genre, the answer easily could be similar to the one given by the language. Very few features could survive the change of function, modality, and so forth, but the need for communication. Every "ingredient" is to serve this very need, and the historical process provides a large moving space to fulfill this. Epical segments are not necessary conditions anymore for a "story"; sometimes the dominant atmosphere is to take over the role of events, voice can be more determinant than what this voice was once for, magical aspects are to replace the dated belief in the structure of reality—the imprint of this new universe is obvious on the literary form, the story incorporated into itself its very own story.

All these "phenomenological" changes (as well as many, many more) are strongly connected to the role stories play in the process of discovering our new universe (in the sense of the epistemology of art), or, to put it more simply: to communicate with the world that surrounds us. This communication determines and influences the language itself and provides a more dynamic potential for stories than anything else for this kind of communication. One basic condition is the untranslatability of stories into anything else: a story is a story is a story.

This is, however, the advantage and the disadvantage of the very literary form. When a story is written, something very important must remain unexpressed; that is part—or rather, condition—of the expressive process. "The one whom God blesses with one hand, he curses with the other," wrote Kierkegaard, the great Danish philosopher, more than 150 years ago. This may be true for this form of art, and yet when Kierkegaard was referring to this paradox, he wanted to explain the biblical story of Isaac and Abraham. Interpretations were given; as for hypotheses and conclusions, however, there was something infinitely more in the story than the best theological analysis could ever reveal. Probably even when God was to communicate something profound and disturbing, like the role of love, sacrifice, and faith, He preferred to use a story—an enigmatic one of bliss and curse. As if He started somewhat like this: "Let me tell you a story."

WORKS CITED

Boccaccio, Giovanni. *The Decameron*. (c. 1351). Ed. Jonathan Usher, trans. Guido Waldman. Oxford, England: Oxford University Press, 1999.

Nádas, Péter. *The Book of Memories*. New York: Farrar, Straus & Giroux, 1980.

Carving the Fruit Stones

Katherine Vaz

My first box-art was a vision of hell, a homework assignment in second grade.
My classmates brought in dioramas with cut-out flames and aluminum-foil
backdrops painted red, but my hell consisted of a papier-mâché mask with
broken green glass in the eye holes and dozens of faces clipped from magazines, impaled on wire surrounding the mask and spewing from its mouth. It
was a luminous jumble of the portentous, too serious by halves for a 7-year-
old, probably inspired by my father's rendition of the Last Judgment, which
he'd painted at the age of 19 on his father's car tarp. It hung in our garage, my
mother's Buick pinning some dervish.

"That's a bit frightening, dear," said Sister Ana Maria, before she bright-
ened. She was no enemy of the morbid. "But I'm sure hell is even more terrible." My hell won its A.

Sister Ana Maria, a native of Barcelona, was a Carmelite Sister of Charity,
which might have remained a cloistered order had not the Spanish Civil War
caused it to relocate in northern California, where the nuns' penance was to
teach school, and where they continued filtering long after the republican
victory. She was among the first genuine storytellers I knew, in that she was
fearless with her imagination if it was in the service of a higher truth that
would captivate her audience. I never once thought of her constructs as conventional lies. All the nuns at Our Lady of Grace in Castro Valley brimmed
with red-edged tales about violence and the power of prayer, eggs broken and
magically made whole after three Hail Marys, uncles machine-gunned against
walls, girls who spent their bus money on candy and were murdered as they
walked home alone at night.

One annual school treat was to file into the convent's chapel to kneel and kiss some 3-D box-art—a small glass dome encasing some pink tin flowers and a black speck that was a particle of bone from the founder of the order. (Why was it black? What part of her body was it from? Who had done the cutting?) Vials of blood that might liquefy once a year, femoral souvenirs of saints said to cure cancer—it seems so quaint and naive to me now, to be taught the powers of first-degree relics, but I cannot otherwise account for my lifelong belief that stories are box-art, hammered together out of a hunger to preserve genuine parts of real people, some construction encasing actual flesh, with shadows to bolster an inquiry of who they were and what they'd say if they could speak and, beyond all that, a sense, as Flannery O'Connor would have it, of enduring mystery, with the framework, the limits, the boxing-in, not signifying containment so much as cheerfully acknowledging the futility of fully encompassing longing, hope, and tragedy. I remember my happiness as an adult when I realized that I loved Alice Munro's stories because they had, for me, a prismatic shape. I could wander into the shadow-box she'd built, with elbow room and dark corners shot through with sex, loss, and the basic impulses of fiction that make it most like life, the awareness that there is always incompletion, fragmentation—in connecting, in reading the bones, in knowingness, in intimacy.

I suppose that is why I construct box-art in between writing short stories, much as I write stories in between novels. I like that definitions of short stories tend toward solipsisms—they're short because they're short, and therefore they're forgiving. Mercy is at the core of their demands, wrenching though the material might be, explicating permanent pain. A story (or a shadow-box) may be reworked over time, but that takes days altogether, not years. Just as the limits of the sestina are what induce creativity, so too does the illusion of the containable and confinable in stories offer consolation. Maybe they're closer to the way we exist, which is daily and anecdotal, out of a calendar's squares, rather than epic.

Select. Arrange. Borges's notion of the Library of the Universe holds that every action or thought, real or imagined, of everyone who ever lived is available in a vast dossier, and the artist's task is to reach into that chaos and connect some elements in order to superimpose a new vision on the familiar world. (Picasso rammed a bicycle's handlebar against the triangular seat, and voilà, bicycles are horny bulls.)

I figured I was adhering to this rule the day I fished through a closet and built a box I called "Dogstar," featuring the sparkle-tipped, cats'-eye bifocals from my grotesquely shy childhood, plus a ticket to Le Nozze di Figaro at La Scala, plus an airline-sized bottle of Johnnie Walker, which I coated in blue glitter. It wasn't too bad a work—sort of a bald amalgam about aspiration and pitfalls—but mostly it was a thrifty use of flotsam, a cleaning-out of junk. I had used what fell to me, what I'd been given, and this fundamental error with my box-art had the reverberating effect of leading me to what I found increasingly troubling, shadow-deprived and hollow, about the way I wrote stories: I'd been grabbing the dazzling, high-gloss elements out of the history lying at hand around me.

And why not? A colleague in a workshop once said, breezily, that she wanted to kill me and "steal my material." My grandmother's housekeeper, from the Azores like everyone in my father's family, could neither read nor write English or Portuguese, and she could not dial a telephone because numbers looked "like fish hooks." My father decided she dwelled in a language of color, and he painted a shade over every numeral on her phone's dial. On a placard, alongside pictures of the police station, the firehouse, and the dairy, he dabbed necklaces of seven colors that would correspond to the appropriate ones on the dial. An uncle who sculpted ice cream took a masterpiece cross-country on a train at the behest of President Franklin Roosevelt. My great-grandfather was stabbed to death by his best friend as they argued over whose son was smarter. An aunt was in a cabal known as the Stain Removers, old biddies in the islands known for making impurities vanish from any fabric and who planned to die with their formula a secret. (We figured they were using American caches of Shout.) A Californian aunt whose husband was having an affair with the neighbor closed the curtains on the side of her house facing the occasion of sin, never to be opened, and my nephews grew up thinking that all homes had a dark and a light side, like the moon.

All highly colorful, all well and good. Carlos Fuentes remarked that one job of the writer is to give voice to those who have none. But how awfully convenient that I could laze over to the family closet and stick a frame around whatever glowed in the dark; though it touched upon me, what canny relief that so little of it demanded the emptying out of my own heart.

My admiration of Joseph Cornell, the premier American box-artist, finally awakened in me an inkling of the cure for this, some of the best instruction I've ever stumbled upon for writing stories. For the longest time, when I looked at his work in museums or photographs of it in books, I enjoyed his swans, clay pipes, gyres, feathers, and baubles from Woolworth's merely because his arrangements took the ordinary and made it singular. Notions of flight compelled him—a simple coiled spring was homage to Bleriot, the first man to fly across the English Channel. He believed in time travel, in linking himself to others in distant eras or places (particularly in France, which he regarded as blue). A virgin for most of his years, he writhed with passions that might have lit into nothing but raw agony had he not directed them into the fount of his shrines to movie stars and ballerinas. His boxes, though stark and unfrenzied, appear ready to buckle at any second with desire.

But only when I read Deborah Solomon's *Utopia Parkway: The Life and Work of Joseph Cornell* did I discover the lesson that must now aid, correct, and rankle me: Loner though Cornell was, he ventured out into the world; he walked in the city. A collector, a pack rat. A believer that the future of American art will rest upon its use of fragmentation. But not someone who grabbed anything whose sole virtue was being apparent or quirky. Items did not leap to his hand unless his sensibility called them out. He'd abjured the ease of surrealism, after all, the idea of juxtaposing unlike objects to create a further impossibility. What interest could there be in heaping glittery this-and-that into impastos? Out he roamed, until something of his insides could be found manifest, and that was when he chose it, and that is why his common flash-cubes lined up in a velvet box feel profoundly devastating—icy diamonds, frozen love exposed and glaring, hardened sexual pain.

His searches were not about selections so much as high, honed selective-ness, examples of Goethe's admonition that writers or artists must reproduce the world surrounding them by conveying the world carried inside them. Some of Edward Hopper's paintings of cliffs are blue-streaked because he'd called out the blue inside them, proof of his eminent realism.

And Joseph Cornell knew how to wait. He waited upon the appearance of truehearted connections. Plunge deep down; guard against whimsy. Some-times it took years to place three objects together in a box.

This waiting-upon is required to write stories, too, a deliberate readiness for the details that will create a person as vividly as one of Matisse's curved lines turns into a whole, living woman. The necklace of black stars worn by the seething Marion in "Babylon Revisited." The slacks on the children's mother in "A Good Man Is Hard to Find" to impart her slack-jawed existence. But it's when this hapless woman puts money in a jukebox and dances with her daughter that she's given higher dimensions of flesh and spirit: what a minute but tabernacular flame she surprisingly carries, at the back of the box of the story. The glimpse of her joy is so slight that readers might easily miss being knocked between the eyes by it. As O'Connor asserted, cagily, any story must have a crucially important meaning, and therefore good "short" stories do not exist, since the best of them have enough depth to make them properly described as long. (To her, of course, that meant piercing every scene until it got nailed onto the anagogical.)

When Lawrence Weschler describes the Wunderkammer or "wonder cab-inets," in his marvelous book *Mr. Wilson's Cabinet of Wonder*, he gives an

accounting of the reliquaries of curios and body parts that were in many ways
the forerunners to museums, but he also documents our endless fascination
with the power of highly detailed smallness, with carving, say, fruit stones
into Flemish landscapes or the Crucifixion. Within the challenge of limits,
the artist administers strokes and cuts only between his heartbeats while he
works, in the hope that instead of breaking everything to pieces, he might just
chisel clear to the universe.

When has this not been the primary challenge for us ants tamping down
the anthill?

I went out, Cornell-like, to wander in the city. The Mexican photographer
Manuel Bravo had an exhibition with the epigram "Extract the precise from
the precious," and I came across a line by Don DeLillo that urged scrap-
ing to the bottom of all we've layered on. I had my lessons about depth,
about excavating to the stones waiting to be carved, but I could not apply
them because there to bury me, instead, was a time of heartbreak, illness, and
looming divorce. I lived in other people's homes when they were absent, a
cuckoo bird in New York, in San Francisco. I avoided friends because I would
have to hear, Where are you? What are you doing? What's going on? (They
might as well have asked, What matters? What's important? What does your
great-grandfather's murder have to do with you?) Solitude didn't have the
decency not to show on my skin; I had the stunned-eyed, porcelain face and
cloth body of Bébé Marie, who resides in a Cornell box behind a thicket of
brambles. One afternoon while walking on Union Street in San Francisco, I
got jostled in a crowd of dot-commers drinking at a pink-slip party that had
spilled onto the sidewalk, and a girl pursued me down the block, offering to
kick "my old lady's ass." Forget that stylish hell I'd devised 40 years ago; this
was Sartrean other-people hell, the real one.

How had I locked step with Gurov in Chekhov's "The Lady with the Pet
Dog" when he fumes, "What savage manners...! What stupid nights, what
dull, humdrum days!"? But the turning point for Gurov is not when he loathes
humanity because he has no clue what to do next, now that he is in love for
the first time. His plunge into anguish is when it dawns on him that he cannot lay claim to any removed, more colorful perch. Everyone else, like him,
is carrying on two lives, the open, conventional one, and the secret realm of
the essential, the core of one's being. (Have I grown so long in the tooth that
a short story encapsulates for me all that could ever matter?)

My search was meant to overthrow whatever was precious and too-pleasing,
and I stumbled right onto the fat lot of my new age: cold fear, the worry
that start-over energies diminish in middle age, seemingly unbridgeable dis-
tances even from those I loved, and a shock and admiration at the capacity of

others—everyone—functioning in grief. As a walker in the city, I had found not gleaming objects, but the fragments of my heart.

I put together a box-art piece centering upon a black-and-white blurred photo of a woman in sunglasses. I'd had it for years; I had to wait until I knew what being haunted looked like from the inside out. I stitched a tiny knight on a white horse emerging from a cutaway I made in her throat, and at her breast I glued a thumb-sized naked girl, originally from a perfume ad, holding a Frisbee that, at the angle she's waving it, looks phallic. Everything is contained in a miniature white frame. It's the simplest but best piece I've devised.

Should I elect to write about that uncle who sculpted ice cream, the story should embody his defeat when he came home to a lifetime of being ostracized for daring to think he was better than his coworkers in the dairy. Forget those neon pistachio and cranberry colors. That woman whose husband was having an affair next door: I'll need to focus in and ask myself, until I'm past wincing, what a man and woman say to one another in those hideously close rooms; the light and dark sides of the house are only the background. Better yet: I've been shoved inside myself to find ways for my own interior to connect to the outside. Characters carved from my own flesh. From the history I own. A depth charge. Stories at considerable cost.

Beyond this business of what is found or not, what raw stuff inside us can attempt to match to the interiors of characters, lie the reaches of imagination, and if we step in bravely enough, we find not the freeze-frames that correspond precisely to memory, but what Gabriel García Márquez had in mind when he protested that he was a social realist. The disease of forgetting in *One Hundred Years of Solitude*, for instance—that's no flight of removed fancy. It's metaphor dreamed alive in counterpoint to the central focus of the novel, a massacre covered up by authorities, obliterated from the record. The writer's job is to dredge up the truth of what isn't there, too, and often it's only the imagination that can lead him there.

Take Edward Hopper's "The Automat," a painting that seems to be, at first glance, the rendering of a scene available to any passerby. Why, then, is practically nothing of the Automat shown? We're not viewing the banks of little windows with their pies, chicken legs, and dishes of custard, or packs of customers; we are given only a solitary woman at a table with a cup of coffee. She's not in distress, but it's possible that not a soul on earth knows where she is or what she's doing right then. What truly arrests me, though, is that through the window behind her, in the black solidity of the distance, a blue dot wavers. The artist subtly but deliberately dabbed it there.

How grateful I am—what a kindness! Gurov acknowledging his fellow universal Gurovites!—that Hopper should offer me a mirror of my current self. I

have been that woman for some time now. I'd like to know what that discon-
nected blue speck is, and why it appears to have no source and no end.

Blue, according to *The Primary Colors* by Alexander Theroux, is the color
of the spot found on all newborn Asian babies, which inexplicably disappears
a week after their births. It is the color Mayan priests caked over themselves
when they cut out the still-beating innards of sacrificial victims. The Egyptian
underworld, of night, hell, moonlight—blue. Cornell's favorite color.

There's a saying that what shows up in the years is never apparent in the
days, but stories, like any well-constructed shadow box, defy that by insisting
that the days be caught and held while we peer into them and imagine their
depths.

It won't be sufficient if I walk about and record only what's for the taking.
That blue dot of Hopper's telescopes onto another plane but will never reveal
completely what it is. It dares to suggest that there's no back wall to anything
I might frame with great care.

I'll have to admit that eventually time and space will fall away from me.

In the meanwhile, to whatever I build now, my imagination will have
to add some blue dot, small and mysterious, but like a hole of sky burned
through the heart.

WORKS CITED

Solomon, Deborah. *Utopia Parkway: The Life and Work of Joseph Cornell.* New York:
Farrar, Straus & Giroux, 1997.
Weschler, Lawrence. *Mr. Wilson's Cabinet of Wonder.* Lincolnshire, England: Vintage,
1995.

2

Relationship of Writer to Short Story

The Short Story and Me

Velma Pollard

People usually ask me why I write. Now someone asks why I write the short story. The answer to the first is easy and is almost always the same no matter which writer you ask. We write because we must. We are driven. In my case the idea hangs like an albatross until I write it in one form or another. The question about form is more formidable, though. I had not thought about it till now. It could have something to do with the size of the ideas that come to me. Perhaps small ideas come to me. So I have written a short novel, a novella, and several short stories. I never seem to want to write about a world war, a political movement, or even the saga of a particular family over so many years. These are important in my writing only inasmuch as they affect the individual. I write about characters caught up in specific circumstances.

By the time I get to writing a story, the situation it explores with the characters caught up in it have been with me for a long time. The point at which I write is simply the point at which I discover a context in which the idea can be played out and find the space/time to sit and write. Let me give two examples.

I could not have been more than seven years old when a young man beheaded my great-aunt-in-law because she did not want him to court her daughter. All through the years I felt that this was a head lost in a poor cause. Fifty years later I could write the story "Carlton" around that tragedy. I had not known the young man. Twenty miles separated his village and mine at a time when that was a great distance. If I had tried to put that event into a novel it might have become an insignificant part of the plot. It could be a beginning or perhaps an end. The short story allowed it to be central. The history of the people concerned, the anger that might have led to the act easily unfolded itself before me as I got involved with realities of class and color that today affect my living in Jamaica and which affected life even more way back then.

Migration has been my pet peeve as long as I have been a teacher. This may well be considered odd in someone like me, from a society whose foundations were laid by migrants both forced and voluntary: people who were bought/brought and people who came. But I have had to note the effect of modern-day migration on children over the years. There are children in Jamaica now called "barrel children": children who survive on barrels of goodies shipped by migrant parents chiefly from the United States. In my school days the phenomenon was still unlabeled because it was much rarer. But even then I was aware of these children. As an adult, a teacher, I was confronted with children of this experience, growing up with grandparents, aunts, uncles, or friends of their parents. Their stories were some of the saddest I ever heard. They have been some of the saddest children I have encountered—trendily dressed, unhappy children.

I had been concerned with barrel children for more than a decade when fate intervened and showed me how to write "My Mother." A colleague had gone to a funeral and returned to report to the office-at-large dialogue between a returning resident and a friend. The former was commenting on her own good fortune in being back in the Caribbean as opposed to remaining in England, possibly dying and being cremated there so the ashes could be sent home. There was a kind of bizarre humor in the interchange, but the more I thought about it the more I realized that something important had been discussed. That night I wrote the first draft of "My Mother."

I had lived in New York myself and knew at first hand how to be a misfit in a foreign land. I could empathize with the migrant mother. I had counseled enough barrel children to be sensitized to their plight. A point to make, a story to write came together in what turned out to be a felicitous encounter. What has surprised me is the extent to which audiences in different countries have appreciated that particular story. Wherever I have read it, people have expressed their empathy if not with the symbol, the barrel, then certainly with the experience of goodwill containers sent from migrants to their more needy relatives.

My behavior on the other side of the page, that is, the reading side, shows that I am consistent in my predilection for the short story. I enjoy reading it. I read on planes, trains, ferries, and I like the assurance that when my journey ends I have come to the end of what I have been reading. Some publishers think that mine is not the popular position, and indeed when I gaze across the aisle in airplanes, the evidence supports them. I note that people are mostly reading novels and settle for a bookmark at the end of a page. They do not seem to have my need for the end of a story.

In reviewing both what I write and what I read, it seems that time is a component to be taken into account. Perhaps time is as important as inclination. My time outside of the home is spent lecturing, reading examination scripts, and writing academic papers. The creative writing I do happens in the odd moments at home between cooking and cleaning and during the breaks I take from academic work. I write a great deal in airline departure lounges. I pounce upon that space to write down a poem or two that may have been moving around in my head or a short story waiting.... Once I have the first draft, the myriad revisions take care of themselves over months and years.

The only novel I ever wrote got off to a fast start at a five-week writers workshop I was privileged to attend. So it could be that my reading matches my travel and my ideas for writing suit the circumstances of my life. But this sounds like a rationalization, and I should not have to rationalize my writing in a particular genre. The short story has respectable antecedents. Was the serialized novel of nineteenth-century England a forerunner? Was the short story that really flourished in America a response to the need to use small available chunks of time for relaxation, leaving the complicated plot, the elaborate setting, for longer tracts of time and the novel?

Short stories have always held a strong place in Caribbean literature. The blossoming of Caribbean prose in the 1950s included memorable collections. Selvon, Naipaul, and Mittelholzer come immediately to mind. The history of the development of this literature includes the place of the BBC program *Caribbean Voices*. The call was for short stories. Perhaps the fact that writing would find an outlet there was one reason for the popularity of the genre. Be that as it may, classrooms of resistant readers have been charmed by stories from Selvon's *Ways of Sunlight*, from Naipaul's *Miguel Street*, and from the others, and through them have been led to an appreciation of Caribbean writing and later of writing in general. These collections were the favorites to which I introduced students I taught in high school in the 1960s.

With the 1970s and on into the 1980s came the several anthologies that were to expose readers to an ever-widening Caribbean experience as people from the different islands and from Guyana and Belize became acquainted with each other's territories through the imaginations of the writers. As a teacher trainer during these years, I have had the pleasure of bringing teachers to an appreciation of the possibilities of the short story in a classroom setting. And they have come to find, as I did in my time, that students of all ages enjoy a reading that can be completed in an hour and leave good time for comment.

And when the Commonwealth Writers Prize came to be won in 1988, it was Olive Senior's collection of short stories *Summer Lightning* that won it.

WORKS CITED

Naipaul, V. S. *Miguel Street.* London: Andre Deutsch, 1959.

Pollard, Velma. "My Mother." *Caribbean New Wave: Contemporary Short Stories.* Ed. Stewart Brown. Portsmouth, N.H.: Heinemann, 1990. 148–52.

Selvon, Samuel. *Ways of Sunlight.* London: MacGibbon & Kee, 1957.

Senior, Olive. *Summer Lightning and Other Stories.* London: Longman, 1987.

Writing Home

Minoli Salgado

"To write," claims Iain Chambers, "is to travel."[1] And for those of us who have experienced displacement from our homes, not once or twice, but so often and so early that it has become a condition of our existence, the process of writing serves as a kind of reclamation of that which was lost. Writing is a process of self-discovery, a means of coming to terms with our being in the world and our place in it. This is true for all writers, but for the migrant writer it becomes not simply a question of self-definition but, more poignantly perhaps, a question of survival, a question of forging a selfhood that, however inchoate and nebulous, allows us a temporary fixity, a transient but welcome wholeness, a position from which to find ourselves and, perhaps, to speak. This is not to say that our writing is necessarily autobiographical. Of course it is not. Rather that the process of writing allows us—no, requires us—briefly but surely, to find our place, our site of imagined unity, our home. And as Rushdie reminds us, our homes are necessary fictions.[2]

My own homes are multiple. They are at once real and imagined, provisional and permanent, deferred into a timeless future and an endless past. This has always been the case. I was born in Malaysia to parents who were themselves migrants. I then spent the next few years of my life in my grandparents' home in Sri Lanka, aware of my other home where my parents, brother, and sister lived. I had two homes from the start. After that, a sense of home—of belonging—was painfully complicated by boarding schools, where I was to spend almost 12 years of my life, first in Malaysia and then in England. In these years home was an imagined construct, one I would re-create during those times when I felt strong, or else, as was more often the case, deny, relieving myself of the burden of the past, the burden of attachment and feeling. During such enforced separation, it was easier to forget home and family, to push it to the margins of awareness, than to bring it into existence by an act of imaginative will and open up myself to the past, to the reality of isolation, to pain. Home was always somewhere I wasn't.

This is still true today, as I work in a country some 5,000 miles from my Sri Lankan home. Fiction allows us the freedom of flight, of the chance to migrate and live where we choose, and I have, so far, chosen Sri Lanka, not because it is my ancestral home, a point of fixity in an unsettled life, but simply (and selfishly perhaps) because I am happiest and feel most complete and "at home" when I return there. Almost all my short stories and poems draw upon Sri Lanka, not as a mere cultural resource, but as a site for habitation, for living and growing in, and it is of course in writing that we truly come alive. Sri Lanka is, for the time being, the land of my imaginative life, and therefore where I would claim I truly live; I merely reside in England.

Yet—and this I believe is important, for reasons that will soon be clear—I seem to be only able to write when I am outside Sri Lanka. At first I thought this was due to the brevity of my visits, their chaotic nature in which family weddings, bookshops, cultural events, lectures, pilgrimages, and touring would compete for attention to produce an untidy jumble of events and experiences, and that I needed time and distance to make sense of it all. While this is certainly true, I have recently discovered that there is another reason too. I cannot write when I am in Sri Lanka because I am too much at home there. I am too comfortable, too secure, too integrated as a human being to write.

This is not of course to say that I feel comfortable with everything I come across there. The turbulent political events of Sri Lanka's recent past have given rise to some of the worst forms of human atrocity imaginable, and it is impossible not to be touched by these. But, in my experience, these events are given historical and cultural coherence and continuity when living in the country. In other words, the charred buildings, burned buses, curfews, lines for gas, power cuts, security checks, roadblocks, and even violent deaths—the discrete, jarring "signs" of war—become integrated seamlessly into the experience of living there, absorbed into a totalizing narrative of which I, as a temporary resident, become a part. When in Sri Lanka, seemingly absurd political events become saturated with contingency and context. They start to make sense. It thus requires (for me at least) not merely a distanced but a dislocated perspective to come to grips with, say, the sheer brutality of extrajudicial killings or the effect of a bomb blast on a neighborhood, not because such things are unheard of in England, but because, when taken out of the naturalizing medium of their specific context, their full moral weight, their strangeness, is felt most forcefully. It is as if we have to experience ourselves at odds with the world in order to write, as if alienation itself were a condition for writing and migration its goal.

Stuart Hall has said that "migration is a one-way trip ... there is no 'home' to go back to."[3] This is true to a degree, but only if you are prepared to believe in the myth of permanence, to see time as linear and chronological rather than spatial and synchronous, to value what Levine has called "clock time" instead of "event time,"[4] to claim "home" is necessarily fixed. The migrant writer can defy—indeed must defy—such laws, for the very condition of her experience is one that is based upon overlapping territories, overlapping temporal zones, overlapping selves where experience remains caught in the flux of the liminal, the in-between, of belonging neither here nor there but also belonging here and there, a scattered identity that is drawn into a nebulous whole in writing.

Little wonder that home is a central motif in the work of all writers who have traveled in search of themselves. From luminaries such as Salman Rushdie, V. S. Naipaul, Derek Walcott, and Michael Ondaatje to those of us who spin our webs in darkened corners, home remains a site of personal and cultural transaction, a locus for our transient selves. Through forming fictional homes, however fragile they may be, we can lay claim to belonging, to indigenousness, to ownership of a sort, and in our recreations find a place to live. The homes in my first short stories have been fairly secure and certain—places of refuge offering shelter from the world. Written during a long interval between return trips to Sri Lanka, I drew upon the large pool of memory that grows in such absences. Writers such as the early Anita Desai certainly helped develop creative expression, but it was undoubtedly an idealized image of the Sri Lanka of my childhood that shaped the homes and homeland found there, traditional, sacred spaces in which history was a noisy intruder.

Over the years and after many visits to the island, I have found the war has blasted its way in, and my homes are now inevitably and unalterably damaged not merely by the effects of dislocation but also by the bombs that break the city. Homes are physically shattered, dislocated, and increasingly borderless, as the boundaries between private and public space, private and public selves, have collapsed. If, as has been claimed, social space shapes and is shaped by our sense of belonging,[5] then these homes bear witness to the way in which civil war—a war defined by territorial contestation—has the paradoxical effect of making migrants of us all. It is as if this war, which gains currency through specifically defining us in terms of ethnic identity, also creates the conditions for the relocation of identity by altering the physical and mental landscape that gives us our sense of belonging, our sense of who we are. This is a potentially liberating effect of an otherwise debilitating political conflict: that the very multiplicity of spatialities that war creates might offer us new terrains for reconstituting ourselves and our land, new locations for restructuring our relationship to the world and, most important of all, for reconciling the differences that would appear to divide us. All Sri Lankans have, in different ways, been made homeless by this war, and such homelessness can offer us the chance to make new connections, give us the freedom to explore different intersections of history and memory from those that formerly constituted us.

An altered geography and displaced history require new modes of writing, and I have found that my work is becoming increasingly perforated as gaps, folds, and tears are needed to explore and expose the dislocation of identity that I feel is now taking place. This last is of course an individual perspective, a result of my own personal voyage helped by the many creative writers and cultural theorists who devote themselves to the study of migrancy. But it would not have been possible for me to realize this broader political truth without embarking on the process of writing itself, and, in this, the short story has proved a good friend. For the short story, with its emphasis on the individual perspective, on the single episode and event, effectively privileges the fragment—and fragments, as every migrant knows, are that of which we are made. The demand for cultural omniscience, for projecting a social and historical totality in narrative, is the burden of the novelist, not the writer of short fiction. And endings in short fiction are porous. They are interludes, moments of respite rather than conclusions, thresholds rather than settled destinations offering us tentative points of departure.

Further, it seems that stories offer us a vital link to our home, our homeland, and our imagined selves. In my case, I have found that every return home is a return to story, not simply because in Sri Lanka storytellers and soothsayers, politicians and priests, all know the power of narrative and the uses to which it can be put, but because on a much more intimate level, every family reunion constitutes a reconnection with a network of narratives in which rumors metamorphose into myth and history is translated into legend. And it is in such reunions that we find we are confronted with our other selves, transformed into a character in someone else's narrative, a figure in someone else's speech, and in such journeys find ourselves placed and displaced once more.

NOTES

1. Iain Chambers, *Migrancy, Culture, Identity* (London: Routledge, 1994), p. 10.

2. See Salman Rushdie, *Imaginary Homelands: Essays and Criticism 1981–1991* (London: Granta, 1991), pp. 9–21.

3. Stuart Hall, quoted in Chambers, *Migrancy, Culture, Identity*, p. 9.

4. Robert Levine, *A Geography of Time* (New York: HarperCollins, 1997), chapters 3 and 4.

5. See David Sibley, *Geographies of Exclusion* (London: Routledge, 1995), pp. 3–10; and Edward W. Soja, *Postmodern Geographies: The Reassertion of Space in Critical Social Theory* (New York: Verso, 1989), p. 57.

A Short History of a Short Story: A Writer's Beginnings

Merrill Joan Gerber

The impulse to write was natural to me from the age of six or seven: live life twice. Live it once in all the confusion and innocence and astonishment of the first experience, and live it again on paper, making sense of it, getting some perspective on it, getting it down, getting it right, getting it locked in for future reference or the recapturing of the pleasure or to punish oneself with guilt or shame or pain. The mind that writes short stories is a worrying mind. Why did something happen the way it happened? Who was to blame? What forces forced the people to act as they did? Why did my mother rage at my father for helping his sisters move their furniture? Why was my aunt in love with my father? (This was not a conjecture: she told me as much, that she would be a better wife for him.) Why did my grandmother tell me that God could see everything I did, so I'd better be good?

All of these questions were embedded in my being from the start of consciousness, and it seemed to me if I thought hard enough, I could find the answers to them.

I looked to my childhood friends to see if any of them had these impulses—to ponder what had happened to them, to reflect and consider why, for example, Ruth had not invited us to her party, or why Alan's mother embarrassed him by screaming at him in front of his house while the rest of us were playing stoop ball with him, or why Linda's father made comments about Linda's mother's large breasts and sometimes made a grab for them. And especially why we hated to play at Linda's house when he was there, with his missing front tooth, and the way he looked at us.

I didn't find in any of my friends a single person who was willing or able to discuss the strange things that had passed or admit that she even thought about them. My girlfriends all charged straight through time, butting forward, cutting through the new day's barriers and boundaries, pausing to enjoy the day's rewards, the ice cream from the ice-cream man, the new skates that buzzed and hummed over the sidewalk, the Monopoly game when all the money piled up on their side of the board. They showed none of the grief I knew I carried with me. (My mother put a poem in front of my glass of orange juice one morning: "If smiles you won't hoard, I'm pretty sure you'll get a reward.") I was far too serious for a child. My friends were jolly, greedy for the next bite, ravenous for the next thrill that was coming toward them. I knew they didn't have a grandmother in their house who had heart pains and who could die at any moment. I knew none of them had a father who went on "calls" at night to strangers' homes to buy antiques and furniture. (My mother always feared he would be mugged or killed for the cash he carried.)

I was sorry not to be like my friends. While they played jacks and marbles and rode their bikes, it was necessary for me to think and worry and wonder and get heart palpitations and finally ... I had to write. My father gave me a dummy printer's book with blank pages—a book as thick as *Gone with the Wind*—with a gray cover and a sailing vessel embossed on the front. Its title was *Mutiny on the Bounty.* I wrote in it assiduously: my dreams, my poems, my questions and my conclusions, my angers, my ambitions, my astonishments, and my jealousies. There was not enough time in the day to do this and go to school and eat meals. I wrote faster and faster. On one of his "calls," my father bought me a small black typewriter, which he set up for me on a bridge table in our basement. After school I typed underground while my friends jumped over hedges in the sunshine. I was happy to be with my typewriter, happier than I was with my friends. I began to pull together events and to see them at a distance with some clarity.

When I was 13 years old, a boy from school named Chuck asked me to go to the movies with him. The day after this notable event I wrote a story called "First Date." I still have it. From what I can make of it now, the date was an interesting torture, the first of many such ordeals and delights. But when I hold this ancient manuscript in my hand, typed on yellowing, brittle paper, I see the first instance, the written proof, of how I would conduct the rest of my life.

Guided Tours of Time and Death

Jayne Anne Phillips

His samples weren't even packed up, and he himself wasn't feeling particularly fresh and active.

—Kafka

In place of death there was light.

—Tolstoy

Companion Stories:
"The Metamorphosis," "Pale Horse, Pale Rider," "The Jilting of Granny Weatherall," and "The Death of Ivan Ilyich"

We could say there is no death in literature, no nothingness, because language bears witness continually, burning its shape into the mind of the reader. In literature, we don't die; we merely think about dying, and darkness is the stark relief against which the light of the words fall.

In stories concerning metamorphosis, death serves as catalyst and witnessed postscript. The long, luminous turning between life and death is the subject of the work. The prison of detail (a form of imprisonment not unlike Gregor Samsa's) shapes the narrative in Kafka's "The Metamorphosis." Simultaneity of time, memory, and the question of faith are mysteries that open and close in the last lines of Porter's stories. In Tolstoy, death exists to birth Ivan Ilyich into an immensity beyond life. Tolstoy hints that the mind cannot comprehend the loss of identity; language can. Language carries within it the soul of identity, culture, and history, and the evolution of the soul is most clearly seen in the process we call metamorphosis.

Kafka, born in Prague in 1883, states in a letter to Oskar Pollack: "The books we need are of the kind that act upon us like a misfortune, that makes us suffer like the death of someone we love more than ourselves, that make us feel as though we were on the verge of suicide, or lost in a forest remote from all human habitation—a book should serve as the ax for the frozen sea within us."

Philip Rahv describes him thus: "It is as if the neurotic sufferer in Kafka and the artist in him locked hands and held on for dear life." Max Brod, Kafka's longtime friend and publisher, writes in his diaries: "Kafka in ecstasy. Writes all night long," and "Kafka in incredible ecstasy." Why was he ecstatic? Because he lived as a creature separated from himself, "full of innate irre-futable feelings, inexpressible urgency and inwardness," *except* when he was writing.

In Gregor Samsa, Kafka creates a clerk whose transformation is an awaken-ing to the full horror of a dull, spiritless existence calculated by others. He awakens also to a terrible self-disgust.

The need to break free of his father and leave the family is transformed by guilt into a revolting punishment. Yet "The Metamorphosis" turns upon itself to provide a spiritual transformation, not only for Gregor, but for the family who have created, consumed, and betrayed him, and for the reader, who becomes familial by the close of the story.

Gregor makes a passage through hellish decay and torture, through a dis-torted darkness not unlike Conrad's jungle in *Heart of Darkness,* a darkness all the more horrifying and grimly comic because it unfolds in Gregor's bed-room. It was Chekhov who said to a critical reader: "You confuse two things: solving a problem and stating a problem correctly. It is only the second that is obligatory for the artist."

Kafka states the problem correctly throughout Gregor Samsa's transforma-tion. The story moves according to specific inconveniences ("to get rid of the quilt was quite easy; he had only to inflate himself a little and it fell off by itself"), pleasures ("He especially enjoyed hanging suspended from the ceil-ing"), and terrors dictated by Gregor's change in form. Gregor has, of course, lived as an insect for many years. He takes the 5 a.m. train every morning to make his rounds as a salesman ("once I've saved enough money to pay back my parents' debts ... I'll cut myself completely loose"), supporting his entire family while living in a locked bedroom in the family apartment. "It was no dream," Kafka states flatly, and the reader begins to understand the author's broad indictment of life itself. The unknowingness of the world is equaled only by the intensity, need, and desire of the "I" to perceive and know that world; the depths of the schism between world and self is nearly holy, and makes the sufferer (Gregor) an avatar. "The rotting apple in his back ... all covered with soft dust, already hardly troubled him. He thought of his family with tenderness and love."

Gregor, like an insect Christ, dies by degrees, spiritually transformed by recognition of love and acceptance of sacrifice. The charwoman briskly disposes of his flattened corpse, the desiccated and rightfully sacred vehicle of his metamorphosis. What "new dreams and excellent intentions" can exist in such a world? Gregor Samsa becomes miraculous, never as a clerk, but as a cockroach. Kafka's miracle can exist only in the turbulent heartlessness of this world, one in which Gregor's sister "springs to her feet first and stretches her young body" into a future rendered spacious by his blessing.

Porter's "Pale Horse, Pale Rider" is a treatise on young bodies rather than insects. The 1918 flu epidemic rises up like a final ghoulish joke to kill off thousands who have (seemingly) survived World War I. In the world of Porter's story, war itself is the insect, and contagion ("that lank greenish stranger") is war's personification and legacy. Metamorphosis of form carries Kafka's story. Metamorphosis of vision, memory, and time carry Porter's. Miranda races death in her delirium, riding the horses she clasped with her body in the lost heaven of home. She decides on Graylie "because he is not afraid of bridges." "Graylie's ribs heaved under her, her own ribs rose and fell," Porter writes, and the words take on a sexual meaning.

Miranda and Adam, her young soldier, are achingly sexual, and as achingly denied. In the story, we see them walk, wait, talk, dance, and look through one another, young voyagers in the same rooming house. They know each other for 10 days; exchange first, searching kisses; and fall immediately into death, moving through fever dreams in which they are joined as angels shut in darkness. Miranda is a bitter angel, and Porter writes this story as an omnipotent, furious mourner. The prose is replete with shadows that cast their shapes both forward and backward in time: Miranda remarks that her headache "started with the war." "My leave is nearly up," Adam tells her, "and it will be the last, the very last." "His eyes were very black," Porter writes. Her young lovers gamely ask one another, "Did you ever see so many funerals?" "It's my turn now," Miranda cries to Adam in her fever, "why must you always be the one to die?" Miranda's movement toward death is a journey through language and the power of metaphor. Death takes the form of childhood terror ("the ledge was her childhood dream of danger"), clarifying Porter's belief that metaphor operates in language as spiritual truth. In Porter's vision, we know death always and live in death as in life: "Oblivion, thought Miranda, her mind feeling among her memories of words she had been taught to describe the unseen, the unknowable. . . ."

Miranda passes through darkness to euphoria to the consciousness of loss. For her, there is no Armistice. She steps into limbo, both angel and agent of death. She has lost Adam and saved him, pulling him into herself as she could not in life. "Pale Horse, Pale Rider" implies a fierce banking of flames, almost a vengeance of belief. Porter has made a lost world ceaselessly apparent and flung that world forward into ours.

In "The Jilting of Granny Weatherall," death is the moment on which the prose turns, the moment that the prose builds.

Granny Weatherall forgets nothing, and the scrambling of time only sets each image and detail firmly into a selective memory that is itself alive, pumping like a heart. Porter is a supremely womanly writer, a kind of Amazon, both fertile and controlled. She is never seductive, yet the energy of her prose moves inexorably deeper, like a bloom opening inward, and the reader is pulled in. The metaphor of death as a bridegroom is ultimately feminine, true to the place and time of the character, but the image of "the white veil and the white cake" and "the man who doesn't come" are religious metaphors that move beyond culture or gender. "That was hell, she knew hell when she saw it," Porter says quietly, and then asks in anguish, "oh surely they were not all?" Her protagonist moves both toward and away from the blinding power of that question by remembering the luminous dislocation of childbirth. The experience of giving birth remains at the core of her being, though the character cannot think of it in language; she turns to details about cards and gossip, in just the way that day-to-day life denies its own reason for being. When we reach the last line—"Again no bridegroom and the priest in the house"—the story tightens to a glass point and the reader slides into the abyss.

To recover, read Tolstoy's "The Death of Ivan Ilyich": "There was no fear because there was no death." Kafka has redemption, while Porter has herself, and infinite awareness. Tolstoy has faith.

WORKS CITED

Kafka, Franz. "Metamorphosis." *Selected Short Stories of Franz Kafka.* Ed. Philip Rahv, trans. Edwin Muir and Willa Muir. New York: Modern Library, 1993. 11–53.

Kafka, Franz, and Mad Brod. *Franz Kafka: The Diaries.* New York: Secken & Warburg, 1948.

Porter, Katherine Anne. "The Jilting of Granny Weatherall." *Flowering Judas and Other Stories.* New York: Harcourt Brace, 1930. 80–89.

———. *Pale Horse, Pale Rider.* New York: Harcourt Brace, 1939.

Rahv, Philip. Introduction. *Selected Short Stories of Franz Kafka.* By Franz Kafka, ed.
    Philip Rahv, trans. Edwin Muir and Willa Muir. New York: Modern Library,
    1993. i-ix.
Tolstoy, Leo. *The Death of Ivan Ilyich,* trans. Lynn Solotaroff. New York: Bantam,
    1987.

3

Storytelling: The Short Story and Pedagogy

The Story as *Su-Su*, the Writer as Gossip

Olive Senior

INTRODUCTION

Talk is what drives my stories; they derive their energy from the desire to speak out. They contain references that are diverse and eclectic: literature, history, myth, fragments of folk songs, sayings, biblical knowledge, and so on. They combine the Queen's English with the Jamaican vernacular. These are all elements of my stories because they are part of who I am.

All of us writers are probably shaped by the place where we spend our earliest years. I myself write the way I do because I spent my earliest years in the mountains of colonial Jamaica. Although at the time schooling was seen as the only means of upward social mobility and book learning was valued, the vast majority of the people were unlettered, and so it was the oral culture that prevailed.

Yet the proverb says, "Before you set out on a journey, you own the journey. Once you have started, the journey owns you." Today, I inhabit both the island and the metropole and feel the pull of both. Part of that tug is between my need to affirm and acknowledge the continued significance of the oral culture and still give appropriate weight to what I do today, that is, engage in consciously "literary" constructions. I am forced to find ways of reconciling the two, to be true to the world that shaped me while creating work that has literary validity and universal accessibility. I realized that as I move further into the journey I am moving closer to artifice; the people I speak to and the ones that speak back are no longer those of my childhood. I don't know if that is good or bad. I intuitively feel that the short story is the mode that most closely connects me to my past yet provides a bridge to the present, since "story" is where the oral and scribal traditions meet. And acknowledging the imperative of the voice is how I pay for my passage.

THE POWER OF VOICE

I learned to write not only from reading Shakespeare, Wordsworth, and the Bible but from listening to what flowed from the world around me. Since I had no literary role models or mentors, my early decision to be a writer was no doubt shaped by an intuitive recognition of the power of words, of language itself; the weight of "tongue"; and the significant roles played by word, story, or narrative in our lives. Voice is the means by which people lacking power in other ways can acquire and exert control. Although I have written from an early age, I didn't find my own writer's voice until I allowed my characters to speak in their own voices.

One of my first adult stories worked only when I allowed the young girl to tell it in her own words. It is significant that this voice was the Creole voice of a little country girl, speaking not standard English, the language of "value" in my culture, but in the cadences of the Jamaican vernacular, which is, after all, her language. Since then, many of my characters have chosen to speak the story in whatever language they would use in real life, often sliding along the continuum between standard English and Jamaican Creole. I say *chosen* because this is how increasingly the story comes to me, in the form of the voice speaking, including the internal voice. Once the character is allowed to speak, then everything else that contributes to story—narrative, scene, setting, description, other characters, and so forth—will automatically fall into place, for speakers do not arrive bereft; they bring their entire worlds with them.

Although I have deliberately chosen to write from the perspective of the many different people who make up the place I come from and not limit myself to any one point of view, most of the time, the voice is that of one who in my culture would still be referred to as the "small man" (or woman), the archetypal bearer of the "little" (i.e., non-European) tradition, expressing "small" concerns—women, children, the rural poor, the "mad," the outcast, the marginalized. I don't find it strange that those regarded as powerless are profound sayers. For, as I will argue below, the voice, any voice, magnifies as it becomes magnified because it is part of a dynamic process in which if you throw words, they are bound to be thrown back at you. Every voice feeds into and takes from a larger collective voice. No man, no woman is an island, but by the means of the voice, a whole island can know your story. And if this voice is captured in that other world of book, then the village becomes the world.

"THROW-WORD": LANGUAGE AS MISSILE

Most of the people I grew up with had no access to books, radio, TV or the cinema, or computers—it goes without saying—but I never had any sense that they were voiceless or silenced. Those perceived as voiceless have always had their ways and means. My education in hearing and overhearing inspired an awe that came from my early exposure to the creative use of words by the real masters of language, the nonscribal for whom words are both tool and weapon. (Of course, as I grew older and encountered the wider world, I recognized how voiceless the villagers were within the larger context of the nation and now even more so within the global village—but that is another story.)

I grew up with a profound appreciation of language as a living object that could be used the same as any other tool or weapon, a possession that in this world is contained (as in writing) or let loose (by the tongue). To create something from nothing is the art of the poor, and to have a mouth full of words is to be endowed with riches.

For instance, where I come from, "throw-word" is a recognized form of relieving aggression—you speak what's on your mind about a person within his or her hearing but without direct reference to them. It is an acting out of the expression "throw a stone in a pigsty, the one who squeals loudest is the one who has been hit."

To this day, I am convinced that no one can curse like a nonliterate person who has to draw from great depths within him or herself the forms of expression needed to demolish an opponent. Creative cursing is called in Jamaica a "tracing match" and is usually expected to attract an audience as the antagonists trace the ancestry, mythical, animal, or otherwise, of their opponents. Women are frequently the best tracers. To have a mouth and use it in this way is to have power, to become the object of fear, envy, hatred, awe, or admiration.

We also learned early that there were "good" words and "bad" words, the latter not simply the kind that made your mother wash out your mouth with soap. No, these were dangerous, big-people, bad-people words, for they came with a price tag attached. These were known as "40-shilling words," for by uttering them you committed a crime, ran the risk of being arrested and taken to court on a charge of using indecent language, and if found guilty you could be fined 40 shillings. Imagine, 40-shilling words! When you consider that up to around 1938 the wage of the average laborer (and "bad-wud cusser") was one shilling a day, you can see how easily *word* and *value* became associated in people's minds. It took me a long time to realize that what was construed as bad language was not the word itself but the threat to a hierarchical colonial society posed by the common man or woman's desire to express him or herself. But express themselves the common people did—and continue to do. It is perhaps for the same reason that as children selected for the privilege of a high-school education, many of us still intuitively felt the need to affirm ourselves, to distance ourselves from the superior class—by refusing to jettison Jamaican Creole, though, in the hallowed halls and playing fields of our colonial high schools, we ran the risk of being punished and denigrated for this identification with the common people—our mothers and fathers.

Even the language that is applied to language itself implies that words are intrinsically powerful and should be handled with care. In my culture, someone who has the power of words, of oratory, of fluent or elaborate speech is said be able to "cut language" or "chop language"—a metaphor derived from the sugar plantations where reaping the sugarcane with a machete or cutlass is a highly valued skill. *Cut* and *chop* are also used to describe the process of clearing a field; hence to chop language is to mow down your opponent with words—a tradition that continues today in some elements of popular Jamaican music, for example, dancehall and dub and in black American culture in rap, the dozens, and so forth. Of course the oral culture also contains sweetness—like the literary culture, it serves to inform, entertain, educate, soothe, and heal. For some people, it is also the only conveyance of their history.

THE LIVING TRADITION OF STORY

When I was growing up, the heroes of books were not people like us. The oral tradition therefore had to carry the weight of our own heroism and our own history. Voice, history, song, and story became conflated. When in a slave society language and other means of communication were repressed by the master class, song remained the most important vehicle for transmitting information and comment for several hundred years. Part of the people's history, the ancestral connections with Africa, were preserved in religious rituals and transmitted orally through music and dance. Even today, songs still tell stories and stories contain songs or are like songs with an implied audience/chorus. To people without book learning, music and song, like the spoken

voice, is an intrinsic possession; it "belongs" to the group. (I quite unconsciously titled the story referred to above, "Ballad," from the form of storytelling chosen by the youthful narrator, since the ballad song with a chorus
was the only model she knew to carry the tale of love and death she wanted
to tell.) Part of the attraction of Jamaica's popular music, reggae, which arose
in the 1960s and 1970s, was not just the rhythms, the sweet harmonizing,
and the danceable beat, but the lyrical beauty of the songs themselves, which,
while often expressing personal angst, were always drawing on, and drawing
in, the collective.

Many of these songs were narratives of the hero who undergoes suffering
and persecution at the hands of a nameless "they," and emerges triumphantly.
Some of Bob Marley's songs in this regard are very widely known, but he is
only the best known of many musicians of his era (now classified as "roots
reggae") who were using song to explore the stories of the past that we as
a people were up to that point afraid to recall or discuss, such as the issue
of slavery. And they did so not as the historian (many of them were largely
unschooled country boys) but by creating a collage of fragmentary images
from various elements that were part of a collective underground or submerged culture that at the time was just emerging and with which people
could identify. Toots and the Maytals' "Never Get Weary" (1981) is a good
example, a story in which a heroic persona suffers persecution at the hands of
the nameless they, yet affirms his triumphant spirit. The chorus of "Never get
weary yet" came from Revival, an indigenous Jamaican Afro-Christian religion. It describes the speaker's experiences of being thrown overboard from
a ship, swimming out of the belly of a whale, and being put in jail with no
bail. Despite all of his trials, the speaker triumphantly responds to each one
by saying he is still not weary.

The use of language as something lived in this way shaped my worldview
and values and—I believe—the way my stories continue to evolve and turn
out. For my characters display their own form of heroism; self-affirmation
is usually more important than the social status that comes from material
"arrival." In the minds of the common people, who have only words as weapons, the rich can be stripped of their vanity by a few well-chosen ones. And
even the most powerful can succumb to the seduction of music, song, or
story, as frequently happens in the traditional Anansi stories where the hero,
empowered by the charms of music and language, will go as far as challenging Death himself. During slavery, the power of the white master class was
constantly subverted by the black slaves who knowingly sang of the swift
vengeance to be wrought by tropical disease and death:

New come buckra / he get sick / he get fever / he be die
Or who chided the white overseer (*obissha*) thus:
Tink dere is a God in a top,
No use me ill, Obissha
Me no horse, me no mare, me no mule,
No use me ill, Obissha
Or the female aware of her sexual power who jeered at her rivals:
  black, brown, or white:
Hipsaw! My deaa! You no do like a-me!
You no jig like a-me! You no twist like a-me!
Hipsaw! My deea! You no shake like a-me!
You no wind like a-me! Go, yondaa!
Hipsaw! My deaa! You no jig like a-me!
You no work him like a-me! You no sweet him like a-me!

Such snatches of popular song, captured by the planter class or visiting Europeans, are the only voices of the slaves we ever hear, the only stories we have of their attitudes and worldviews, the only notion we have of their heroic outspokenness, which subverts the received picture of passive, animal-like acceptance of their fate. Only by knowing these stories can we contextualized ourselves, and understand that we are the inheritors of a powerful tradition of subversion through language.

THE PREVALENCE OF "VERSION," THE POWER OF "ANON"

Growing up in a society where the oral is still more significant than the written is both enriching and sobering for one who would claim the title of author. For what is valued is not authorship but the power of the story, which can exist in as many versions as there are individuals willing to tell it. This means that while language is highly valued, the accepted components of the book—word, author, artifact, commodity—are meaningless. Instead, in this worldview, the language of literacy is co-opted and new values are assigned to its lexicon.

While the ability to communicate ranks high on our list of admired skills, it is the writer who is not widely read. In my own country, authorship and publishing are put in their place by the saying "If you want to hide something, put it in a book." Magic inheres in the words themselves, whether collected or isolated and alone. In traditional religions where healing ceremonies are important, talking in tongues or using esoteric language derived from the spirit world is an intrinsic part of worship. The unspoken is as feared as the uttered, for example, the numerous euphemisms in the language for the black magician or *obeahman* and associated practices. Singer man, storyteller, preacher, speech maker, or religious specialist—all are honored for their juggling with words, not how they put them together in linear fashion. The honor is not so much for sense as for effect and efficaciousness.

Weight is given not to the author or originator but to the art of the telling. The most influential authors in these societies are known only by their first names—for example, Matthew, Mark, Luke, and John. And even they are recognized for their role not as creators but as "sayers," through their writing of letters, speaking to multitudes, addressing their mates, teachings, instruction, and so forth, the same role played by popular radio evangelists today.

The book itself is valued as commodity only for the purchase of a better life for one's children who master it. It is perceived not as art but as symbol or talisman. Due recognition and respect is, however, given to the fact that the most powerful words are the ones that are written down and contained, in the same way that malignant spirits must be ritually contained to subdue their power. The greatest power is believed to reside within books and on paper, so much so that the Bible and the dictionary are valued in many oral societies because they are tools of conjuration. An open Bible placed near a baby is a form of protection, not necessarily as an expression of Christianity but as recognition of the symbolic power of the Church, and as a powerful prophylactic against evil spirits that might come by to harm the child. Books are containers of multiplicities; counting magic forces an evil spirit to stop and count the letters or words inside a book, a task that will keep it occupied till morning, when its own power dissipates and it is no longer a threat. Or well-known passages will be selected for use in other forms of word magic.

As for paper, its real significance is that it is symbolic of state power. *Paper* is used to refer to official documents such as birth certificates, land titles, doctor's prescriptions, or the paper that one is given to enter the hospital, the paper one hopes one's child will get after years in school as the passport to a better life. Nowadays of course, paper would include that higher passport: the green card to America.

Reading is also part of the co-optation of the language of books and its use to signify something different from the perusal of words. The true reader is the see-er, the one with the power to see right through someone or something and reveal the truth. Thus a healer's "reading" can result in cutting through the blockages causing illness; the *obeahman* or sorcerer's practice rests on "reading" a bad situation and selling countermeasures. The religious specialist who receives messages from the spirit world wears one or several pencils stuck in his or her ritual headdress in order to signify readiness to "record" the messages.

Even today, despite many decades of much wider access to education, the socially and economically disenfranchised see books and paper as the weapons of the ruling class, and continue to value the democracy of the tongue over pen or voting paper as the ultimate expression of personhood. This can be read as a kind of resistance to the forces of domination contained in the global culture to which the majority of people know they will never have access, since in the past 400 years they have still not had access to universal education. But they have nevertheless taken charge of the metaphorical pencil, the means of getting the message across. Hence in Jamaica the most popular means of expression continues to be music, a music that has gone global yet still affords avenues for individual entrepreneurship and expression. And—despite the proliferation of television, still a largely foreign medium in terms of content—the most popular medium of communications continues to be radio, with its largely local content, especially the dominant programs of talk shows and call-in programs that command vast audiences.

It is amusing to contemplate that the popularity of some talk-show hosts arises from their parading their learning and erudition, "reading" out a part of their own book learning day after day in an almost talismanic way, to the point where the discourse makes little sense but resonates with the profundity of quotations from the world's greatest books that no doubt impresses the listeners (or the speaker) as the loquacious master of ceremonies at tea meetings and country weddings and wakes once did. The purpose of talk radio in general seems to be the reading of significance into events by both host and listeners, as day after day they examine the same events or issues from every angle, exhaustively and to exhaustion, in the process weaving a story, each adding something to the collective voice that, like traditional storytelling, has no real end but endless permutations. Thus, "version," as it is called in Jamaica—that is, variations on a theme—is a recognized art form in popular music and an unrecognized but potent one in public discourse.

Today, while traditional storytelling has almost died out and the traditional music is preserved largely by folk singing groups, talk (on radio, roadside gossip, or in songs) remains the poor person's primary medium of communications, and serves as a way of mediating his or her encounter with the world and, even more important, a means of securing justice. Talk can lead to rumor, which can and does lead to universal outcry of such magnitude that it will soon enter the media and lead all the way to official commissions of inquiry (as has happened in the recent past). While the latter might not secure justice or satisfaction, it will secure an airing. As such it is a counterpart to silence. This is absolutely essential in small societies where literacy levels continue to be low, the media are not engaged in any real investigation, and the justice system has become suspect. People in such situations know how powerful a medium the mouth is. It is the vocal equivalent of the literary Anonymous, a reflection of the voice that cannot be traced but can be duplicated in endless versions. "Anon" has a long tradition of expression through work songs, songs of derision, political and "parson" jokes, and so on. Anon is also present subliminally in my short stories, the community that comments on the action either in the story itself or stands looking over my shoulder and reading me as I write.

THE WRITER AS GOSSIP, STORY AS *SU-SU*

A society where the oral culture continues to be powerful puts the written (and the writer) in its place, a place that is not above or below, perhaps, but just different from how we as literary persons conceive of our place. To be a writer in a culture that elevates the oral is both humbling and enervating, since *writer* is not a recognized profession or activity. Often in Jamaica when I tell people I am a writer, the response is likely to be "Yes, but what do you *do?*"

What I do as a writer is, I think, mediate the worlds I have inherited. While writing is a private act, orality is a communal one; it implies a teller and a listener, as traditional song consists of call and response. It implicitly invites the community to participate by approval, disapproval, persuasion, or by contributing different versions of the event.

In Jamaica the word *su-su* conveys the sound of a whisper passing from ear to ear, the vehicle of gossip. While gossip in our time has come to mean idle chatter, the word's original meaning is much weightier. It derives from *God* and *sib* and referred to the godparents of a child, who, presumably, were the ones that announced the event. Gossip therefore denoted a spiritual affinity between the baptized person and his or her sponsors. Thus a gossip was not only a close acquaintance but one who has a vested interest in the event and its outcome. Even today, we know that the godparents are duty-bound to have a hand in the shaping of their godchild's character. Gossip then presupposes a loop that connects teller to listener, binding both to the subject of the story.

As a short-story writer I consider myself a gossip, the godparent of the story that enters the world to the shout of "I have a news," as a folk song announces. Not *news*, but *a news*. "I have news" is the shout of the newspaper with its varied stories stacked beside each other like a flight of rooms and arrayed in vertical columns like a many-storied building. Or it might be the clarion call of the novelist who cements many stories together in a (hopefully) substantial structure, plastered over seamlessly so we cannot tell where one story begins and the other ends. "I have *a* news" is the announcement by the gossip of the individual story that arrives with the implication that it is only the latest of an endless line of stories. I like to think it sometimes arrives with the force of a thrown brick. Or, better still, a stone; in traditional cultures, word and stone are symbolically interchangeable.

Short stories are still close to their lowly origins, traditional tales as well as *su-su,* plucked and shaped out of the raw material that is circulating freely on the air. With the trend to globalization, it is important that small voices and small concerns continue to be heard. The short story is the medium of "small" concerns (we are often told), as is the oral culture, the culture of the voice. Where both are combined, the story partakes not only of a literary tradition, but of a longer tradition of vocal expression.

The short story gives me a kind of satisfaction as a participant/observer as I set out in search of truth, though not "the truth." My desire is not to tell an overarching story (the novel) with closure as the goal. I am rather like the examining magistrate or the doctor or the psychiatrist who is involved in the search for meaning, one strand, one witness, one session, one version at a time.

I can only try for honesty of representation, a kind of truth telling where the narrative might be flawed; where details might be inaccurate, inconsistent, or subject to correction; but where the core meaning must be recognizable. The ultimate judgment will not be based on veracity but believability. What keeps me honest is the consciousness that there is always an audience peeking through the windows, "reading" my mind as I write, the community that will affirm, at the very least, "If a no so it go, a nearly so."

The oral culture has to be seen not as ossified, decayed, or dying "traditional" culture but as the continued bearer of a whole way of being. It privileges the writer by giving access not just to one world, that of the scribal, but to a second world that continues to exist and thrive apart from it. To claim the influence of the oral and assert its continued potency is not to devalue literary endeavor, but to enhance it. I myself would sleep easier at nights, have greater confidence in our collective futures, if I were able to imagine the globalization of culture not as the imposition of technology from above, but a welling up from below, a pouring into that increasingly depersonalized "master culture" of that creative flowering that is rooted in the tongue. In Pablo Neruda's words, "Tyranny cuts off the singer's head," yet the storyteller's voice overcomes tyranny and "rises out of nowhere in the mouths of the people."

Wholeness and the Short Story

Billie Travalini

What is most impressive about the modern short story is its sense of Wholeness. Recently I have read dozens of short stories in contemporary magazines and collections that are less concerned with convention and mechanics and more concerned with telling a story and getting it right. The result is stories that flow easily and don't sound contrived. Gone is the formula story where plot is everything and each word, each sentence, each paragraph has a distinct purpose and leads to a singular conclusion. Gone also is the formula of the unresolved impasse where plot is secondary and each word, each sentence, each paragraph has multiple meanings and leads to no conclusion and no resolution. What has taken their place is a sensible approach to storytelling where both subsurface thinking and surface action work together, without losing one or the other, to create a sense of Wholeness. Where does Wholeness come from in the short story? Wholeness comes from causality of subsurface thinking and surface action or vice versa. What becomes important is not whether a story focuses more on the mental process or physical but if such focusing works towards Wholeness. A tree is a tree and is familiar and useful in its own form regardless of whether it is an oak or weeping willow or magnolia. So, if a short story is to be successful, readers must recognize in the working a familiar and useful sense of Wholeness.

To make sense of all this I will talk about my own writing. Most of my stories come from somewhere deep inside of me that I may or may not be aware of. But they are there just the same, incidents from my past that are stored in long-term memory like high-school yearbooks that gather dust on a shelf and are rarely opened. The mind, however, is much more than a yearbook. As if to prove this, every so often one of my long-stored memories breaks free and springs onto the computer screen with little or no effort from me at all. As my hands move along the keys, I watch, amazed, as a single memory evolves into a short story. I am tempted to slow down, but a rhythm has established itself and the rhythm is king. It refuses to slow down so I can hammer in the proper subjectivity and plot and all the other things I was taught to include in a short story to get it right. The result is an exercise in storytelling. And like its oral predecessor, it is unbound by rigid and, often, artificial expectations. Without such expectations the story, then, becomes a frame on which characters and surface action are stretched onto a page until both gain a new shape and meaning. Still my story is not Whole. Wholeness is achieved through writing that presents people with all the raw-boned honesty one can muster. This takes work. It requires knowing what your characters are comfortable doing and what they are uncomfortable doing but seem to do anyway. Flannery O'Connor demonstrates this over and over in her stories. The grandmother in "A Good Man Is Hard to Find" is a good-hearted fool but no match for the quick-witted Misfit who, true to his nature, shoots her dead. Such an ending would have seemed distasteful, even irresponsible, to popular writers like O. Henry, who gave their nineteenth-century audience dovetailed incidents that served two distinct purposes: (1) to shed light on the mental and emotional states of their characters, and (2) to bring a plot a complete (and always happy) resolution.

Whether the primary intention of the modern short story is to reveal some great truth about human moods and motives or simply entertain, writing must, first and foremost, be Readable. No writer is a successful writer if no one wants to read his or her work. As an emerging short-story writer, I have studied O. Henry and O'Connor with great interest. Each contributed to my view of the writing process. O. Henry wrote formula stories that relied on literary convention and happy endings. O'Connor ignored literary convention and went straight for America's jugular. O. Henry taught the importance of pace and action. O'Connor taught the beauty of originality and the impact that writing can have on the social conscience. Recently I wrote a story that ended with no resolution. After complaints from my peers and family, I rewrote the story so that the much-underappreciated wife leaves her controlling, self-absorbed husband for a new life on her own. Is the former ending, the unresolved impasse, truer to life than the latter? Probably. Which ending will I stick with? I don't know. What I do know is the story is not done. Will it ever be done? Yes. It will be done when the rhythm of each word, each sentence, and each paragraph moves the subsurface thinking and surface action towards Wholeness, and I cannot imagine telling the story any other way.

WORK CITED

O'Connor, Flannery. "A Good Man Is Hard to Find." *A Good Man Is Hard to Find and Other Stories*. Orlando, Fla.: Harcourt Brace, 1955. 1–22.

Not Taking the Bait: A Brief for Uselessness in Short Fiction

Lucy Ferriss

The short story today is under a peculiar sort of threat. I am not talking about the threat of dwindling readership or diminishing financial rewards—those disappointments exist, but thus far they have not adversely affected the quality of stories themselves. (If anything, the oft-quoted threat of workshop over-kill does more to injure the vitality of the form than puny payments or scarce readers.) Rather, the danger to the continuing evolution and excitement of the literary short story lies in a less expected quarter: its usefulness.

The short story is handy in a number of unseemly ways. Being short, it can be used in high schools to introduce lackadaisical students to prose fiction. Similarly, its length is conducive to introductory creative-writing classes, so that college students who want to write fiction find themselves willy-nilly writing short stories. Both these approaches view the short story as a junior novel, an apprentice work and perforce simpler to create or analyze than the longer form. If an apprentice writer is lucky, he or she can massage a group of stories into something a publisher might call a novel, and thus make the form more palatable to a presumably averse reader. In the nonacademic world, the commercial handiness of the short story is evident in the string of Absolut vodka ads featuring stories by such notables as John Irving and Julia Alvarez—the idea being, in what the vodka company's spokesperson calls "an entertaining way to reach a potential target audience," that the short story is a pleasurable vehicle for "product placement." The stories all mention Absolut, but they are not always identified as ads, and in some cases their typeface matches the magazine's editorial font.

Finally, there is the jackpot of the film option. Novelists have long bemoaned (all the way to the bank) the oversimplification of their multilayered texts to make a screenplay. They fear that people will see the movie rather than read the book, and they rejoice when the movie instead leads readers back to the book, to glean the greater literary wealth found there. The translation of the "simpler" short story to film faces no such dilemma. Presumably the text will be expanded rather than cut back in the screenplay. No one will have read the story in the first place, so there is no danger of losing readership, and journal publication means that the story will have outlived its day already, so there is usually no literary text for readers to return to. (And, one suspects, be disappointed by.)

Why are these uses of the short story dangerous? Do they not gain wider recognition for the story writer, put money into his or her bank account, broaden the appeal of the story beyond the elite self-serving readership of the country's M.F.A. programs? Yes, yes, and yes. They also dismiss the value of the short story as an experience in itself—which is a little like saying that rhymed poetry is great for song lyrics and greeting cards, or that 85% cacao chocolate is handy for making brownies. I do not believe that we denigrate lyrics, cards, or brownies by suggesting that Keats and Godiva are intense experiences unto themselves. Similarly, I have no desire to take up arms against Alfred Hitchcock, but I believe we are in danger if we say we are grateful to Cornell Woolrich for having written *Rear Window* so that Hitchcock could put Jimmy Stewart in it.

The most blatant example of this last, touted use of the short story is Francis Ford Coppola's magazine *Zoetrope,* founded in 1997. The word *zoetrope* has no literary connotation but refers to the old-fashioned slitted, spinning cylinder through which one can view a succession of images so fast that they appear to move—literally, a moving picture.

Coppola was canny about the reception of his new magazine. In his opening editorial letter, he admitted to the usefulness of the short story for the screen, confessing, "I have never met a person in the film business who enjoys reading a screenplay," but he claims that his magazine belongs foursquare in the literary world. Nonetheless, the very notion that Hollywood types are reading this magazine (and how many of them read the nonpareil, recently defunct *Story?*) puts a spin, if not on editorial selection, at least on submissions.

For a short-story writer, the temptations here are enormous. The only other high-paying outlets for short stories—the *New Yorker, Harper's,* and occasionally *Esquire*—run at most one story per issue and tend to prefer writers with whose work they are familiar. Coppola pays approximately $5,000 for a story, and he doesn't seem to care who wrote it. The magazine has solid funding, and its initial, nonsubscription distribution was 30,000. The only catch, decried by many, is that for the $5,000, the story's author must sign away his rights to the story and its adaptation in all media, in perpetuity. Were the story to be optioned under normal arrangements—a film or TV producer somehow finds it, reads it, and contacts the author or agent to make an offer—each expiring option might bring $15,000 or even $20,000. Coppola, then, is getting the story on the cheap. This hitch, though, doesn't bother many story writers, who are clear-sighted enough to see that, first, the chances of a short story's being optioned under normal circumstances are that of a camel passing through the eye of a needle, and second, that the exposure provided by a film adaptation will more than pay off for other stories they will publish.

The problem is that writers who submit their work to *Zoetrope* are writing, as it were, for the small print, the disavowed purpose—that is, they are composing stories in terms of screenplays, planning epiphanies in terms of camera shots. The handiness of the short story turns it into a vehicle for content and does away with the aesthetics of the form itself. The results are, in some cases, unreadable. Take Melissa Banks's "The Worst Thing a Suburban Girl Could Imagine," in *Zoetrope*'s summer 1999 issue. The story begins with the promising if not entirely original line "My father knew he had leukemia for years before telling my brother and me." Banks is a fine writer, with a much-praised volume of stories under her belt. But after several pages, we suspect that we are not reading a story about a daughter's encounter with her dying father, or about the intersection of that plot with her glass-ceiling job, or another intersection with her May–September love affair. We are reading—in short takes, cuts, jumps of time, decontextualized dialogue—the précis of a novel, its reduction to a sort of pre-screenplay narrative form. The "story" goes on and on, filling some 35 pages of the magazine, but its length is not the disturbing factor; "The Death of Ivan Ilyich" is longer. Rather, as the protagonist tries to ingratiate herself with her boss, gets involved and reinvolved with a powerful older man, handles her dying father and complicated family, and takes her first, lonely steps into the solitude of adulthood, the reader hangs onto the narrative thread only by imagining, say, Winona Ryder in the part. This will make a good movie, you find yourself thinking. If it had been a novel, it would have had a shot at being a good novel; Banks has a way with characterization and the telling moment. Undoubtedly producers find the text as it appears in *Zoetrope* easier to read than a screenplay. But that statement is like saying cold corn mush is easier to eat than dried kernels. We are reading something usable, yes. But the reading of it gives no intrinsic satisfaction, and it is not a story.

One might argue that "The Worst Thing" is simply a bad story, the editorial choice to include it a bad editorial choice. I don't think so. Rather, whereas the story writer, like the poet, has heretofore had as his or her main business to make a story, Banks's very well-executed purpose has been to make material. And why should she not? She has been trained, as have so many of us, from an early age to understand the story form as being good for something else—for a painless introduction to literature, for a satisfying two-hour workshop, for advertising, for the movies. It has become almost impossible to retain the value of the short story as a unique, solitary, irreplaceable reading experience. And yet this is what we must do if we are to prevent the literary story from going the way of the verse epic or the public epistle.

What, then, can a story do, on its own, that none of the secondary purposes it so handily serves can offer? I have been pondering the question for some years and have several vague and probably refutable answers—but I shall offer one here, in the hope of keeping a finger in the dike. There is a kind of hunger created in the reading of a certain kind of story (and I should allow, lest I be accused of narrowing the field, that I have no strict definition for what constitutes a short story in terms of either length or style)—a hunger that cannot be satisfied by a profluent resolution but must have recourse to a different kind of information that only the characters within the story can provide. This hunger for the unknowable ingredient cannot be sustained over the course of a longer work like the novel, nor does it translate well to film, where the nonstop rush of images precludes our gnawing awareness of the thing we cannot see. At its best, this kind of story—which I'll call, without much relish for the cinematic connotations, a *flashback story*—performs a kind of high-wire artistic act that leaves us holding our breath. As a short-story writer, I aspire to this risky act of literary creation the way I imagine a dancer aspires to a triple grand jeté. Two examples I'll look at briefly here are James Joyce's "The Dead" and Charles D'Ambrosio's "The Point."

The recounting of a Dublin party and a moment of truth between man and wife afterward, "The Dead" is a masterpiece of setting and allusion, of course, and holds its rightful place as Joyce's greatest short story. It has been translated into film more than once. But neither the film versions nor any summary of the story can yield the emotional impact of the unforeseen punch that Gretta Conroy deals her husband. And yet without not only Gretta's confession but the supremacy of her voice at the end of the story, "The Dead" would be a collection of superbly spun and loosely woven threads.

Here are the seeds Joyce plants. At the beginning of the story, supercilious Gabriel Conroy is taken aback by his encounter with Lily, the maid at his aunts' party, who responds to his teasing question about marriage with "The men that is now is only all palaver and what they can get out of you," a line that not only causes Gabriel to blush but anticipates his own demeanor toward the end of the story. His wife Gretta, scarcely introduced, would, according to Gabriel, "walk home in the snow if she were let," suggesting a wildness and love of rough weather in which he does not share. Lily, says Gabriel's Aunt Kate, is "not the girl she was at all," as if some heartbreak has led to her cynicism. Later, during Gabriel's strained conversation with the radical Miss Ivors, we learn that Gretta is from the "primitive" west coast of Ireland ("Her people are" is all Gabriel will admit), and when the idea arises of visiting the west, Gretta leaps at it whereas Gabriel goes cold. In his much-anticipated dinner speech, Gabriel refers sentimentally to "sadder thoughts that will recur to our minds: thoughts of the past, of youth, of changes, of absent faces that we miss here tonight." Finally, perceiving his wife alone at the top of the stairs listening to "distant music," Gabriel comes close and hears the tenor Bartell D'Arcy singing an old Irish air about the death of a young.

Still, none of these moments appears to anticipate the epiphany of the story. Rather, we are caught up at once in the warmth of the party and Gabriel's insecurity, with Irish politics as a constant undercurrent. Whatever the resolution of the story, the first time we encounter it we do not expect it to turn to the intimate relation of husband and wife. Yet turn it does, with the suddenness of a whip, when Gretta, in response to her husband's lust in their hotel room, tells him about the boy Michael Furey, who died long ago for love of her. Not only did we not anticipate this information, we did not anticipate hearing anything from Gretta at all; and yet of course, by the time "a strange, friendly pity for her entered [Gabriel's] soul," the effect of the past on the new relation between man and wife has become the end-point of all the story's action ... and more.

If the twist of Gretta's confession in "The Dead" were the final resolution, we would have what's known in the trade as an O. Henry story, a surprising but fitting ending. Joyce goes further, however, leaving Gabriel alone after Gretta goes to sleep so that his thoughts may expand momentarily beyond the "distant music" of his own past to encompass the impossible snow "general all over Ireland" and the human mortality in which he shares. The fleeting insight he gains is not really reducible to words, and yet the form of the short story allows the juxtaposition of this particular narrative and this particular conjugal dialogue to make the same insight, or at least a glimmer of it, available to the reader. The experience of "The Dead" is the experience of what words can convey and what they cannot, and as such it is neither translatable into another medium nor useful as a springboard to that wordier form, the novel. It is wholly of a piece with the art of the short story.

Charles D'Ambrosio's elegiac "The Point" is a more contemporary example and one that relies on a different conveyance of words and silence. Here, the action of the story concerns a teenage boy's escorting a drunken friend of his mother's home along the beach from a party. From the start we know that Kurt's father, a Vietnam vet, has committed suicide; that the wild parties began before his death; and that his mother's continuation of them is in part an extended expression of her suicide as subtext. As a "seasoned veteran" of these drunken escortings locked in an extended encounter with a needy middle-aged woman, the virginal Kurt veers toward a classic albeit updated sexual coming-of-age story. Will they or won't they? We wonder; and when they don't, Kurt's lingering awareness of the woman's hand having brushed his crotch still serves as a rite of passage.

And then we get the letter.

Like Joyce, D'Ambrosio has woven unseen threads into the story. Kurt knows no bedtime stories—so what does he read at night? Twice he informs the reader that his father shot himself, and when the woman he's escorting claims that her boys would never forget her if she committed suicide, he observes, "That was certainly true, I thought, but I didn't want to get into it." The shrine Kurt's mother has made for his father, including his med-school diploma and a souvenir baseball, suggests that theirs was a marriage of mutual support and sympathy. But what D'Ambrosio does is riskier, more startling, and more specific to the short story than telling us that Kurt has squirreled away a letter his father wrote to his mother from Vietnam. He reprints the letter in its entirety, even though the letter makes no mention of suicide or of Kurt and is, as Kurt observes, not "about love and family and work" but just "about war." The letter recounts a raid on a village, during which a young soldier was killed horribly by a land mine despite Kurt's father's medical attentions. In the aftermath, Kurt's father expresses some concern for his own fair-mindedness and sanity—or anyone's sanity: "I think in this condition," he writes, "men open themselves up to attack." He addresses his wife as "sweetie," and tells her it's a comfort to write to her even as he hopes she will never have to "really understand."

In terms of war correspondence, the letter is almost ordinary—and it is that ordinariness, the warm, sane normalcy of relations and mutual respect between husband and wife, that redirects the story toward the aching damage sustained by Kurt's parents even before his father's suicide, in the superficiality and self-destruction of their post-Vietnam life on the Point. Without further direction from D'Ambrosio, we move way past Kurt's nascent sexuality to mourn a happy marriage killed by war.

And then—again, like Joyce—the story turns back to the narrator and to the larger theme that knits together both the action and the surprise information. "It was me who found Father, that morning," Kurt confesses. As if in a natural segue from the letter, he describes sex, or "just to go salmon fishing out by Hat Island and not worry about things, either way, but I also have to say, never again do I want to see anything like what I saw that morning." It is the awful burden of choosing and protecting life, the final passage implies, that separates Kurt from his mother and also accounts for his poignant "job" of rescuing her pathetic friends. What we owe the dead, the story suggests, is to disallow their claim on us.

This kind of turnabout and larger revelation is surely unique to the reading experience of the short story. I am speaking not simply of the time-honored "epiphany" that goes with the story form, but of the large ripples that its economical language, like a compressed pebble, can set off when tossed into an unexpected pond. Those ripples are what set stories like "The Dead" and "The Point" off, not only from other stories, but also from any other use to which their narratives might be put.

There is risk here. The hunger for the flashback may not be keen enough to propel a reader from the necessarily greater energy of the present action into the past scene or artifact. The gap between narrative and flashback may be too great to allow the crossover of meaning, or too narrow to make the buildup seem worthwhile. The larger metaphysical implications of the juxta-position—awareness of mortality in "The Dead," responsibility to choose life in "The Point"—may seem unwarranted, bloated, or sentimental. But even these risks are exciting, because they are specific to the form, to the challenges of the form and the claims the form can make as literature and art.

The type of story I've explored here is not the only one inimical to its own "usefulness" for other, more commercial purposes. Other writers can surely list other story patterns, other features unique to certain stories' openings or conclusions or use of leitmotif that make them as difficult and inalienable as any other perennial art form. What concerns me in the present climate is that writers accustomed to thinking of the story as a "junior" form or as "material" will not go to the lengths that Joyce and D'Ambrosio have gone to, because there is no payoff to those lengths except on the story's own ground.

Do I not, then, wish the writers and editors of *Zoetrope* well? Am I not pleased when an acclaimed short story is adapted to a lucrative film? Or when a collection of linked stories is adjusted and edited and marketed as a novel and so garners readership and rewards? Can't I see the writing on the wall, smell the coffee?

Well, of course I can, and I do. And perhaps the safest thing to say to such editors and the writers who tailor work for them is, Godspeed, and quickly too. Whatever its worldly reward, the true short story, like Dylan Thomas's "sullen art," is written "for the lovers," for "the common wages / Of their most secret heart." The faster and farther its useful variants travel from the deep well of satisfaction that the story itself provides, the more apt we all are to recognize and return to that well. And even a film producer or two, if they be thirsting, may stop there on their way to the next idea, to refresh no one but themselves.

WORKS CITED

Banks, Melissa. "The Worst Thing a Suburban Girl Could Imagine." *Zoetrope* 3 (summer 1999): 1–22.

Coppola, Francis Ford. "Letter to the Reader." *Zoetrope* 1 (Feb. 1997). <http://www.all-story.com/about.cgi?page=letter>.

D'Ambrosio, Charles. "The Point." *The Point.* London: London Flamingo, 1997. 21–62.

Joyce, James. "The Dead." *The Dead: Case Studies in Contemporary Criticism.* Ed. Daniel R. Schwarz. Boston: St. Martin's, 1994. 21–62

Tolstoy, Leo. "The Death of Ivan Ilyich." *Great Short Works of Leo Tolstoy.* New York: Harper & Row, 1967. 245–302.

4

Culture and the Short-Story Form

Making the Invisible Visible

Marion Bloem

Translated from the Dutch by Wanda Boeke.

"We're in a P.O.W. camp. My friend, a Moluccan guy, is able to make himself invisible to the guards. At night he secretly visits his wife and children. Others also want to visit their wives and come to him for help. He makes sure that they, too, are able to leave the camp without being seen. That night the Japs get us out of bed. Roll-call. He counts, *adu* ... seven are missing.

"The next day all seven have to stand before the firing squad. The Japs shoot. All dead.

"Except my Moluccan friend, he remains standing. Again they aim. They fire. But you can see the bullets veer off. *Betul.* They can't hit him. The Japs get angry. One cries, 'OK, not you, but instead of you, 50 others!'

"My commanding officer says, '*Kasihan*, though, innocent people will have to go in your stead.'

"That Moluccan, a good guy, a friend of mine, says to the Japs, 'OK, give me a glass of water. But I'm doing it for my comrades, not for you.'"

My father pulled an imaginary glass out of the air, looked inside it, sniffed, and drank it down, gulp, gulp, gulp ... empty. He wiped his mouth, proudly tossed back his head, and said, "Go ahead. Shoot."

I grew up with a father, uncles, and a grandfather and grandmother who were good at storytelling. The stories they told, even if they remained true to their experiences down to the last detail, were like fairy tales to me. They used words that were for me sometimes no more than sounds and that did not refer to objects that I knew from daily life.

These stories, which also happened to be conspicuously magical, concerning mysterious and inexplicable events, were situated in a country I did not know. Born in the Netherlands, I was only familiar with their albums of black-and-white photographs. Everything they told me stimulated my fantasy.

My parents were born in the Dutch East Indies, one of the overseas colonies belonging to the Netherlands. My mother had spent the Second World War in a Japanese camp for civilians on the island of Java and my father, a member of the Royal Dutch East Indies Army, had been in a prisoner-of-war camp and worked on the Railroad of the Dead on the island of Sumatra. They were 2 among 300,000 Dutch East Indians, or Indisch Dutch, who, after the independence of Indonesia—a colony of the Netherlands for centuries—chose to maintain their Dutch citizenship, instead of becoming Indonesian, and who moved to the Netherlands in 1950.

Due to my Asian as well as European background, I looked different from others my age. Until 1945, despite its mercantile spirit that caused all kinds of areas of the world to be visited and countless colonies to be taken over, the Netherlands was a white country with an almost exclusively Caucasian population. After the Second World War this situation changed somewhat.

Although the administration did its best to convince the Indisch Dutch that it was better for them to stay in Indonesia, the country of their mothers and grandmothers, these mixed-bloods did not feel safe there. The dark-skinned Indisch Dutch men, usually called Indos, had almost all fought in the Dutch colonial army. They were therefore hated by the Indonesian freedom fighters. Right after the Japanese capitulated, Sukarno called for the independence of Indonesia and called the Indos "the dogs of the Dutch."

In many respects the Indos looked like Indonesians, but the group distinguished itself more from the Indonesians than from the white colonials particularly on the social and cultural levels. They were not Islamic but Christian. The requirement in order to be recognized by a European father and thereby acquire Indisch Dutch citizenship was being baptized. From that moment on, the Islamic mother also lost all rights to take care of her own (Christian) children. Marriages between Christians and Muslims were prohibited, and marriages between Indonesians—Christian or non-Christian—and Europeans were allowed only around 1900.

Thus I know that my Polish great-grandfather officially recognized the children he had produced with his Indonesian maid only when he wanted to send them to school, because they could only receive European-oriented education if they were baptized and recognized, and only as such did they have any opportunity in the tough caste system of the colony.

Alongside the small group of white colonials in the Dutch East Indies, often referred to as "the Emerald Girdle," a group of mixed-bloods arose who had their own culture and their own evolution within that diverse colonial society. In addition to the many different Indonesian ethnicities—including the Moluccans, who were Christian and had been put into action in the colonial army in order to fight the rebellious Islamic people of the province of Atyeh—there were also Arabs and Chinese, the merchants of the colony, living there.

The popular language was a language of trade, Pasar Malay, on which the current Indonesian language, Bahasa Indonesia, is based. Pasar Malay was a language with a simple grammar using only the present tense, where the subject was often left unspoken and where onomatopoeia lent extra emphasis to what was said.

You could split Indos into roughly three groups. First of all, there were the Indos who were born in the barracks as the children of soldiers. Then you had the Indos who were born in the *kampongs,* the result of many secret visits by the colonial gentlemen. The third group consisted of Indos produced by marriages between the European, Arab, Chinese, and native rulers and marriages between colonials and Indos. Indo children usually married one another and formed their own community. Both of my paternal grandparents as well as my maternal grandfather come from this group.

The status of an Indo depended completely on color and education. The colonial society was a racial society, where class difference correlated strongly with racial difference. Many Indo children ended up in orphanages, residences that often closely resembled merciless training camps for obedient soldiers in the colonial army. And I can easily imagine that the sleeping ward was a hotbed for Indo stories.

The colonials were embarrassed by the existence of the Indos because they were seen as living proof of Calvinists who had committed sins.

This is why, despite the fact that the number of Indos far outnumbered the white colonials, there is little to be found about them in Dutch East Indies literature. The little that was written about them at that time was based on stereotypes. The men were gamblers, the women prostitutes. At that time their existence was usually denied in print. Indos were divided up according to their color. With a light skin color they had a chance at a reasonable job in the government sector; with darker skin they could really only enter the colonial army. Dark girls, in contrast to their by-happenstance whiter sisters, were given housekeeping duties and tasks in the kitchen starting at an early age, because they probably wouldn't be able to find husbands who could afford help.

The white colonials lived in large homes on the paved main streets. Behind these lay the homes of the rich Arabs, Chinese, and Indos, not always on paved roads, and behind these again, haphazardly, with narrow paths between the bamboo houses, lay the *kampong,* the native village. The closer you lived to the *kampong,* the more you were looked down on. As a result, Indos were often ashamed of their native mothers and acted as if she were some aunt or servant. Colonial society was one of divisiveness and shame.

In my opinion, my opening story is one of the many tales from my father's and uncles' lips that sprang from the need to be proud of their heritage, in spite of their subordinate position in the army and in spite of their humiliating repression by the Japanese. It is striking that the most important thing that comes out in these stories is magic. Their Asiatic origins provided them with the capacity to deal with that magic, whereas it filled the white colonials with nothing but fear.

In the army, Moluccans ranked lower—received lower pay—than Indos. The Indos ascribed supernatural powers to the Moluccans, feared their communal power and the mutual solidarity of the Moluccans, and at the same time secretly admired them. The divide-and-conquer policy of the colonials made it possible to pit the Indos and the Moluccans against one another, both inside as well as outside the army. By explicitly labeling a Moluccan as his friend, my father broke through the divide-and-conquer administrational policy of the colonials with his typical Indo story and, in this particular story, the power of the Japanese as well. He participated, as it were, in the strength that the Indos keenly admired in the Moluccans.

As a child I liked to do nothing as much as write. For me, writing was the equivalent of fantasizing. Reality fascinated me less than my own imagination. At school, writing essays about spring, fall, winter, or summer were the most obvious assignments. In spite of the realistic nature of compulsory assignments, I managed to give my stories a certain kind of twist so that reality no longer mattered.

When they discovered my passion for the written word at school, I was allowed to take old reading books home with me, books that hadn't been used for years because they still had the old spelling. These schoolbooks were bursting with stories about Catholic saints—short stories that were all structured around the appearance of a saint to some poor, disconsolate, lonely soul. They stimulated my fantasy just as much as the stories my grandfather, grandmother, father, and other family members used to tell.

Around my cousins I was allowed to tell stories endlessly. Nobody would say a word; they would stare at me, even the older boys, and by their faces I could tell how they were surrendering to my imagination. What I liked best was pretending that I had been the one to experience it all, the way my father always told us stories. My sister and younger brothers, my cousins and second cousins would hang on my every word.

I wasn't supposed to tell stories as if they had really happened, or present them as stories of what my father had been through, or else they would label me and my family fit to be committed. During recess, even if it were raining and we were doomed to spend recess inside the classroom, there was no need for me to open my mouth. They had their own chatter and I didn't belong. During class, however, if I passed a piece of paper with my fictions to the girl sitting next to me, it would eagerly be passed around the classroom, with no competition whatsoever coming from the teacher, who was explaining long division.

Initially my essays were strongly influenced by my background and the stories in my family. Also, the characters in my stories were exactly like the people in my family, or my parents' Indisch Dutch acquaintances. This changed later on. In the tender beginnings of my writing career, my Indo background and the Dutch world were pretty harmoniously integrated into my stories.

At the age of six, I wrote a short story that exemplified how belonging to two cultures was at that time already being expressed in my fictions. In this relatively realistic story, I am already quite clearly conscious of the fact that I belong to two cultures that don't always understand each other very well. I also knew about the existence of the common belief that Indisch Dutch people were supposed to be more hospitable than the Dutch themselves. Indos prided themselves on their hospitality. Everybody, even the mailman who rang the doorbell to deliver a package, as well as the police officer who warned of excess noise, having come at the neighbors' request to say that the stereo had to be turned down, would be invited to come have a bite to eat, or would at least get an exotic little snack, like *lemper* or *bapu*, pushed into his hands. Indos disdained the stingy Dutch, who let you leave without anything to eat and who shut the cookie tin after they presented the cookies once. There were all kinds of stereotypes with which I grew up, both the clichés Indos projected onto the Dutch as well as the other way around. I heard them both and had to weigh for myself to what extent reality correlated with them.

The very first little story that I committed to paper as a six-year-old and tossed into the neighbors' mailbox—in other words, my first bibliophilic, self-illustrated publication—exhibits that colorful element in our Indo use of language and provides an insight into the manner in which stories came about for me at that time, and still do now.

Auntie Nonny is home alone.
   A thief sneaks in through the window.
   "Your money or your life," says the thief.
   He has a gun.
   Auntie Nonny says, "You can have all my money! But don't you want some coffee
tubruk?"
   "Tubruk? What's that?" asks the thief.
   "That's Indisch coffee," explains Auntie Nonny.
   He feels like having some.
   She gives him a big mug of coffee.
   The thief raises the mug *rakus* [greedily] to his lips with both hands.
   Auntie Nonny asks, "Do you want ompong?"
   The thief is happy.
   How kind this lady is, he thinks. She's probably talking about an Indisch snack.
   "Yes, please," says the stupid thief.
   Auntie Nonny hauls out with her fist.
   The thief has no teeth left in his mouth and lies knocked out on the floor.

In order to be able to evaluate this story, the reader would need to be
familiar with the stereotypes of generous Indos and eager, greedy Dutch. The
reader would also need to be cognizant of the spoken custom among Indos
of mixing Malay words in with their Dutch. In this story, which I wrote in
all my six-year-old innocence, I moreover assume another stereotype, of the
stoical Asian who smiles, but might be hiding another emotion behind that
smile, and the straightforward Dutch person who gets straight to the point,
but who, because of greed, is easily taken in.
   An Indo would have to smile at this story, but a Dutch person, if I didn't
obviously ridicule our so-called hospitality and the other stereotypes, would
at most laugh like a farmer with a toothache.
   The first literary story of mine that was published in a magazine was about
a white girl. I was 15 when I wrote it. My Dutch teacher insisted that I send
the story to a literary magazine, but I didn't know the ropes and sent it to a
glossy monthly magazine with a literary page. I was 16 when I saw it in print
and received my first honorarium for a story. Filled with pride, I looked at the
illustration of the protagonist, who didn't bear even the slightest resemblance
to me. I was used to ridding my stories of my Indo background. It happened
seemingly automatically; it became second nature. Only when I was asked
to write stories for the children of Turkish and Moroccan migrants when I
was in college, something changed for me. In my need to transplant myself
into their world of experience, I remembered the attempts I had made in my
childhood to erase from my stories all traces of being Indo. Listening to the

parents of these children, curious about what interested them and what they would like to read about, I recalled my father's, my uncles', my grandfather's and grandmother's stories.

Aside from the stories for foreign children, I began like one possessed writing stories whose protagonists were Indos, as if it were some kind of catching up process. And in these stories I sometimes incorporated the often-mythical stories I had heard as a child. I became aware that many stories would remain incomprehensible to others besides Indos, or one-dimensional if readers weren't familiar with a few archetypes or at least familiar with the situation of the Indos in the colonial past. So the stories required being embedded in another framework that would give the non-Indo a chance to understand all the meanings behind the words.

The direction in the oral tales was essentially different from those of the short stories that belonged to Dutch literature. My grandma's stories never had a punch line, but ended in an almost questioning way. They were stories of amazement at her past. As if she still didn't understand much of the injustice with which she dealt day in day out.

My grandpa's stories were descriptions of his feeling of powerlessness in a world of black magic and his attempt to protect his beautiful daughters from an evil society. The stories always had happy endings where Indonesian magicians (*dukuns*) would help him out of some predicament. These stories exhibited a great respect particularly for the involvement with magic in Indonesian culture.

My father and uncles, the really masterful storytellers, told tales of soldiers that sketch the position of the Indo in society, and whose function seemed to be to teach Indos, in spite of such stories, how to live with their complicated position in between two worlds.

One critical story is the story about the crocodiles. Indos were also made out to be *buaya*, or crocodiles, and this is why this story has extra meaning for me.

Belanda was the Indonesian word for the full-blooded Dutch. The word supposedly derived from the Dutch words *blanke* (white) and *Hollander* (Dutch) and was used by natives as well as by Indos. My parents had forbidden me to use the word *Belanda,* but once the adults got to telling stories, they would make use of the term.

"It is war," said my uncle:

War of the Indonesians against us Dutch.

We are Indisch, and serving in the Royal Dutch East Indies Army. We are fighting for the queen.

We have been stationed in a little village.

On leave. Everybody can do what they want.

I always stay with a friend.

Some Dutch soldiers, real Belandas, they know for nothing after all, go out boating. One of those little rowboats.

Maybe they want to go fishing.

I don't know.

In any case, our leave is over, and they don't come back.

We have to look. Everywhere.

Another Dutch soldier knows that they went out on the water in a little boat.

Our commanding officer thinks that the Indonesians from the village have maybe picked up the two men, or killed them. So house searches.

And of course the officer is angry.

He waits for two days. No news.

Then he says, "Take 20 men prisoner!"

Twenty Indonesians we have to put in the lockup.

But first they have to stand in a row. In line.

All the inhabitants of the *kampong* have to watch.

He just went and took those men, young boys, too, though, out of the houses.

"If my two Dutch soldiers aren't found, then all 20 men are dead."

Yes, that's what he says.

The *kampong* is afraid, of course. *Kasihan.*

Innocent, in fact, these 20 men. But that's what reprisal is. It's always like that, in war.

The inhabitants of the *kampung* come to me.

They always come to me if something's going on.

They say, "*Adu, bapa....*" They're always calling me *bapa....*

"You have to help us, those Belandas weren't killed by us, they went out in a little boat. The boat was found. Crocodiles did it, after all, not us."

I talk with the commanding officer.

He says, "Then I give them 12 hours to prove that the crocodiles did it."

But how are you supposed to prove that, eh?

Those people from the *kampong* come to me. They are nice.

They give me rice, sugar, mangoes.

Not bad people, you know, they know that officer is angry.

They say, "There is somebody who can talk with crocodiles."

"Okay, bring him here," I say. "Maybe then I can talk with the officer."

They have to get this man from far away.

But the officer does not want to grant any more hours.

If they're not found after 12 hours, those Belandas, all 20 Indonesians will be shot dead.

So I help them with my Jeep. I know I'll be punished later, but I don't care.

We get the *dukun,* you know, the man who can talk with crocodiles. *Dukun* is what we call this kind of man. He walks barefoot.

In the Jeep he's chewing *sirih.* Red crap. That junk is bad for your teeth, you know. Many there chew the stuff, though.

We all follow him to the water.

The whole *kampong* and us, all the soldiers and our commanding officer, are standing there.

But the *dukun* won't let us get too close.

Those crocodiles get scared, you see.

He stands there. All dressed in white, he is.

He has changed his clothes, washed, doesn't have his usual *kain* on anymore like in the Jeep with me, no, white, he's all in white.

Betul, I see him standing there.

I am allowed to come close, because I can be trusted, you see.

I stand right behind him, not as far away as the rest.

He calls the crocodile. The chief of the crocodile he calls. Just like this, calling.

First he mumbles something, Lord knows what, and then he just talks with him.

You wouldn't believe it, but this crocodile comes up to the surface of the water and swims towards him. Looks at him, like this, very calmly.

You can see him coming towards the shore, that crocodile, very calmly.

He swims over to the *dukun* and the *dukun* asks, "Where are the Belandas?"

Then the crocodile goes underwater again. We have to wait a moment.

Not long. You know, don't you, that when a crocodile kills somebody, he doesn't eat him right away. He waits three, four days. He hides his prey.

And here comes the crocodile. One by one he brings the two Belandas up to the surface and lays them on the shore.

By immersing myself more thoroughly in the oral storytelling art of my Indo heritage, my stories changed. I want to write about what is unspoken in the dominant society. The function of oral Indo tales was for people to give one another the strength to be able to be proud, despite the fact that they felt themselves forced into a position of shame.

With my stories I attempt the make the invisible visible. I feel the need to surprise, and also have a need to lend the migrant, the forced traveler, the person without a home, a feeling of self-worth through my stories. In my stories I call attention to the need, through humor, relativizing, and exaggeration, to bring misunderstandings to light. Something I was already starting to do tentatively when I was six.

My Sister—The Short Story

Karen King-Aribisala

As a woman, as a black woman writer of the African diaspora, I consider the Short Story a dear sister; one with whom I can empathize, share thoughts, and through her and with her revolutionize and transform not only my situation but those of others similarly defined in terms of a supposedly derogatory physicality.

There is no need here to relate that peculiar angst of racial and gender oppression to which the black diasporan female is often subjected—given her historical legacy of slavery, colonialism, and neocolonialism in many areas of the world. Suffice it to say that the worth of the black female of the diaspora is more than often not determined by her physicality, and that her sister the Short Story shares the same dilemma. When placed alongside her other generic relatives, such as the Novel, Drama, or Poetry, the Short Story is deemed inferior, simply because she is short; which is surely an injustice when one considers that one of her sisters, Poetry, as a genre, is usually shorter than the Short Story; but this particular poetry-sister (or possibly brother) is not seen as a kind of apology, as an excuse for being short. Her inherent poetic value as a genre is not questioned. No one, so to speak, feels the compunction to argue her poetic case, or indeed, justice; she has an unquestioned right to "poetryness." Not so her short sister, the Short Story.

It is interesting to note that in the United States short people prefer to perceive of themselves as being "vertically challenged" as opposed to "short," the latter definition containing within it a sense of importance, meaning, "combative" worth, and defiance of presumed inferior status.

Vertically challenged as we are and very conscious of our limits and limitations, the Short Story and I use ourselves and perceive of ourselves as weapons of liberation and of survival. Taking our cue from both literary and human ancestors, we speak to save our lives, and in this we salute Scheherazade of *The Arabian Nights,* who, cognizant of the murdering intent of her husband, the king—a man who had killed his previous wives because he was bored with them—proceeds to tell the short stories that save her life and perhaps his. She utilizes suspense—a key trait of ours—and exercises a keen sense of judgment in the relation of her tales, including only enough material to enable her to drive her points home, controlling him thereby with her words. Like my sister, the Short Story, she employs symbols, imagery rich in its explosion and implosion of meaning, which reverberates long after the story had been read and heard.

Heard and listened to because the Short Story's voice is grounded in the Oral Tradition that even in this so-called modern age of ours it continues to resonate in conferences, on the television, the video, and the radio. My sister, the Short Story, being essentially oral, has the capacity through tone, rhythm, and voice, to liberate not only the teller of the tale, but her audience, and to persuade others to her own point of view——and quickly too.

Grounded as she is in the Oral Tradition, the Short Story harks back to the very source of creativity, of spirituality of human kind when the world was created by God's voice and words in just seven days. Later, after the Fall of Man when Adam and Eve of the Bible were expelled from the Garden of Eden, the Word made flesh was sent to us in Jesus Christ that mankind might be reconciled with God. And Jesus Christ utilized the vehicle of short stories to proclaim His message and thereby gives to us the choice to save our lives and other lives. As such, the Short Story provides selected food for the soul and the spirit of man and links us with our spiritual side.

In our numerous discussions, she has told me that each person is in fact a short story with a beginning, a middle life, and an end or death; but there is a continuance after that death in that there is an afterlife, or if you will, a further reverberation of the lives that we live, all constituting a collection of short stories in the Book of Life.

You see, my sister the Short Story recognizes that there is a generational continuity in the life of man, that ours is an oral source and legacy on which we can build in a number of connective units of several short stories that can be read either singly or as a collective entity. It is the Short Story that early man told around their fires after the day's work, and it is the Short Story that nurtures the children on the values and principles that should be adhered to for the efficient running and guidance of a society.

And yes, the Short Story, this sister of mine, is efficient, a quality that is reflected in her perfect figure. Like any of her other genre relatives, she proves a specific premise within the created world of a setting or situation. Unlike her relatives (say, the Novel), she has an inherent purity of line and structure in that she utilizes the minimum number of characters and/or situations, honing them to a fine edge, a polished gem that makes a complete statement—startling sometimes with aggression, sometimes with a calm quietude, but always with strength. Indeed, I have often expressed admiration for my sister Short Story's body consciousness, of the "truth of limitation." The truth is that each and every one of us has limits. If you cut your finger it will bleed. The trick is to know how to work, exist, survive, within these limits. So I appreciate my sister for revealing this to me, for showing me that I can create and overcome those limits to such an extent that new freedoms are realized. Limits force the friends of the Short Story to create with precise deliberation, new freedoms.

Perhaps because at her best the Short Story is spiritual, she, more than any of her genre relatives, encourages flights of fancy, of the imagination, which her aforesaid genre relatives would be hard put to render in as convincing a manner as she does.

There is so much more I can write about my dear Short Story sister—that's one of her invaluable assets, that she makes you think and reflect and ponder and rethink again. She has a big powerful *RE* in her. Rebirth, reclaim, revolution—resurrecting power in her. I don't think anyone would mind if I reaffirm her greatest gift to me. "Acknowledge," she says. "Acknowledge the limitations of life, the confining prisons of gender, race, anything that imprisons you, that makes you enslaved, but work within those limits with imagination and boldness and the fear of God and you will see my little Short Story seed will transform; reconnect you with a mighty force; empower you; save lives—your own and others; make of you a genre, a species to be reckoned with." With this—do you wonder that she is my favorite sister?

WORK CITED

Haddaway, Husain, and Muhsin Mahdi Haddaway, eds. *The Arabian Nights*. Boston: Brill Academic, 1995.

Giacometti's Foot and Proust's Madeleine: The Short Story of Desire

Janette Turner Hospital

Years ago, in some magazine (I can't remember which, but it would certainly not have been a sports magazine), I read an article that fascinated me, and which now seems to me relevant to the hazardous attempt of a writer to talk about her craft. Here is the gist of the article, refashioned, no doubt, and embroidered a little, by the cunning unreliability of recall.

A young American pole-vaulter had just won a gold medal at the Olympics. A Soviet athlete, one of his competitors, asked him a question: how many steps did he take between the starting line and that moment when he lofted himself into the air? The American was baffled. He had no idea. He did not count his steps. He leaped at precisely that moment that his body told him was the right moment.

Some time later, the Soviet athlete passed on classified and volatile information: eastern-bloc coaches had analyzed multiple tapes of Olympic trials and performances. The American medal-winner took exactly the same number of steps every single time—let's say, 43—never more, never fewer. This was deemed ideal by the analysts of peak performance. The Soviet athletes were subsequently drilled in a 43-step routine until it become natural to them, until it became a bodily instinct, until they no longer needed to count. Their pole-vaulting records were measurably improved.

Of course, if I were fashioning this account into a short story, the American would be the protagonist. At his next international meet, self-conscious, aware of the video cameras and counters, aware of his body as template, he

would be unable to *unknow*, unable to ward off the sense of his body as met-
ronome, of his feet as integers, of numbers thudding along his nerve paths
to his brain. (*Every single time? And have I always? But what would happen if
I...?*) He would no longer be able to perform instinctually. All too conscious
of the magic formula, he would miss a half-beat, he would stumble....

That is where the story would end.

Caveat lector.

Caveat *scriptor*, for that matter.

It seems relevant, also, to cite at this point another artist trying to talk
about his art: the painter Georges Braque speaking of his canvases.

The only valid thing in art is that which one cannot explain.... In my own work
there are mysteries and secrets which even I do not understand, nor even do I try. The
more one probes the situation, the more infinite the mystery: it constantly escapes.
If mysteries are to preserve their power, they must be respected. Art is to disturb: sci-
ence is to reassure. If there is no mystery, there is no poetry, the quality which I hold
highest in art. (13)

If there is no mystery, I will attempt to show, there is no short story.

I write both novels and short stories, and I am addicted to the creation of
both forms. The latter is not a condensed version of the former, and is never
a draft or a trial run for a novel. They are two distinct genres, as unmistak-
ably different from one another as painting is from sculpture, as poetry from
prose—though, occasionally, perfect short stories can be found embedded
within novels, much as a sculpted image may be incorporated within a painting or a lyric poem within an epic cycle (for example, the song of Wealhtheow
within *Beowulf*), or indeed within a novel (the poems in A. S. Byatt's *Possession* and Carol Shields's *Swann* come to mind). There is a genetic narrative
link between novel and short story, but the forms are distinct in ways more
absolute than the simple issue of length. For me, the difference begins with
the very nature of the initial impact.

Impact.

I have to use that term, since all my created works, both novels and short
stories, first announce themselves like a hurled baseball on the side of the
head; no, that is less than ideal as a metaphor, since it captures only the force
and the suddenness of the sensation, but not the excitement, the pleasure,
the moment of desire. Something strikes and burns the way love does. I am
seduced. The shadow of a shape is conceived. From that moment of fertiliza-
tion, through the delicious turmoil of gestation, to the labor and the birth,

there is no point at which I would ask myself: Will this thing be born as a short story or a novel? The glowing smudge, in its uncreated state, arrives as one or the other, just as surely as the future child's gender is fixed from the instant of the collision of ovum and sperm.

For me, the novel arrives as a riddle, urgent and compelling. It seems unanswerable, but demands an answer. The riddle obsesses me. It inhabits me. Its grappling hooks lodge themselves in my thoughts and dreams. I will not be free until I have embarked on the voyage toward the answer—that is, the writing of the novel—a journey that I know will take from three to four years. Though my response involves intense emotion, I would say that the primary nature of the enterprise is cognitive and analytical and teleological. My search will rarely be linear, but it does have a goal. I am heading for an answer. I may never find it, but I will eventually reach a point of repose when I have exhaustively explicated the question and have established, perhaps, that there *is* no single answer; in which case I will write until I am able to posit several, possibly contradictory, ones. For me, the novel begins in *not knowing,* and the writing of it proceeds from *having to know.*

The short story, on the other hand, *begins in knowing,* in radiant apprehension, in revelation, in a heightened sense of having gone direct to the core of some experience. *This is the essence of loss,* one knows instantly, overhearing a stray comment, or seeing a face in a window. It is loss before the terms and conditions of loss take on a particular configuration and before loss has words to express or define itself. Or it might be the essence of confusion that one apprehends, or of anxiety, or of the simultaneous awareness of the sharp little nick of desire and of panic.

(*Oh, where will this lead?* the eyes of that woman are asking. She is a total stranger, two feet away at a cocktail party, accepting a glass of wine from a man who leans over her. The man has his back to the watcher. Neither the woman, nor the watcher, can read the expression on his face. A fog comes off the woman, visible to the watcher. The fog is highly charged with both sexual excitation and the fear of humiliation. *Where will this end?* ask the woman's eyes, flecked with caution and recklessness. The woman and the watcher, like Yeats's Leda, see everything instantly: the beating swan-wings, the hot sheets, the exaltation, the fall of Troy, the wrecked marriages, the desolation. *Is this worth the risk?* the woman's eyes ask. *Yes. No. Yes. Is this euphoria or despair?*)

Or perhaps what one suddenly knows, as though one were a god, is the essence of something ineffable, something one is unable to name. One is seized by the desire to hold onto this intense and godlike perception, but it has no fixed shape. There are no words for it yet. It is like catching a handful of light. What net can it be kept in? One wants to be able to pin it down, to keep it and look at it again. One wants to be able to show it to others: see how poignant, how profound this is! *O, what a piece of work is man … !*

The moment of revelation itself is the object of desire, obscure, diffuse and unstable as light-and-shadow beneath leaves, and this moment seeks an incarnation in words: as lyric for the poet, as short story for the writer of prose fiction.

Let me try to describe the process of incarnation by way of reference to Giacometti's foot and Proust's "petite madeleine."

In his biography of the sculptor Alberto Giacometti, James Lord recounts a curious and revelatory incident from the young Italian artist's early years at the Geneva School of Fine Arts. Students were set the task of drawing the human figure from a live model, the curvaceous and naked Loulou. Giacometti worked obsessively. He did sketch after sketch, angle after angle, consumed with intensity. To the bewilderment and chagrin of his professor, however, every single sketch was a more and more detailed study of Loulou's foot. He never got higher than her ankle.

But what a sensual foot!

For Giacometti, this incident suggests, the essence of Loulou's sexuality was condensed and contained within her foot: in its perfection, in its arched tendon, in the provocative way it pointed and suggested invitation. If he could manage to draw what he perceived in that white-hot moment, the foot, obscure object of desire, would reveal all.

The short story works comparably in its sharp focus and density.

The moment of a mystery incarnating itself in words has never been more exquisitely described than by Proust in his overture to the long journey into the recovery of lost memories and lost times. I would argue that his tale of dipping the madeleine into lime-blossom tea is a perfect short story embedded into one of the longest novels ever written, one of many lyric Proustian moments in an epic. (If this possibly controversial assertion sends short-story theorists back to the overture to *Swann's Way,* I shall be well pleased.) It is, perhaps, a view of the short story as quasi-religious mystery. Marcel-the-narrator lures us in to the state of heightened esoteric awareness:

I feel that there is much to be said for the Celtic belief that the souls of those whom we have lost are held captive in some inferior being, in an animal, in a plant, in some inanimate object, and thus effectively lost to us until the day (which to many never comes) when we happen to pass by the tree or to obtain possession of the object which forms their prison. Then they start and tremble, they call us by our name, and as soon as we have recognised their voice the spell is broken. Delivered by us, they have overcome death and return to share our life.

And so it is with our own past. It is a labour in vain to attempt to recapture it: all the efforts of our intellect must prove futile. The past is hidden somewhere outside the realm, beyond the reach of intellect, in some material object.... And it depends on chance whether or not we come upon this object before we ourselves must die.

Many years had elapsed during which nothing of Combray ... had any existence for me, when one day in winter, on my return home, my mother, seeing that I was cold, offered me some tea, a thing I did not ordinarily take. I declined at first, and then, for no particular reason, changed my mind. She sent for one of those squat, plump little cakes called "petites madeleines," which look as though they had been moulded in the fluted valve of a scallop shell. And soon, mechanically, dispirited after a dreary day with the prospect of a depressing morrow, I raised to my lips a spoonful of the tea in which I had soaked a morsel of the cake. No sooner had the warm liquid mixed the crumbs touched my palate than a shudder ran through me and I stopped, intent upon the extraordinary thing that was happening to me. An exquisite pleasure had invaded my senses, something isolated, detached, with no suggestion of its origin. And at once the vicissitudes of life had become indifferent to me, its disasters innocuous, its brevity illusory—this new sensation having had on me the effect which love has of filling me with a precious essence; or rather this essence was not in me, it *was* me. I had ceased now to feel mediocre, contingent, mortal. Whence could it have come to me, this all-powerful joy? I sensed that it was connected with the taste of the tea and the cake, but that it infinitely transcended those savours, could not, indeed, be of the same nature. Whence did it come? What did it mean? How could I seize and apprehend it? (47–48)

The story proceeds with an account of the arduous process of apprehension, and then the revelation incarnates itself in words:

Ten times over I must essay the task, must lean down over the abyss....

And suddenly the memory revealed itself. The taste was that of the little piece of madeleine which on Sunday mornings at Combray ... when I went to say good morning to her in her bedroom, my aunt Léonie used to give me, dipping it first in her own cup of tea or tisane....

And as soon as I had recognised the taste of the piece of madeleine soaked in her decoction of lime-blossom ... *(although I did not yet know and must long postpone the discovery of why this memory made me so happy)* immediately the old grey house upon the street, where her room was, rose up like a stage ... [and] all the flowers in our garden and in M. Swann's park ... and the whole of Combray and its surroundings ... sprang into being ... from my cup of tea. (50–51; italics mine)

That is where the short story ends and the novel begins. Proust's "Overture" is the incarnation of a revelation. The novel that follows it, as the parenthesis I have italicized indicates, is the long journey undertaken to answer a riddle, a reconstruction as much cognitive as emotional. But the madeleine ("so richly sensual under its severe, religious folds") on Proust's tongue, and Loulou's foot in the eyes of Giacometti, are obscure and elusive objects of desire. The search for a distilled form to incarnate them, first for the self, and only secondarily for others, is allied to ritual and magic.

"The potion is losing its magic," Proust despairs after a third mouthful of lime-blossom tea has given neither name nor form to the exaltation, and has in fact diminished the intensity of the "extraordinary thing." He resorts to atavistic ritual. He is not certain that the task of finding words and narrative shape for this inchoate knowledge is possible.

Often it is not.

There are short stories still unborn that have lived, entire and glowing, for years inside my head. I may never find the form or the words to write them. Once a story does begin to take on narrative shape, I spend much more time on it, per page, than I do on a novel. I am not sure that my novel-writing self and my short-story-writing self even know each other.

When I am writing a short story, I am in it for the magic.

WORKS CITED

Braque, George. *Illustrated Notebooks: 1917–1955.* Trans. Stanley Applebaum. New York: Dover, 1971.

Lord, James. *Giacometti: A Biography.* New York: Farrar, Straus, & Giroux, 1985.

Proust, Marcel. *Swann's Way.* Ed. C. K. Moncrieff and Terence Kilmartin. New York: Vintage Books, 1982. Vol. 1 of *A la Recherche Du Temps Perdu.*

5

The Short Story and Politics

Writing Tough—Staying Honest: Challenges for a Writer in Singapore

Kirpal Singh

Writing is never easy. I mean real, good, honest writing. Writing that lives. Writing that gives a new dimension to the way we breathe, look, see, view the world. And ourselves. Through the ages men and women have written about their agonies in wanting to write the great poem, story, book, play, and all of these provide valuable lessons for the new seeker of these elusive glories. What follows is a personal narrative, a narrative that many of my fellow Singaporeans will not tend to agree with, but a narrative worth recording, if only because it illuminates, I think, one fundamental dimension of the Singaporean literary experience.

Singapore is a tiny island nation, so tiny that on most world maps it tends not to be too visible. Once, in an angry response, a former president of Indonesia (a republic of over 7,000 islands with more than 360 million people!) referred to Singapore as "that irritating red dot!" So, what does living in a dot-like environment portend for writers? Well, I am not sure what it portends for other writers (and there are at least four major recognized languages in which Singaporean writers write!—English, Malay, Chinese, and Tamil), but for me—lots.

Living in a small place, I am told, often breeds small minds. This is where even gossip kills. A small place invites us to be petty, suspicious, narrow-minded, closed, arrogant, and smug. Most of these apply to us, I think. Of course we would be the first to protest if these epithets were publicly stated, as we did when the Malaysian—our northern neighbor's—ambassador to Singapore criticized us for being an arrogant people ... perhaps his diplomatic status did not sit comfortably with his frank observation, but some months after Singaporeans had protested about this, the former Chinese ambassador said the same thing—and this time Singapore kept mum! And the point of this recollection is that memory and defensiveness become crucial to the observing eye in Singapore.

Well, memory is tricky business here, where a graveyard one day could become a KFC joint the next and a children's and women's hospital the day after. Of course I am exaggerating, but the essential point is not sensationalized: memory is not something most Singaporeans are very good at. Because old houses, roads, buildings, spaces, are constantly being brought down, leveled, refurbished, made anew such that it becomes extremely hard for anyone to remember precisely where to locate either a precise moment, or a precise venue. And because memory is not something readily available to the Singaporean writer, recollection is frequently flawed, or at best, tentative. That "recollection in tranquillity" that the great Wordsworth said made for the spontaneous overflow of powerful feelings is often wanting here. In its place we have, most often, a cunningly constructed recollection, a framed spot of time that allows for expression and comment but which can sometimes confuse because its precise locale is unclear. Well, I imagine the literary scholars of the future will have a lot of excavation work to do as they burrow deep and unearth some pleasant and mostly not-so-pleasant records of memory and its many distorted manifestations in our stories, poems, plays, narratives. For instance, anyone doing biographic work on me—and such work has already begun!—will find it difficult to understand that when I was young and in primary school, my school was a very significant educational institution, because it was one of the few used by the newly elected Singapore government to showcase the brilliant pedagogy at work! My school—Jalan Daud School—ceased to exist so many years ago that many don't even ever recall it these days. The school made way for the Pan-Island Expressway (known as the PIE in our republic of acronyms), which now brings travelers to and from the world-famous Changi International Airport. I used to live, then, along a street named Jalan Mangga (Mango Street)—this, too, went the same way, for the same PIE. The secondary school I went to—Tanjong Katong Secondary Technical School—also went, as did the Raffles Institution, a school founded by the "founder" of Singapore himself, Sir Stamford Raffles. This school, originally known as the Singapore Institution, was begun in 1823. In 1969, the old school was demolished to make way for the brand new Raffles City, which still houses the world's tallest hotel! Even the old university where I studied left its original site! So, where does one begin placing events alongside personalities, moods, feelings, dreams, visions?

A friend said, "Try fantasy."

So do we all write fantasies in Singapore? Or, do we write fantastically? Well, both, actually. Several of my writing colleagues (Stella Kon, Catherine Lim, Kelvin Tan) often seem to flit between one or the other or even between so-called fantasy and so-called reality. I certainly do. I come from a tiny minority ethnic group: the Sikhs. Even in this tiny group I belong to yet a tinier community: that variously referred to as hybrid, mixed-race, *rojak*. Having a Scottish mother and a Sikh father put me in a unique spot—there are so few of us around of this combination. How do I, therefore, adequately "represent" Singapore when I cannot even pretend to belong to it in a more sustained, specifically noticeable kind of way? Luckily, I wear what is called the turban, a long piece of beautiful cloth wound round my head to cover my long, long hair. But wearing this, this thing on my head brings with it other, more complex problems and challenges....

Thus many of my stories are about my childhood, the world I grew up in, a world now forever lost, even in memory. From an etch to a patch might be one way of summarizing the transformation, but no description can bring back the sounds of laughter; the screaming of young kids as we wrestled in a wild, abandoned manner; the quiet of those dark and terrifying nights when only the stars seemed to bring us any light, when the curfews were imposed because we didn't know how to live in harmony with each other on account of our religious, racial, and linguistic differences. The patch my fiction covers is spread along a very thin line crossing real history with imagined geographies. Somewhere in the dimness of my now unclear past lie very powerful passions that have demanded a hearing as well as a knowing. In writing my stories with titles like "Jaspal," "Ah Kong," "Laprik"—names of friends, people I knew/know—I am only too aware that many of the allusions will be easily lost unless these narratives are kept burningly alive by those for whom the literature of their country marks the start of a *real* encounter with Truth.

It is tough to be a writer in a small place like Singapore. Especially if you want, also, to be honest. I have long suspected that one reason why our writers have not made more of an international impact is the fact that we are too shy, too afraid, too fearful, too embarrassed, too ashamed, and too cowardly to engage with even our own small honesties (let alone the *big* ones!). For too long, to be honest was to betray: betray family honor, personal integrity, public morality, and so forth. For too long our writers thought the best way out of this quagmire was not to write about anything remotely verging on what really happened, on what actually transpired. Consolation and stories were sought for in fictionalizing, in trying to tell something by pretending it was something else. Yes, we all knew/know about metaphor and symbol. But this deep-seated issue goes well beyond metaphor and symbol. How could I write a story about a man, roughly the age of my father, who was a boxer as well as an inveterate womanizer, without bringing shame upon my tribe and layers of guilt upon my soul? How could I write about the sexual intercourse I witnessed between a brother and a sister in my old *kampong* without threat that curious readers will pry and try to pin the pair down and in the absence of memory will attest falsehoods, pretending they have discovered the old truth? How could I write about that strange incident when the ex–prime minister of Singapore confronted my late Uncle Bill and told him to decide which way the wind was blowing for him? How could I?

I chose poetry and fiction: poetry for my more personal truths and fiction for my more public truths. I used to reflect much on those terrible lines of Wordsworth's, lines that most prefer not to recall:

> The deeper malady is better hid
> The world is sick at heart.

Yes, "The Recluse"—from which these lines come—is little known and these days hardly read, I suspect. But, yes, my world was very much akin to Wordsworth's. It did seem sick. The more I mulled them over the more I was struck by their homily—the world and the people the world is made up of don't, really, want to know our truths. Why should it? Does it matter that much if on a bright and moonlit night in the middle of prosperous Singapore I proposed to a fairy and was accepted? Does it really matter if I revealed that once upon a time in my school there was a headmaster who used to kiss every female student who went to seek his advice about the larger concerns of life? Does it matter if it was confirmed that "to ask mercy from the merciless / is to exact a sentence of silence?"

In my most published short story—"Monologue"—I invite readers to share my inner landscape, a landscape where there is much to bear and little to enjoy. If this alludes to Johnson and his odd writing of *Rasselas*, yes, good, because my own story resonates with allusions. Many of my readers have found it to be "intensely passionate and moving," "bewilderingly complex," "highly demanding." Its style (similar to but not equal to the so-called stream-of-consciousness) has left many confounded and some confused. A friend told me she found it "irritatingly difficult" because I had no paragraphs! Whatever its deeper preoccupations, most readers got bogged down by the oddness of expression. Manner took over matter, much as I feared. This first "Monologue" was written in the warmth of a beautiful setting in the campus of the University of Papua New Guinea in 1980, in Port Moresby.

My host—that most humane of human beings, Elton Brash—had invited me to teach there for two years and had made sure I had a good house to live in. In my mind I talk to him, listen to his naughty chuckle as he briefs me on what to do when the "rascals" call (the rascals were/are the inhabitants of the not-so-nice world of Port Moresby—they come by and demand things, and if they don't get what they want, they do bad things to you and your family…) or where to go up along the enticing Brown River. Yet not this entire story, in fact only a very small part of it, belongs there literally. But it was there that I wrote it. Do these two disparate statements matter? In my mind, naturally, they do, or I would not have stated them here.

Twenty years after that first monologue I wrote another one—in similar style but entirely different vein—and put the two stories together into one small book separated by a prose poem, a poem, and a blackened page, and I dedicated this small book to my daughters, Sarah, Areta, and Misha. In my little prefatory note to this small book (a limited edition was published specifically for the First Hong Kong International Literary Festival, to which I was invited and where it was launched), I drew attention to the very, very transparent line that is drawn between truth and fiction. Much as Melville said, "I write fiction but my readers want it to be 'realistic'!" Well, I say, we should all take cover under the large stature of Whitman: "you say I contradict myself? / that I speak in opposites? / well I am large, I contain multitudes." I pray that when my young son Christopher, who is now only about five months old, grows up and reads my stories, he will know just how tenuous it was for his daddy to keep writing in the face of veiled and not-so-veiled threats. And, the most damning threat of all—a benign indifference!

Right. I am convinced that all stories contain multitudes—of meanings, significances, nuances. But we don't have the time—or, more accurately, the luxury of time—to discover these. A pity, because embedded in the multi-layering of the stylized fictions we write are the sad and tragic kernels of our truths. Writing tough but staying honest is not everyone's cup of tea, coffee, *milo,* or milk. Neither is it everyone's glass of brandy, whiskey, gin, or wine. Whatever. But it *is* my position. It is where I site myself in the overarching universe of our literary heritage. Without my own understanding of this, I will never be able to hold my head high when my time comes to meet my maker. Male or female; Chinese, Caucasian, or Indian; young or old; beautiful or ugly; whatever shape and form my maker takes, finally it'll be me whose head will be on the stand. My witnesses will all be somewhere, mostly hidden, silent in their fear, wicked in their knowledge, small in their humanity. But my writing will shout out loud and bear testimony to a life lived at the expense of exclusivity, because I have attempted to include as much as I can, particularly with reference to my home, my nation Singapore and its multitiered and multicultured society. My mistakes are my own—I have to take ownership of them, because no one else is going to. When old Aristotle said we are all "political" animals, he was thinking of me. For all my work is political in the sense Aristotle meant it. Because I try to be total, I try to remain intact, I try to stay sane. My writing is tough, but that, dear reader, is the price or reward, the blessing or the curse, of being honest.

Apartheid in Literary Criticism

Alfred Birney

If someone were to ask me about setting records, I'd look at how long it took me to write a short story or a novel. My speed record for the sprint lies at three days, for the distance run nine months. So, not unusual. My records for slowness are more interesting. I worked for twelve years on my longest novel and needed just as much time to write one of my short stories. It's somewhere in the middle of my only collection of short stories, one of my finest books and also the only one that was really hard for me to get published. My publisher was impressed by the style and the variety, but didn't publish it without reluctance. Why? Because short stories barely sell in the Netherlands. Is that true?

Short stories have their history. If you wanted to become a writer in the mid-1970s, the rules were set. It was ideal to start with poetry, consequently to devote yourself to the short story, and then make the jump to the novel. Almost all of the current arrivés, they said, had taken that route. Poetry as an exercise in style, the short story as a finger exercise. In this context, poetry was of course dutifully considered the highest form of literary art, but it was particularly novels that were talked about in the literary salon. Between these genres lay the no-man's-land of the short story.

If a positive aspect did cling to the writer's traditional route, it would be that particular attention was paid to style. Unfortunately, style was primarily understood to be an erudite way of writing. If you could manage to suggest that you knew your classics well, in playful references for instance, you were sitting pretty. In any case you proved you weren't just somebody off the street. Of course, with the Western classics as your stock-in-trade, the rest of the world didn't count.

It was a time during which people no longer spoke of short stories, but of texts. Thus you submitted a text to a literary journal. The editors of these journals, usually writers themselves, reviewed the text and returned it to you with a comment about your style, and, in the best-case scenario, the invitation to submit something else sometime. A short story in which something was related was called anecdotal, was a shame and a sin, and went straight to hell, the wastebasket. Only with a short story in which nothing happened did you prove you were able to write, precisely by having nothing happen.

Making a debut in one of the literary journals was important. After all, they were published by the big publishers in Amsterdam. There they could keep close track of your evolution as a writer and see whether something had already been written about you in the papers, whether the most influential reviewers already had you in their sights. If that were the case, then you could come by to talk sometime. Quick to publish, they were not. You were the wine that had to age in their cellars. And then in such a way as to evolve somewhat along their norms. After all: you were destined for their stable; awaiting you was the seal of approval of their label, your passport to the literary press.

At that time you saw no writers from minority groups making their debut among the established publishers. Those writers spoke another kind of Dutch, and, what was worse: they really had something to relate, particularly stories that people in the Netherlands preferred not to hear or that simply left them indifferent. These writers could go to the smaller, idealistic publishers who would later see them leave in turn for the wealthier publishers, once these last started smelling money.

In the 1970s, a novel or a collection of short stories could wait around on the bookstore shelf for seven years to be discovered by the public. At the moment, it's seven weeks. The process was first reduced to two years during the 1980s, when literary publishing was starting to become big business. Writers were no longer judged on their work alone; their image began to be seriously taken into account. Images have faces and, if necessary, can get by with even less content than a literary finger exercise. So the barrels in the cellars of the literary journals began to rot. People had to come out from behind their editing desks and go out to cast their nets. From now on, the fish had to be brought ashore right after the catch, salted and ready to eat.

This was a hard blow for poetry. From now on people would be flipping through the literary journals in search of short stories. Was the short story reevaluated because of this? No. Just the opposite, since you only had to write one, as a kind of test. One good short story had to carry an entire collection full of hackwork and crap. More than ever before, the short story was a jump to the novel: the genre it was ultimately all about and is nowadays practically exclusively about.

As such, it is strange that precisely now, in this day and age, when information is increasing by the day and people want to consume more and more information through various channels, that the short story is not being taken very seriously. It wouldn't surprise me that all the buyers of those fleshy mega sellers and all the reviewers who discuss those books also watch television in the evening, surf the Net for an hour or so, go down to the local bar, and go to concerts, or museums, exhibits, and whatever belongs to a so-called cultural life. With such a way of life, it would appear the short-story genre would fit in excellently.

It seems strange, but a fleshy novel lets itself be read faster (for the purposes of interpretation, that is); it allows for flipping through the pages that are not as convincing. A short-story collection presents a much tougher conquest: the reader has to start a new book, as it were, with every story. Plus, a good story has no sentences and certainly no pages that can be skipped. It doesn't allow itself to be easily consumed; if it's good it demands rereading. A collection of short stories by one writer requires more time and attention from the reader as well as from the reviewer's capacity to say something sensible about it. Evidence of this is the greater attention paid to anthologies. The reviewer plucks out a couple of writers and leaves the rest for what it is. When my collection of short stories was brought out on the market in the spring of 1999, reviews all but failed to materialize. This happens to other writers too, authors of best sellers aside, but I really wasn't ready for such a poor showing. In spite of this, the book sold no worse than my other work, so who would still want to argue that the Dutch public doesn't like short stories? My publisher must have meant that the publishing house could also use another hefty dose of reviews to bolster its image a bit.

When I started writing seriously—which means to say, writing with an eye to publishing—I had a problem. This may sound a bit ambiguous, but I had a pretty large arsenal into which I could delve. Complex, too. My father was born in the former Dutch East Indies, my mother in the Netherlands. They met each other in the Netherlands after the Second World War and there gave me life, or life me, an unspoken question that resonates all through my work.

Let me touch on my parents for a moment. In most cases involving an interracial marriage, the relationship was as follows: the husband was Dutch; the wife, of mixed descent or not, was from the Dutch East Indies. With my parents, it was the other way around. My mother, as a white woman, was regarded with suspicion whenever she went down the street with her brown brood. And my father, an Indo, was thought of as an exotic creature that had better beat it, back to his country of origin, and best keep his paws off a white woman. That in the Dutch East Indies he, a man of mixed Eurasian descent, already had a European passport and had fought in that patriotic capacity on the side of the Dutch during the Indonesians' struggle for freedom, is something about which people here in Holland knew nothing. They had had the German occupation, and anybody with a different history wasn't listened to, certainly not if something "colonial" clung to that history. That the Netherlands owed its prosperity in large part precisely to that former East Indies colony, they simply neglected, for the sake of convenience, to teach in the schools.

The war in the Dutch East Indies—first the Japanese occupation, then the Indonesian fight for liberation, and finally the exodus of 300,000 Eurasians who took refuge in the Netherlands—had traumatized my father to such an extent that it was no longer in the cards for him to lead something like a normal family life. Problems with the social life in Holland, so different in the country where he was born; the communication problems with his wife, even though they spoke the same language; the racism that his children also had to undergo; and particularly the persecution complex, of which he suffered spells, made him impossible to live with from time to time. He persisted too much in the idea that raising his children with a hard hand would make them tougher later on. His rigid physical punishments hardly fit in with the culture in which he had ended up. And his craziness didn't at all. I was 13 when our family fell apart. We, the children, had to spend the rest of our youth in homes.

A bad childhood is a gold mine for a writer, they say. This doesn't mean that you can just wipe your hands on the paper, though. People who want to tell their life story can, possibly without much love of the writer's craft, casually toss that story off on paper and enter the top-10 book lottery with it. The novel is an excellent vehicle for this. Certainly these days, when a book primarily has to be fat, not to mention fleshy. Lots of words about a catchy issue for an attractive sales price. Such books will get even the foremost critics off on the wrong foot. You tend to find these books a lot among the current best sellers. Some of these, fortunately, come from immigrants and second-generation immigrants and are applauded not so much for their literary value, about which they otherwise can't say enough, but presumably for the counterpropaganda that such books implicitly contain. Dutch critics are pretty much all white, and I can hear them quietly cheering: You see what a beautifully democratic and open-minded country we are? They devote entire pages of newspapers to one book like that, profiling themselves as progressive or at least culturally correct, and the next day they get back to producing their drivel with their traditional Western thinking and, in particular, feeling.

Of course stories do still get published. But then primarily by novelists who want to keep their fingers warmed up in between enterprises and callously slap their collections of metroprose on the market, stories that, like a hamburger, you consume between stops 1 and 3. Stories that are bland, but at any rate have a famous name printed at the top. If writers themselves don't take the short story seriously, then reviewers could hardly be expected to be lagging behind.

I am not jumping to rally behind the overworked, mostly wooden exercises in style that once made the literary journals all but unreadable. Linguistic art without a clear story line can be fascinating, particularly to those who want to learn how to write or to those who have read so much by now that virtuosity is the only thing that can still enchant them. When I started writing my first stories, I was very preoccupied with form and style. This way of working offered me the great advantage of not having to busy myself with the past, my own, my mother's, or that of my father and his Dutch East Indies plantation owner's family, and certainly not with something like the color of my skin. So, I, too, learned to write a text with a disdain for the narrative element. I didn't make a habit of this because I wanted to tell tales; they had to come out. So I began to look for a balance between form and content. Was I looking for something akin to the literary golden mean? No, I try to unite talent and baggage, and in essence I'm talking about something completely different.

Reviewers seem to have at their disposal a left eye for form and a right eye for content. With the left eye they view the stories of "autochthon" writers, with the right eye stories by writers referred to as *allochtones* in the Netherlands (in order not to have to use the word *immigrant* or *second-generation immigrant*, which is evidently not done and as far as I'm concerned is pretty hypocritical). Now, that right eye is pretty lazy. It has no trouble seeing the works of immigrants from non-Western cultures. It sees, but this is different from recognizing. Still, both eyes have difficulty with the work of writers who harbor a mixed Western and Caribbean or Western and Asian culture. Indo writers fall under this last group of mixed-bloods. So do I.

Stories in Dutch literature that take place in the low countries are usually boring. The themes hardly differ from those in other European literatures. Interesting in itself, but many Dutch stories miss *brille,* have no *schwung.* Colonial and postcolonial literature is far less boring, and stronger: stories from this quarter can oftentimes be described as spectacular. It is not by chance that the Dutch masterpieces wholly or in part take place in the Dutch East Indies. These are the pilings on which all of Dutch literature rests.

Ultimately, content always rates. Life was simply less boring on the other side of the ocean. The colony tempted the Dutch to excesses that would have been unacceptable back home. You only need to read a few stories from colonial literature to run into lawlessness, immorality, corruption, misogyny, murderousness, hunger for power, the practice of magic, racism, sexism, linguistic conflict, ridicule, and slander. Are these then also the motives they expect of a postwar, postcolonial Indo author? I'm afraid so. I believe people at any rate want to see a sequel, although preferably one captured by a problematic perspective. If you have a mixed-race background, then you must have a problem. If not, you're not playing the game. So a familiar dilemma arises: do you represent your father's group, your mother's, or both? And: if you represent both groups, does it naturally follow that you are doing the most right by yourself and your craft? I'd rather turn it around and say that I somehow represent both groups, as long as I remain true to myself. This seems to me, at any rate, to follow naturally.

Why didn't you give your story a Eurasian setting? I was asked this question when I published my first story in a particular journal that had space for stories in which something could be related. My answer was that for me there was no reason to decorate the story with Indisch wallpaper, because the story didn't need it and didn't demand it. When I later published a story about a roots-trip to Indonesia in a newspaper, the question ran: Why are you writing about your being Indo now? That's not what you started out doing. In short: Staying quiet about my background raised questions, and the opposite did as well.

Before my first collection of short stories came out, I had published only novels. Going on how my novels were received, one thing had become clear: there were reviewers who only discussed the novels I wrote with an obviously contemporary "Dutch" orientation and there were those who were interested only in the novels with a clearly "Indisch" or postcolonial orientation. Exceptions to this apartheid were not to be found in the Netherlands, but in Belgium, where people speak the same language but are at any rate not saddled with a colonial past in Asia, putting aside their own colonial past in Congo for a moment. Thus the reviewers who managed to put their finger on one overall theme that recurs in all my stories and novels were living abroad. They called it simply "alienation," a theme that can be found in the whole of world literature. This theme can be linked to issues surrounding someone's origins, past, sex, sexual preference, neuroses, fantasies, or craziness—in short, everything you could possibly imagine. Alienation knows no mainland; alienation seeks it. And as long as one hasn't been found, alienation itself is the mainland.

Of course the reader does have the right to be able to place the alienation that dominates my protagonists. At least I give the reader the mainland of language and story. However, reviewers, professional readers, want more. They in turn want to show the reader that they totally understand if not see through the writer whom they are discussing. This is why writers who clearly profile themselves, in whatever way, are easier for reviewers to discuss than those whose work breathes a personal synthesis of the diverse cultural influences they have undergone.

When I write a story without an explicitly Indisch accent, then this story will still always have been written by someone who carries Indisch accents inside. Coming from my background, I naturally place different accents, even without bringing that background explicitly to bear. And this is precisely what people do not have or do not wish to have eyes for. I don't think that I have to place a ghost story or whatever against an Indisch background in order to make it more believable for a Dutch reader. A ghost story is not unusual in Indo circles, but in Dutch circles it still is. This is why ghost stories preferably have to come from abroad. Or from a writer like myself, but then it is in fact situated in an Indisch framework. Then they can give you a place and you pose no threat to the autochthon authors, who have their own themes that people evidently wish to reserve for that group. We get magic; they get love.

In the Netherlands of today, where people are brimming with "multicultural remarks," a separatism is utilized that goes way back in the country's colonial history. It is not something like a mutual influence that people here wish to arrive at. No, they want everybody to keep their own cultures behind closed doors. You can tell from the books by (here we go again) autochthon writers who, during the time when the discipline of "philosophy" was in vogue, were bursting with references to the most far-flung Western philosophers. The stuff of Asian thought, in the best scenario, has been considered to be a nice expression of another culture, befitting *allochtone* writers. They can go ahead and write fairy tales, divert Dutch rivers, and have spirits floating around over the Amsterdam canals. The autochthon writer who does that is punished or else excessively applauded, particularly if he or she has actually experienced those "good old Dutch East Indies" as a white person, and is once more, the umpteenth in four centuries of literary enterprise, illumining it with his or her Eurocentric gaze. I wonder what the reviewers would do with a love story situated in the Dutch polder country written by a Moroccan. Perhaps very loud applause, because now at last that long-awaited multicultural dream has taken shape in the literature of the Netherlands? They will most certainly want to convene a symposium on this first. Briefly sniff at one another to see whether there's a whiff of shame lingering around their seat.

As a writer of Indisch background, born and raised in the Netherlands, in fact neither autochthon nor *allochtone*, I am burdened with both my father's as well as my mother's heritage: an Indo from the former Dutch East Indies and a cobbler's daughter from the southern Netherlands. I remember that my Dutch grandfather let me weigh nails in his shoe-repair shop as a child. They were sold in little paper sacks for five cents to poor people who had to fix their shoes themselves. After 12 1/2 years of being a practicing writer, I still see no need for a boy who's weighing nails in his grandfather's shoe shop to be given an explicitly Indisch background. I do have the choice, it's true, depending on what I want to show. However, in this day and age each choice entails a disqualifying factor. If I give the boy a brown face, I no longer rate with Dutch letters. If I give the boy a white face, I don't rate with Indisch or postcolonial letters.

Until now I have usually gone about it this way: I give my protagonists no face. What I do give them is a certain feeling of alienation, with the underlying question: What am I doing here? As a writer I want to be judged by my craft and not by my background, which gets printed in big bold letters on the jacket text of my books. White writers aren't treated this way when they feel like situating a story in the former Dutch East Indies. Sure, they are permitted that kind of thing, no questions asked, and afterward they can cross back to the order of the day. Yes, why don't you read those last four words one more time.

The Long and the Short of the Story

Vicente Soto

None of the numerous descriptions thus given of the short story can be considered final. Editors, critics, authors, all say something valid and none of them, apparently, since new attempts at description or definition keep emerging, says all there is to be said. At the same time something remarkable is happening: the ease with which short stories are compiled to make up a book and the spontaneity with which the author gets down to writing a short story without stopping to consider what the dickens it may be. Everyone knows with a kind of inspired knowledge what a short story is, and no one manages to say quite what it is.

Despite its limitations, the work of the editor-as-anthologist is still fine. Necessary, I daresay. The very fact that stories of several storytellers are brought together in a book is positive. Stories are better preserved this way than they would be otherwise. Should they remain dispersed, it would be harder for the reader and the critic to discover—and keep!—them. For practical purposes, some might even disappear in an odd sort of disappearing act: as if they had never existed.

The fact remains, nevertheless, that the short story has indeed a quality of unknown quantity that demands to be found. To no avail. Curiously, arriving in the world of literature after verse like a thread of cold, clear water, prose has always refused to be measured. This has been true ever since it appeared as an oral form, in the tradition of tale telling—glimpses of which can be caught from time to time in books such as Harold Courlander's *The Crest and the Hide and Other African Stories,* or through some of the extraordinary, wonderful passages of Samuel Feijóo's *El Negro en la Literatura Folklórica Cubana* and *Mitología Cubana,* as agile and alive as cave paintings, looking at some of which Picasso once said: "We've learnt nothing."

Verse, instead, nearer to song, is measurement by definition. One heptasyllable, one octosyllable, one hexasyllable, or a quatrain, a tercet, a hexameter, are exactly what these words say they are. Even if the name does not imply measurement, the meaning is always unequivocal.

Azorín, that well-known figure of the Spanish Generación del 98, says that the short story is to prose what the sonnet is to verse. I do not know. I respect and admire Azorín, but I really do not know. Needless to say, despite the mathematical flavor of his sentence, he is not trying here to define the short story or the sonnet, but simply to emphasize the intensity and concentration that both literary expressions may offer by virtue of their brevity. And who would deny the wonderful possibilities the sonnet has on that score. But aside from the fact that while a sonnet will always be *catorce versos* and a short story will always be shorter or longer than any other short story, surely there are poetical compositions briefer than the sonnet that can be equally as touching, to say the least. I cannot remember offhand a sonnet that surpasses in quiet nostalgia and intensity this *endecha* (quatrain) flying through time like a lonely, forgotten leaf, by Antonio Machado:

> Tengo a mis amigos
> en mi soledad.
> Cuando estoy con ellos,
> ¡ qué lejos están! (ll. 15–18)
> I have my friends
> in my solitude.
> When I am with them,
> how far away they are!

It takes a poet to say that—sorry, couldn't help the comment.

No, Lope de Vega's precise definition of the sonnet, for instance, "Catorce versos dicen que es soneto" (the third line of his well-known versified description of the poem), has no equivalent in prose. Impossible to know beforehand the length of any narrative, short or long. Good! I am tempted to add. For this limitation frees prose and is its privilege. The work of art is a miracle towards which the artist, irrespective of his or her chances of succeeding, instinctively moves. With a feeling and a hope, rather than a reason and a plan—these come later. Of course the writer has at the outset of his task an idea of what he intends to do, but he does not care a damn about his narrative perhaps one day being called a long story, say, or a short novel, or even both by two different critics. His own initial assessment will be subject to incalculable alterations carried out by himself. In 1906, Joyce told his brother Stanislaus that he was thinking of adding to *Dubliners* another story: "Ulysses."

Especially as far as the short story goes, my experience for quite a number of years now is that either one begins writing it soon, while the motivation to write is still alive, or one will never do so. I am not talking of plot, which can be remembered (dead) for years and years, I am talking of the motivation that is short-lived and has to be taken with both hands while it is still throbbing and then translated into written words. V. S. Pritchett defines the short story as "something glimpsed from the corner of the eye, in passing." But as well as that glimpse, it could be the sparking Raymond Carver wants for the poem (he himself tells us that "short stories are closer in spirit to poems than they are to novels"). Or a cry, an echo, a smell, a flash, the vanishing of a song... in short, anything that by grazing the string of memory will trigger the vibration that demands words, words, words, the magic and the madness of writing. This is what makes literary creation possible.

Which then has to be communicated, transmitted to someone. Nobody writes for the desk drawer, and if somebody did, nothing would happen in the world of literature, no matter how good what he wrote. Art does not exist in itself, it exists in you and me and that girl and that fellow over there, in all of us readers, viewers, listeners: cocreators with the author. Nothing is born, literarily speaking, without the gaze that is not of the author, without the gaze that reads. Only in solitude—which may be in the midst of roaring company—can the writer find the truth he needs and is searching for, but only someone else, the reader, will know if he has found it.

To communicate with spontaneity and warmth, as if in confidence, the essence of the motivation:

The old man leaned closer and whispered:
"A tree. A rock. A cloud."

There it is at long last, transmitted to the boy with a kind of secrecy, the beginning of love for the old man or rather the realization that such a beginning can be hidden in anything—"a goldfish" as well as (why not) "a street full of people," "a bird in the sky." Whatever. Carson McCullers has tumbled upon these three words as if they were physical. Things. So intensely felt through the thrill of the old man that she grabs them and plants them at the top of her story as an ornament and a title. Only once will the three words appear in the narrative. Bare, without a single detail. How tall is a tree, how big a rock, how dense and big a cloud ... how many words or pages make up a

short story or a long one, where does a long story end and a short novel begin
... what's bigger, a lake or a sea....

I have just crossed out those last words, "what's bigger, a lake or a sea," I put
them down again, I cross out not less than 30 lines, and I will try to forget
them. Carried away by a sudden and very old memory—prompted in turn,
I guess, by the association of cloud/water/lake ... —I caught myself beginning to write a kind of short story. One day, when I was 12, I learned with a
shock that a lake may—just may, but may all the same—be bigger than a sea.
I learned that at a lecture with slides and maps and things at the old Instituto
Luis Vives in Valencia. There, at the very place from which one day long ago
I sailed toward my future and where all the fabulous things, bad and good, I
know even today have their first root. One such lake was Lake Baykal. Which
may have, we were told, a sort of swell and even a sort of storm. Besides being
bigger, for instance, than the Dead Sea. What? I immediately went through
lots of big blue plates in my own atlas and came across the American Great
Lakes and discovered that they are bigger than Lake Baykal, with Lake Superior being nearly three times as big, so to hell with Lake Baykal, but just a
minute, what's bigger, a lake or a sea, that is the question, and I went on looking, feeling a sort of seasickness. And what an odd relief when turning a page
I discovered my Mar Mediterráneo

No, I am not rewriting the story—but it was not fair, was it, to kill it so
abruptly. Frankly I am trying to forget it because it would be out of place
here and, more importantly, because I have always believed that in the field of
creative literature one's mother tongue is one's mother and that whoever runs
away from it (from *ella*) gets lost. There are exceptions to this, some brilliant,
but just exceptions, the consideration of which would take us too far. There
is one, nevertheless, that fascinates me: Beckett. Who wrote masterpieces in
French because, as Martin Esslin (himself another brilliant exception) explains
in *The Theatre of the Absurd,* he felt he needed the discipline that an acquired
language would impose upon him: asked by somebody why he did that, Beckett replied: "Parce qu'en français c'est plus facile d'écrire sans style." To put it
bluntly: because he did not know French as well as he knew English.

One understands how a linguistic limitation can intensify the purity of
expression, how, by wiping out the disturbing presence of too many words
and word associations that tempt the writer like toys and games dragging him
away from the essence of his thought, the naked truth can best be reached.
Like transplanting from the world of architecture to literature Mies van der
Rohe's radical principle: Less is more. Not a single unnecessary frill. With
what marvelous results. Nevertheless, and despite the stunning example of
Beckett—and now I am looking at the achievements, not at the theory—we

all know that world literature owes its masterpieces to the command the great writers have had of their respective languages.

At the same time, despite what I have just said about one's mother tongue, I admire the translators of literary works. They enrich our lives on this multilingual globe. David Lodge feels that "you never really experience a writer when you read him in translation." Of course every language hides in its innermost recesses words, idioms, untranslatable puns. At most they can be explained—thereby losing their freshness. Which is why, I confess, I have always refused to translate literary texts; I have more than enough with the task of translating my own ideas into words. But these untransferable "secrets" are very few compared with the mass of the language, the benefits of translation far outweighing its limitations. In transferring pure narrative, whatever the length of the work, from language to language, decisive influences are transmitted that would otherwise be lost. As if inexistent. The chance of seeing through the transparency of translating another language while looking at your own is magic.

You know, Italo Calvino confessed that he did not finish reading *Ulysses*. And he used to grumble about modern novels being swollen by the attention given to needs that, as addressed by nineteenth-century writers, had already been satisfied.

Borges, and we know this by his own confession, read very few novels, in most cases reaching the last page out of a sense of duty, "un sentido del deber." He was on the other hand an avid reader of short stories, and those by Stevenson, Kipling, James, Poe, Conrad, as well as the tales from *A Thousand and One Nights,* formed part of his usual reading, he would say, "ever since I can remember." (Not in contradiction with this, I think, I hope—life is very strange—I remember suddenly and have to point out that, besides everything else, Borges translated Faulkner's *The Wild Palms* into Spanish.)

Let's go on. Saul Bellow adheres with delight to something Chekhov said: "Odd, I have now a mania for shortness. Whatever I read—my own or other people's work—it all seems to me not short enough." No doubt Chekhov will always be included among the genuinely representative great writers of the nineteenth century, but at the same time he is modern in the strictest sense of the word: an influential writer of modern writers and a favorite of modern readers. And I am convinced that he owes this to, inter alia, his "mania for shortness," a kind of good taste against the bombastic.

Raymond Carver showed himself to be a bit more radical. He did not refer just to "writing short" but specifically to the short story. "Has there ever been a time like the present for short story writers? I don't think so," he wrote not so long ago, I daresay, as his premature death did not occur until 12 years ago. "To my mind, perhaps the best, certainly the most variously interesting and satisfying work, even, just possible, *the work that has the greatest chance of enduring, is being done in the short story.*" And: "The current profusion in the writing and publishing of short stories is, so far as I can see, the most eventful literary phenomenon of our time."

Why?

Among the numerous reasons Saul Bellow sees for the present tendency towards shortness, he mentions one that to my view embraces all of them: "We have no time."

Technological achievements and the mass media keep stuffing us at terrifying speed with masses of information and distraction we cannot assimilate. Take television, for instance, a major cause of the situation. By just clicking the remote control of the old set, we open a window to an unimaginable variety of entities that can thus invade our very private loneliness. I will not list the possible intruders, from ET beings, more often than not horrendous and always, miraculously, Anglophone—at least, so far as I can tell, from those that visit British and American homes—to certain butterflies or certain lizards—I think they were lizards—perhaps caught in the problematic act of mating. Anybody can effortlessly visualize a long succession of plausible images flowing in the sort of fluid scenario provided by the small screen. I will only touch upon a rather dull and yet, I hope, telling experience I had a few days ago. I was surprised to find myself facing a table of foods classified according to their cholesterol content. I don't know if my father (but I am sure that my grandfather) never said the word *cholesterol.* Nowadays a teenager running away from this word can end up reading "anorexia." Fair enough, that may be progress. Seriously. But as it happens, I love shellfish. Perhaps more than any other food. A hell of a temptation, king prawns. Lobster. Now, however, I know that depending on the variety I choose, hidden in any portion of 100 grams of shellfish, I will ingest up to 220 milligrams of cholesterol. This, I am told, is bad. Never noticed a thing, but there you are. I think I will carry on loving shellfish, but very likely I will make an effort to avoid this kind of food and to some degree this will sadden me. Now, will this bit of new knowledge prolong my life a little bit? I still do not know, but it is certainly already stealing time away from me.

This is it. In this small example the "bit" can at least theoretically be compensated, but what about the hours and hours lost in soap operas, rotten chat shows, rotten sitcoms with canned laughter.... Enough. "We have no time"—to read, to write—because someone is taking it from us. Not the creator of progress, of course (do I need to add "needless to say"?), but the sly parasite of progress. Our time is his staple food and he has a voracious appetite. In every country, in every language. Which is why though we live longer than ever before, we have less time of our own. Relentlessly, as the number of years we live rises, our time shortens. As we approach the moment when—perhaps, just perhaps—we will live so many years that we will have no time at all.

I am going to find it hard now, I know, to praise TV. I am not going to alter, however, what I have just said. Neither will I start talking of the immense potential everyone knows it has for the good of humanity in terms of peaceful coexistence and culture. On top of that, and this is all I want to add, from a humane point of view, I find it moving. Good, in the most humble sense of the word. It gives company to innumerable loners who do not love loneliness. All over the planet. I am willing to welcome the bloody parasite of progress so long as with his rubbish he makes the loner laugh, weep, scream. Even from time to time sleep. Dream. So blissfully immersed in himself that if somebody turns the set off, the ensuing deafening silence wakes him up. And there is something else TV can do, something perhaps hard to believe: it can shed light for at least a few blind persons, as I know thanks to a true story I cannot go into at the moment.

Now, even if we leave out the negative aspects of TV, the fact of the matter is that as an audiovisual medium, right from the start it came with the irresistible invitation to learn with minimum effort. No need to read or write as much as before. And there are other technological achievements that have taken place in the twentieth century that offer even greater "economies" of time. We are trapped by a series of invisible nets that besides posing a threat to the right to a private identity and anonymity (the walls of our dwellings are already translucent) are transforming the world of letters. I have a feeling people will end up reading more on dazzling screens than in books. Even that they will cease to know how to write by hand. That they will write only by typing or perhaps speaking to something. Handwriting, so idiosyncratic, as much a part of one's self as one's blood, voice, gaze, will be lost in an unstoppable standardization of signs.

All the same, here we are talking again of writing and reading. Technology may transform them yet needs them, could itself not evolve without them. Maybe I am beginning to miss already the vanishing ink and pen and the smell of print and all the rest of it. And the world does not care a damn about this sort of "prenostalgia" of mine. Thank goodness. The only thing that counts is that the need to write, along with all creative needs, will prevail.

Summing up:

I tend to believe that in this hectic and truly changing world of ours, with time at a premium, for the foreseeable future the norm will be writing short. Of course, traditional, more substantial—bigger—books will also keep appearing. I see quite a few around me on my bookshelves. I do not always know the moment when or how they arrived. I have a feeling we are on nodding terms, that we know each other by sight. Like shy old neighbors. I respect them and admire their authors, most of whom I already know. I keep promising myself that I will read all these books. Meanwhile, I mainly keep writing short, and reading short writing. Short stories, long stories, novellas. I do not care if it is just a taste or a need, I love it. As a matter of fact, I wish to God I could trim down, prune several of my old writings. Nothing doing now, I know. As the old saying goes, "Too late, mate."

WORKS CITED

Courlander, Harold. *The Crest and the Hide and Other African Stories.* New York: Putnam, 1982.

Feijóo, Samuel. *Mitologia Cubana.* Havana: Editorial Letras Cubanas, 1985.

———. *El Negro en la Literatura Folklorica Cubana.* Havana: Editorial Letras Cubanas, 1980.

Lodge, David. "Finding the Time." *Guardian* 14 Jan. 2000.

Machado, Antonio. "Gems of Wisdom." *New Songs.* Madrid: Latin World, 1924.

McCullers, Carson. *A Tree, a Rock, a Cloud.* New York: Creative Education, 1997. 15–18.

6

The Role of Gender in
Short-Story Writing

Telling Stories about Falling Men

Ivan Wolfers

Realizing that he corrupted probably the only place on earth that could compete with paradise, Rudolf Kippenheim jumps down from the 17th floor of a bank building. A bicycle rack breaks his fall. He has to live the remainder of his life as a fallen man in a wheelchair. Rudolf Kippenheim is the protagonist in my novel *Het Zout van de Doze Zee.*

All my stories are like that. They are about falling men, and really, I don't know why I write them.

We tell our stories for many different reasons. Maybe, like Scheherazade, to save our lives. Or, like Hollywood scriptwriters, to tempt, please, and sell. We want to convince, to provoke, to surprise, to amuse, and in addition we feel the need to add our views of what happened with us, insignificant human beings, to the big, big collection of versions of the truth. We tell our stories to catch that one moment that moved us and to cage the flow of events in a controllable stream of words.

Desperately, we want to make visible what we think is not perceived and understood fully by others.

By telling stories we make an effort to catch what is escaping us now, to cherish it later. We want to control what cannot be controlled. By doing so, we turn what happens in our lives and has no connection whatsoever into a story with a logical order of events that gives meaning to what we do not understand and that satisfies our autobiographic needs.

Like stammerers, not able to react at the very moment that we are threatened by the intimidating realities of our daily lives, we know in hindsight what we should have said, and we write that down in our stories. What just occurred by coincidence turns into fate. And bad luck becomes a drama where we had to make choices on a quest without a goal. By telling our stories we explain our suffering, we forgive, we are comforted, we accept, we become the leading characters in the movies that are made about our own lives, which is denied to us by what really happened.

By weaving networks of words we interpret the world around us and give meaning to what was meaningless. Human beings cannot live with the idea that what happens to them is indifferent and coincidental. That is why we are religious, why we love to believe in conspiracies, and why we have become storytellers. We use adjectives to explain and make parentheses to plead not-guilty for what happened.

However, storytellers should not know all that. They have to believe that they are trying to describe reality and to unveil the truth. If we are not convinced of the validity of what we tell, we may as well give up storytelling. Unconvincing storytellers are never popular, because those who listen and read want to believe in the story too. That is why we—the storytellers—better not analyze our stories. We risk discovering that the myths we create are just air. Let others look at what we wrote and let them decipher the secret codes that we are blind to.

When I, nevertheless, look in an analytical way at the fiction I have written in my life and realize what it is about, it is slightly threatening. Again and again, I write about falling men. For example, I just finished the first draft of a story. Reading it, I am not surprised. It is about a man who is well known for writing sex education for teenagers, and on a perfectly normal day in spring, he is charged with having intimate relationships with 13-year-olds. In the newspapers, journalists reveal that he exchanges sex for copies of his books. The nice uncle that counseled generations of teenagers to help them discover their sexuality is caught with his pants down. He falls from grace and is evicted from his house and family. His publishing company does not want to be associated with him any longer. The radio shows he was doing are discontinued. Finally he ends on the streets with the prostitutes and homeless, to rediscover who he really is and to be finally healed by love—true love, not the one made of words.

I don't even want to think about what this means and what is resting in the depths of my mind. The theme of the falling man is something that keeps on coming back in my stories. The men in my stories are successful, but something unexpected and simultaneously predictable happens and their lives change. Initially they seem to have success, because they have everything under control. Passion is a strange word to them. They are even afraid of it. But then the inevitable happens. They find the dark underworld of temptations and desires, and like Lucifer they are thrown in their own subconscious world, where violence and sex guide their behavior. Rationality is replaced by lust.

The fall of man. Am I afraid to fall? Do I fear the irrational ways of feelings? Am I afraid to be seen by others like I really am? Do I fear that I have to recognize that I am a creature that is close to nature like other mammals, and that disregarding all the studying, reading, and writing, I am only superficially covered with a thin layer of civilization?

Perhaps I have to explain something about myself. I have been a writer since the day I could hold a pen. Writing is a way of living and results in an attitude of continuously transcending observations and experiences into words. However, I have also studied medicine and did a Ph.D. in medical anthropology. Because of that, I work in development projects and programs in Asia and Africa. When I turned 50, I realized that I had never made any choices in my life. I had been greedy and wanted it all. That is why on one side I am a scientist who meticulously tries to copy versions of the truth and makes effort to influence it. On the other side I am an artist, trying feverishly to get away from reality and fly to the world of my imagination. More and more I think that I should stop going to places far away and retire behind my desk and describe the world from there.

Over the past 30 years I have traveled extensively in Southeast Asia. That part of the world often provides the decorum for my falling men. My protagonists are white intellectuals like myself, because they provide me with the easiest alter ego to hide behind as a narrator.

One man is a development worker bringing progress and market economy to a near paradise in the Indonesian archipelago, finally turning it into a tourist center with prostitutes and a casino. He is Rudolf Kippenheim, the one who jumps from the building. Another is an expert in family planning, working in central Java, who manages to impregnate the only woman on the island that *misses a vagina,* and he is killed by a jealous lover. A third is a journalist that is supposed to report on what happens, but has become the cynical creator of the truth that people love to believe. A fourth is a successful medical specialist feverishly looking in the slums of Surabaya for a transsexual, who—when the night falls—is picking up men in the graveyards to have sex with them.

While writing I sometimes try to understand what I am creating, to be able to control the process. It is difficult. Beyond the level of my story I am afraid to analyze too much, out of fear of losing the innocent surprise of the storyteller who discovers while formulating his words.

Perhaps human beings are all storytellers, and we tell them to each other about a past we share. Our stories differ because we are only able to stick to our own memories and interpretations, incapable of seeing our own blind spots. In *American Pastoral,* Philip Roth describes a meeting with former schoolmate Ira at a high-school reunion, where people are telling their memories, and it seems as if the participants all have their own cherished stories and versions of the past. Roth writes:

So you don't have to look much further than Ira and me to see why we go through life with a generalized sense that everybody is wrong except us. And since we don't just forget things because they don't matter but also forget things that matter too much—because each of us remembers and forgets in patterns whose labyrinthine windings are an identification mark no less distinctive than a fingerprint—it's no wonder that the shards of reality one person will cherish as a biography can seem to someone else who, say, happens to have eaten some ten thousand dinners at the very same kitchen table, to be a willful excursion into mythomania. (55)

Therefore, I accept that I am not able to fully understand my own myths, but I see right through the fantasies of other storytellers. But what do I read? I read colonial and postcolonial literature, and I am especially intrigued by the stories of white men in the tropics. I like to read about the cynical Humphrey Bogart men, who hang around in sleazy bars, where they drink too much and don't know where to go anymore. They are disillusioned about what they actually do in the tropics, but there is no place for them anymore in the country where they come from. It is a bit like Gauguin, who went to the Pacific and became famous for his paintings of Tahitians. He wanted to return to France, but his art dealer and friend Georges-Daniel de Monfreid did not want that, because it would disturb the picture of the white man having found happiness in the primitive world. Gauguin, infected with venereal diseases, died lonely and bitter in 1903 with on his easel the picture "Villages in Bretagne under the Snow." Those disappointed romantics I like to read about.

White men come to the tropics and think that they own the world, because their education taught them they were special, they were winners. They think they have the right to use everything on their path and that they are responsible for all that happens. It is the Kipling attitude, best expressed in his words:

Take up the white man's burden
Sent forth the best you breed
God binds your sons to exile
To serve your captives' needs. (12)

However, after a few years most white men have fallen from their self-constructed thrones and have become slaves of their passions. It is no longer possible to maintain the belief that they are something special. Dramatic decline of the moral behavior of white man is one of the main themes in colonial literature. Colonizers must have told stories about certain behaviors to set them apart as examples of what happens if you do not uphold your European background. And the fear of gliding down has been worked out in many colonial novels.

Joseph Conrad beautifully tells his stories about it. *Lord Jim* is the story of the immoral white man who goes down in the jungle of Borneo. And *Heart of Darkness* is the story of Kurtz, the degenerated European in the heart of Congo. In both these novels it is Marlowe, the narrator, who tells us these parables about good and bad in the tropical context and about the need to stick to European values. Sailing up the Congo River, Marlowe goes deeper and deeper into the wilderness. The sound of the drums becomes stronger and stronger. It is foggy and dark. Marlowe goes into the primitive world, and he admits that it is like a trip into his own soul. At the bottom of the white soul, the subconscious, where the primitive instincts are hidden, Marlowe finds Africa. And what are these primitive instincts? They are violence and sex, but mainly sexual lust.

In Conrad's *An Outcast of the Islands* we find the theme back in another form. The Dutch trader Willems destroys his own culture when he can't resist the temptation of the local woman Aissa.

"Ah! She is a ferocious creature." He went on. "You don't know ... I wanted to pass the time—to do something—to have something to think about—to forget my trouble till you came back. And ... look at her ... she took me as if I did not belong to myself. She did. I did not know there was something in me she could get hold of. She, a savage. I, a civilized European, and clever! She that knew no more than a wild animal. Well, she found out something in me. She found it out, and I was lost. I knew it. She tormented me. I was ready to do anything. (269)

Such stories I like to read, fascinated by the misunderstanding that people had to maintain their cultural identity and if they did not do that, they became outcasts. Dutch colonial literature is full of stories like that.

In the Dutch colony Nederlandsch Oost Indie, it was not good when people said that a person was *verindischt* (had become *indisch*). In the colonial hierarchy one could not get much lower. The stories from colonial times are like mirrors. Perhaps the bottom line must be that I look for myself. Reading the stories from that time I try to find out how different I am from that colonial white man. Because, let's be honest, colonial times may be over, but the idea that Europeans and North Americans represent superior cultures, because their economies do so much better than others', has not changed much. Development workers have similar ideas about the superiority of Western thinking. They explain to people in Africa and Asia that they have to wash their hands, have to breastfeed their children, have to wear condoms while making love and try not to overpopulate the world.

Stories about white men in the former Dutch colony Nederlandsch Indie who fall from their artificial world of civilization into that of simple lust are somehow comparable to postcolonial literature about countries like Vietnam. I want to share my thoughts and experiences while reading a collection of short stories and watching a musical about Vietnam.

Since the end of the 1980s I have visited Vietnam many times. It was special, because like everybody who was an adolescent in the 1960s, the history of the Vietnamese-American war had its mark on my development. Each of us has memories of news programs from the 1960s and 1970s that made us familiar with this small Asian country. The report that impressed me most was that about the last plane from Da Nang in 1973. Fighting Vietnamese try to conquer a place on that plane before the Vietcong arrive. For me it was a frightening image of survival, and it gave me restless nights. In my nightmares I saw men pushing women off the stairs to the plane and mothers trying to get their children in the plane.

Every time I landed in Da Nang I looked around to find something that could be related to these haunting images. There was nothing but a lot of concrete and a small arrival and departure building. It was not at all suitable for the drama I remembered. Only because of the memories, the images, the novels, the movies, and the stories we tell does the concrete landing lane in Da Nang get its meaning. That is for us, because in Vietnam the 1970s are over. There are new generations, and what remains of the imagination created by our dramatic newsreels are the old Zippo lighters of American soldiers, for sale in the souvenir shops in Dong Khoi in Ho Chi Minh City. In these Zippos dates of battles are engraved and texts like "Give me your heart and soul or I'll burn your hut down" and "If I had a farm in Vietnam and a home in hell, I'd sell my farm and return home." The Vietnamese are not interested in buying them. They live in a developing country and are busy surviving a state-run third-world economy.

Winning a war is easier than losing one. That is why in the West people still write stories about this strange cold-war conflict between the United States, champion of the rich and powerful, and the third-world country that was determined not to be dominated. We write novels, make books full of stories, and compose musicals to reinterpret history in order to make it bearable for those who lost. Those who lose are comforted by movies like *Platoon* that tell us that the Americans did not lose from the Vietnamese but from themselves, or like in the first *Rambo* movie, in which they are told that the war would have been won if only the politicians in Washington would not have betrayed the soldiers. We need such stories to understand and accept why Saigon had to fall and its defenders with it.

In 1993, Robert Olen Butler received the Pulitzer Prize for fiction for his book *A Good Scent from a Strange Mountain*. Butler's book contains 15 stories, and the protagonists are all Vietnamese migrants in the United States. I have the feeling that Butler writes stories about Vietnamese Americans in the United States at this moment to give meaning to the Vietnamese American conflict in the past. He tries to harmonize the United States and Vietnam with each other. Butler's stories are all told in the first-person singular, and as a matter of fact the majority of the stories even starts with the word "I." Sometimes the I is a man; sometimes the I is a woman; sometimes the I is old; sometimes the I is young. It is an exercise by Butler in being Vietnamese. The protagonists in Butler's stories discuss the importance of fish sauce for a good meal, and a woman speaks with her unborn baby in Vietnamese, because it does not make sense to do that in English, as in America they do not believe in such things. It sounds very authentic, but reading the stories I kept on wondering how Vietnamese the stories really are, or whether they are Vietnamese in the way an American author or reader likes to see them.

In one of the stories, "An American Couple," a Vietnamese woman travels to a five-star hotel in Mexico, because she has won the television game *Let's Make a Deal*. The woman sees other couples and guesses immediately that they also must have won the trip through a television show. She tries to figure out what couple won the trip in what show. Is it *The Price Is Right; Wheel of Fortune; Tic, Tac, Dough;* or *The Newlywed Game?* What happens is the following: I, as a Western intellectual, am amused about the funny way this Vietnamese woman ridicules American television shows, without her realizing it.

Another story in the book tells about a successful Vietnamese businessman who was not able to bring anything from Vietnam when he left, but who has bought at an auction the right shoe of John Lennon. Now he wants to buy the left shoe, so that he can put on John Lennon's shoes and walk as far as it needs to find the place where he belongs. The story has all the imagination and reflections of different realities in it. I like it because it fits Western expectations that migrants are always looking for their roots, that they never feel completely at home in their new country and that they feel a bit lost. We may say that it is universal, but I wonder what Vietnamese think if they read it.

In another story—again starting with "I," telling the reader that a genuine Vietnamese is speaking—we meet a faithful Vietnamese prostitute who migrated to the United States. Her purity is proven by the fact that she has remained loyal to the Americans who gave her apples in the time they were in Saigon.

All 15 stories are views of Butler on Vietnamese migrants, and through them he tells us his version of the history that Vietnam and the United States share. Butler was in Saigon in 1971 and claims that he felt at home there. In his novel *The Deep Green Sea,* Butler creeps alternatively under the skin of American veteran Ben (approximately 50 years old) and the very young Vietnamese girl Tien. In that novel it becomes clear that Butler's stories are an attempt to make happen what never occurred: peace and understanding between Vietnam and the United States. Tien, the innocent virgin, born after Ben left Vietnam, has been waiting in a hotel bed to give herself to this stranger from America. Imagination is finally conquering reality. The fall of Saigon and all the Americans with it never happened.

Butler's story about Ben and Tien made me think of a young Dutch soldier who was sent to Indonesia to fight against the Indonesian revolutionaries. It was just after the Second World War, and in Indonesia the soldier decided to desert the Dutch army. In the 1980s, the man lived somewhere in one of the poor suburbs of Jakarta with his Indonesian wife. He could never return to the Netherlands because he would still be arrested for desertion. When he was young, he had read a book called *Tropical Nights,* and at that moment, he fell for Indonesia. He volunteered for the army, and in the period before he had to leave the Netherlands in 1948, the man was sitting for days behind the organ, singing "Once upon a time Indonesia and the Netherlands will be one family again." Through his song he wanted to undo the war and hoped that his imagination would be stronger than reality.

A song, played on a solo saxophone, a crazy sound, a lonely sound, a cry that tells us: Love goes on and on. Played on a solo saxophone, it's telling me to hold you tight and dance like it's the last night of the world. (act 1)

That is the song that white American GI Chris and Vietnamese bar girl Kim sing in the musical *Miss Saigon,* by Alain Boublil and Claude-Michel Schonberg. Chris has fallen for Kim. It is April 1975, and the defeated Americans fly from Saigon before the Vietnamese will enter the town and rename it Ho Chi Minh City. This sweet song is part of a fairy tale that these young people want to believe in. Love wins over war. Love wins over racial differences. Love wins even if you don't speak each other's language. Love wins even if one is a prostitute and the other a middle-class American.

The creators of *Miss Saigon,* Boublil and Schonberg, found their inspiration in news images. In their case it was a picture taken in 1985 of a Vietnamese women who sees her 10-year-old daughter leave Vietnam to go to her American father. The child is crying and the mother, who will never see her daughter back, looks away, seemingly emotionless.

Miss Saigon starts with a scene in a nightclub in Saigon in 1975: "The heat is on in Saigon." The girls are waiting in the bars for the soldiers to come. Because of my research I know that the women hanging around in such bars are often those with limited opportunities in life. They have little schooling, come from rural areas where there are few employment possibilities, and often already have one or more children. Sex work is increasingly a career for women with few chances, but with many responsibilities. I see them in our projects. At 16 they are sent by their families to the UNTAC soldiers in Vietnam to earn some money to support the family. They are infected with HIV when they are 20. Without doubt, some of them want to get away from Saigon, but most Vietnamese women want to stay there and care for their children and parents. However, in the musical the women are made to sing in a sleazy nightclub frequented by American GIs. The engineer, acting as their pimp, instructs the women to believe that their passports to Europe or America are the men in the bar and that each day, with more and more people leaving Saigon, their money-making power decreases.

We communicate through stereotypes—otherwise we would not understand each other—and this is one of the well-known stereotypes: the Asian whore. She wants to get away and go to Europe or, even better, the United States. It is Aissa who took Willems by surprise. He did not even know he had something in him on which she could get hold. She is a savage and he a clever European.

Our heroine, Kim, is one of the girls in the bar. A real prostitute is often not effective as a protagonist for storytelling. An audience has to identify with them. At least with Chris, who cannot be portrayed as a man who picks up hookers in obscure bars. No, on that evening—at the end of April 1975— Kim is for the very first time in that bar. She is a virgin and innocent. Kim and Chris fall in love and get married in the Vietnamese way, but they are separated because of the sudden fall of Saigon. Just in time, Chris manages to escape with the last helicopter. He has been looking desperately for Kim, but she was not allowed to pass through the embassy gate. Kim remains in Vietnam.

After wars the hatred does not stop immediately and a lot of bills still have to be paid. After April 1975, many people felt insecure about their safety and future, and wanted to get away from Vietnam. An extra argument for leaving was the communist attitude towards entrepreneurship that made many businesspeople decide to try their fortune elsewhere. The West encouraged it because this exodus had the function to demonstrate how barbarian the North Vietnamese regime was and that the American efforts to protect the inhabitants of South Vietnam had not been for nothing.

The stories of the refugees were needed to reinterpret our own history. However, when there was no longer a need for that, the heroic boat refugees changed overnight into economic opportunists and had to be sent back.

Do not misread me. The government in Vietnam does not respect our glorified human rights. If I teach at the university in Hanoi, Hue, Ho Chi Minh City, or Can Tho, all my handouts are checked, at each workshop a spy is listening to what I say, and my wife's faxes are only given to me at the very last day, because the man of the university's intelligence department cannot read Dutch. But for the rest he is all right. Sometimes we drink a BaBaBa beer together.

Miss Saigon is about the Bui Doi (the dust of life), American Vietnamese children. To my surprise, in Vietnam I met Americans who were actively looking for them. More than 50,000 Bui Doi have already left Asia, though only one percent have found their natural fathers. In Vietnam, children without fathers have less chances, like in so many other developing countries. Probably they also were teased a bit extra because they reminded the population of the war. However, it was no easy time for any Vietnamese (nor for returning Americans).

Reading *The Sorrow of War* by Bao Ninh, we know that even returning North Vietnamese soldiers were not welcome home anymore.

To single out the half-American children and "bring them home" is outrageous. In 1948 the Germans did not go to Poland, the Netherlands, France, or Hungary to save their offspring produced in the war. What is so special about American blood, that if there is 50 percent of it in a child, he or she has to be taken away from the Vietnamese mother? It is especially interesting because in the documentation that journalists received about the musical *Miss Saigon,* we could read: "Their background is marked undeniable on their faces. They have a dark skin but blue eyes. Blond hair frames their Asian features."

This brings me back to my falling white men. They fall for the women in the Vietnamese brothels, but when they realize how low they have gone, they come back to bring their 50 percent kids home.

Chris is back in Atlanta and already married for a few years to Caucasian Ellen. John, a former friend from "Nam," tells him that Kim has been able to escape to Thailand. She has a child and Chris is the father. Kim had to get away from Vietnam because Thuy, the bad Vietcong officer, wanted to have her, but she remained faithful to Chris. The faithful whore must be one of the favorite themes to express total love.

John takes Chris and Ellen to Bangkok. For whatever reason, Kim finds out that Chris is in town and goes to his hotel. Meanwhile, he has gone looking for her, and Kim meets Ellen. Ellen tells her that she is married to Chris and the dream is over. When Chris returns to the hotel, Ellen sings "Her or Me," and the underlying theme is that you have to choose your own kind. As already mentioned, that is not a strange theme in colonial literature.

For instance, in 1880, there were 471 European women against 1,000 European men in the Dutch Indies. There were many mixed relations, some official, but mainly unofficial. It was even promoted by the authorities for difficult areas like north Sumatra, because these places were supposed to be unfit for white women. Around the turn of the century more European women came to the colonies, and they saw it as their responsibility to save the fallen men, who were often consuming a lot of alcohol and living with "native women." The European women became the protectors of Dutch culture and prevented the former colony from developing into a melting pot.

In the same way Ellen seems to save Chris, and he explains to her his affair with Kim: "Let me tell you the way it was. Saigon was crazed, but she was real and for one moment I could feel. I saw a world I never knew and through her eyes I suffered too" (act 2). It all happened because of the circumstances, and only when Chris met Ellen did his life really begin. "East is east and west is west, and never the twain shall meet" (also written by Kipling). For a moment the dream seemed to come true, but it lasted only as long as the saxophone played.

The end of the musical makes it all even clearer. Kim commits suicide because Ellen has told her that her son can come to America, but that Kim is not welcome. However, according to Ellen, it is better when a child remains with the mother. Before committing suicide, Kim sings to her son, in act 2, telling him that she knows her purpose on earth was to help her son find his place and his way to America.

The Vietnamese woman is not even a savage, like Aissa, but only the vehicle to bring a child to its white American father. The musical is a compilation of stereotypes of Vietnam, developing countries, the relation between East and West, and migration. It reflects and reinforces unconscious ideas of Western people about those with a different ethnic background. It has racial motives.

It plays on clichés about the sexually attractive Asian women and their dangers for white men. Apart from its impossible love story, its popularity is due to the fact that it contributes to the idea that white people are superior. They can fall from their high place, but if they stick to their own kind and culture they do not have to fear.

I write this essay during the evenings of a mission to Cambodia, where I train Cambodians to do behavioral research in the framework of AIDS prevention. In the bars I see white men. The *mamasans* offer them their young girls. Virgins are expensive. They cost up to 200 dollars. I see adolescent girls in adult evening dresses hanging against these men, talking in Khmer with high-pitched voices. They have barely breasts, probably no pubic hair, and the only English they know is laughing. I try to understand the fall of these white men who believe that they are so special that they can do whatever they like, even if the girls are only 13. I try to understand why it intrigues and irritates me, and what it is that makes me write about it.

I have come to the conclusion that there must be two separate reasons why I write stories about falling men.

The first is related to my life as an academic, because I want to provoke and irritate my fellow compatriots and confront them with the reality as I see it. I want to deconstruct their fantasies about how wonderful they are. I want to show them that man is not so very special and equal everywhere in the world. In the end, all culture comes down to a few things: interpretations of power and sex in order to control them. Let me be honest: I love to rub those stories in.

WORKS CITED

Boublil, Alain, and Claude-Michel Schonberg. *Miss Saigon.* London: Cameron Mackintosh, 1988.

Conrad, Joseph. *An Outcast of the Islands.* Garden City, NY: Doubleday, Paige & Co., 1896.

Kipling, Rudyard. "The White Man's Burden." *McClure's Magazine* Feb. 1899. 290.

Roth, Philip. *American Pastoral.* Miami: Vintage, 1997.

"Not about Me"—Autobiography and the Short Story

Janet Kieffer

Apparently there's a new literary term these days: "autobiografiction," meaning "fictionalized" autobiography as a serious subgenre. Hemingway and others wrote famous "autobiographical" pieces, and there are contemporary writers, like Pam Houston, who gladly claim a large share of personal experience regarding their stories. Houston's contemporary stories seem to have a real value and appeal for readers in that personal experiences are shared. The appeal was so great that Houston subsequently published a collection of essays, *A Little More about Me*—but her contribution to the writing of fiction, insofar as it reimagines the general human condition, doesn't seem to be what these writings are about. The Pam Houston stories are "self-identification" stories for a legitimate readership interested in the transformation of a particular writer's life into aesthetically charming stories, and in that way they certainly contribute. These stories are primarily rooted in who Pam Houston is. But far more admirable are the stories that illuminate the characters of other human beings. We do not read James Joyce's *Dubliners* to find out about James Joyce, but to have reason to think about ourselves and others who either are or who might have been.

The first problem with a term like *autobiography* is, of course, a matter of semantics and degree. In a loose philosophical or etymological sense, a writer can argue that all of her fiction is autobiography since her stories are written via her unique perspective and experience—which is in turn an amalgam of her impressions: the anger or confusion she felt when the boy looked up her dress, her mother's snatching of her felt hat, the warm or elusive settings she has enjoyed by the fire with the mutt or the green pepper, the eerie camp-ground, the apartment full of spiders. Yet most fiction writers know that there is a great deal of variance within the definition of autobiography, and a very good short-story writer knows that the variance can be crucial and that the balances between variances are even more so. It's not so much a matter of what was real or where one was. It is the lateral connections the writer makes within any certain story: between a certain character and setting, for example, that looks far beyond self and discovers new insight. An autistic individual (who was inspired by someone the writer met years ago and who may not have been autistic at all) and a New England setting the writer experienced or read about might merge under the right circumstances of lateral thought to create a whole short story, precisely and artistically rendered. It's the ability to combine impressions, with the writer always looking outward, that lends itself to the best stories. The short story is a sacred little form. It teeters in various places between the poem and the novel like an owl between the oak and the rabbit. And the best short stories know how to preserve themselves: They are always looking around! They had better be, too, because the economy of the form insists on this. There is neither time nor space to waste when one is stuck between a poem and a novel. The short story is not about "me."

The interest in autobiographical fiction stems from many sources. Recently, some popular ones are sociological and/or political, as in the concern with gender and ethnicity in the short story. There are those who would condemn a writer from writing from a point of view that is not native to him. But this interest seems to be coming more from a sociological interest than a literary one. A literary one is far more liberal, as long as the writer looks outward and does it well. So often, given the concentrated form of the story and (per-haps) the limited imagination or experience of the writer, stories wind up flat, lacking detail and spirit. The current sociological/political emphasis, coming from a critical perspective, can be an inadvertent aid to this disability.

By "self-identification stories," I'm not referring to the work that reveals histories and contexts of different cultures. These are important and enrich-ing, like the works of James Baldwin, Julia Alvarez, Ernest Gaines, and so many others who write from within their cultures, but not from within the exclusive perspective of self. Interesting also are the stories of writers like Lucia Berlin, a racially Northern European woman who grew up in a Span-ish-speaking country; these are mirrors, when I think of them, and Lucia's stories, the mixed-culture stories, are empathetic and spiritual ones. As our various cultures merge, stories like these will be all the more valuable. It's also important that a writer of one culture be able to render another culture in art, as long as the writer knows something of what she's doing and handles this with a genuine respect. Berlin has done this so well that she has been invited to panels as Chicana. She has had to explain that she is not, but they wanted her there anyway—who wouldn't? Her stories look at the human spirit in many of its ambiguous forms.

There are so many delightful stories that unearth the lives of others. A marvelous story by Alyson Hagy, "Graveyard of the Atlantic," begins this way:

His wife was a poet who, in cruel and important ways, was becoming lovelier and more gifted as she aged. She was close to fifty now, her hair threaded with a tarnished silver that looked warm, unkempt, in photographs. She was also thin, as whittled down as she'd ever been, and so argumentative that her friends forgave her, thinking it must be part of some performance she was putting on for herself. He knew better. Something deep had taken hold of his Lucy, a grip which felt relentless even to him. Each morning she set off on her walk through the neighbor's fields limping with tension. He followed her progress along the sun-spackled path, watched her shrink to the size of his thumb, then disappear.

This introduction to Lucy and her husband leads, among other things, to an image of newly hatched turtles on their way to the sea, and to Lucy's being "curled up like a dried wasp" in the midst of her distress. It is the opposite of egocentrism or emphasis on who the writer is.

I greatly admire a classic story by Stephen Crane, "The Blue Hotel." There is a Swede in the story, among other people, but what particularly intrigues me is this sentence about the Swede: "In his eyes was the dying swan look. Through the windows could be seen the snow turning blue in the shadow of dusk. The wind tore at the house and some loose thing beat regularly against the clap-boards like a spirit tapping."

Regarding Ernest Hemingway, one of his best stories is not an "autobiographical" Nick Adams story; it's "Wine of Wyoming." Set during Prohibition in the United States, this remarkable story includes a major character, Madam Fontan, who speaks broken English/French. Her dialogue is a wonder to read. Maybe Hemingway had some connection to this place; it is impossible to tell, but he was looking outward as he wrote it. Here is an excerpt:

"They're drunk," she said. "That's what makes the trouble. Then they go somewhere else and say they got it here. Maybe they don't even remember." She spoke French, but it was only French occasionally, and there were many English words and some English constructions.

"Where's Fontan?"

"Il faut de la vendange. Oh, my God, il est crazy pour le vin."

"But you like the beer?"

"Oui, j'aime la bière, mais Fontan, il est crazy pour le vin."

She was a plump old woman with a lovely ruddy complexion and white hair. She was very clean and the house was very clean and neat. She came from Lens.

"Where did you eat?"

"At the hotel."

"Mangez ici. Il ne faut pas manger à l'hôtel ou au restaurant. Mangez ici!"

"I don't want to make you trouble. And besides they eat all right at the hotel."

"I never eat at the hotel. Maybe they eat all right there. Only once in my life I ate at a restaurant in America. You know what they gave me? The gave me pork that was raw!"

"Really?"

"I don't lie to you. It was pork that wasn't cooked! Et mon fils il est marié avec une américaine, et tout le temps il a mangé beans en can."

This is one of the best Hemingway stories because he is going away from himself and emphasizing a little culture in Wyoming in the middle of Prohibition, and he is showing great care for his characters as he does so. How can one help but to adore Madam Fontan?

> ... nor till the poets among us can be
> "literalists of
> the imagination"—above
> insolence and triviality and can present
> for inspection, "imaginary gardens with real toads in them," shall we have
> it.... (Moore, "Poetry")

Aside from the fact that autobiographical stories can fall flat because of a perceived egocentrism, they can fail from a lack of fictive detail, a matter of craft critical to a good short story. What are the specifics of character, setting, or mannerisms? How do characters talk? And which details are the best revelations of particular characters in this situation? Are there cracks in the walls of the house? The situation often flushes out as follows. A writer recounts a thinly veiled, actual occurrence—her summer vacation, or a fight with her spouse. But the events in the story, when recounted (though they might be slightly different to lend a "fictional" aspect to the tale), lack the fictive specifics necessary, especially in such a small space as the short story offers, to render the story's essence. The writer is looking at the story so much from her own experience that the details are a given in the writer's mind. The cup is on the counter, the moth is on the wall. But she will not mention these things. Everything's there. Her fiction does not demand that she provide the fresh and intricate details so necessary to the short story. When asked about certain aspects of such a story, the writer will often respond with comments or questions like this:

"Well, don't you get it? You must not be reading well enough. The old man leaped to one side of the fireplace because there was a snake in there."

"What snake? There's no snake in this story. You must be tripping. There is no snake in the story at all."

"Sure there is. It's a blue racer snake and it went into the fireplace to get warm. Maybe you missed it. It was definitely—"

"Well, it might have been there, yeah, but the problem is that it's not in your story."

"Really? I forgot to put the snake in?"

"Yes. I guess you forgot."

"Oh."

Providing fictional detail, using imagination, is a mental organ. If not engaged, it won't get stronger. In this way the writer does not progress, and churns out unimaginative short fiction, chunk after chunk, about his ex-wife, his crotchety uncle, his dog, what have you, but most usually about one or two aspects of his life in particular. The good creative-nonfiction writer realizes the demand for detail, but in short prose fiction it's even more essential to construct a story worth reading in such a small space. Details provide a sense of reality, but even more importantly, they provide fodder for the connections made in the process of lateral thinking. Without these connections, a story lacks movement, a kind of atrophy sets in, and like an inviable fetus, the story perishes before it even has a chance to start.

Finally, heavily autobiographical stories often fail due to the simple difference in definition between history and fiction. History is the recounting of events; fiction is construction of them with an eye to the revelation of some kind of truth, no matter how simple. With history, the facts are there, and cannot be selectively picked over for the better morsels (though in our own personal histories, we often like to do so). Fiction involves the deliberate discrimination of what should or should not be in a story—and again, with such a demanding short form, these decisions are critical. So an "autobiographical" short story, if we attempt to use the term literally, is a contradiction. (A literal translation, "self" and "life" and "write," is actually vaguer and paradoxically even more contradictory.) A writer is forced to make decisions of what details will and will not fit into that little space, and he's certainly not going to opt for his first vomit rather than his first painting; whether "fiction" or "nonfiction," autobiography has its limitations. Most people understand that autobiographical fiction is not a literal term; the term opposes itself, but it is for this reason that the term becomes instantly suspect. An actual occurrence does not become a good short story simply by bending a few of the details. Besides, autobiography itself is a fiction (who can include everything?), and when a writer piles another fiction onto the one that already exists through what he chooses to remember about his own life, the form gets very messy indeed.

How, then, can such writers as Alice Munro, who relies heavily on settings she remembers, or writers who write from a certain cultural or sexual sphere, write stories unaffected by such complications? How can Lucia Berlin write intriguing stories containing impressions from her background? How can they write imaginative, lasting stories without contradictions? The answer, as I have suggested, is that they are not essentially writing with the self in mind. When that is taken out, many of these problems with what we think of as autobiographical fiction are eliminated.

Any sense of egocentrism cannot exist.

There is a greater demand for fictive detail, because although the writer may remember a certain setting or event, her characters do not. She is forced to provide them, often from the point of view of another human being.

This, in turn, provides the food for lateral, associative, and abstract thinking, which sets off a thriving chain of possibilities for the story: plot, theme, character, setting, initial situation, all of it.

The writer is not mired in the details of what to include (about herself) or what not to include, because the story isn't about her. She includes only those details that belong in the story, the details that reveal the toad in the garden.

Autobiography, as it applies to short stories, is hardly a dirty word. Probably the best sense of autobiography in fiction is that it's always present, simply because the writer's work, after all, defines him, and because he shares that work intimately with his readers in a way that explores the world from his perspective, no matter what point of view he opts to use. So when one reads *A Long Day in November* by Ernest Gaines, one is discovering Ernest Gaines more effectively than talking to him directly. And one reads Hagy's "Graveyard of the Atlantic," from the point of view of a man and his concern for a woman, in the same way. The perspective, as the writer becomes more and more involved in his story, is bound to surprise him. It makes him explore areas he hadn't thought of before. If he does so carefully and unflaggingly, avoiding self-centeredness and valuing his characters over himself, he'll find and reveal all of the toads and snakes he cares to find, and more.

Imagine that.

WORKS CITED

Crane, Stephen. "The Blue Hotel." *The Norton Anthology of Short Fiction.* Ed. R. V. Cassill and Richard Bausch. New York: W. W. Norton, 2000. 376–96.

Hagy, Alyson. "Graveyard of the Atlantic." *Graveyard of the Atlantic.* Minneapolis, Minn.: Graywolf Press, 2000. 81–106.

Hemingway, Ernest. "Wine of Wyoming." *The Complete Short Stories of Ernest Hemingway.* New York: Macmillan, 1987. 342–355.

Moore, Marianne. "Poetry." *The Norton Anthology of Modern Poetry.* Ed. Richard Ellman and Robert O'Clair. London: W. W. Norton, 1988. 457.

What Comes Next: Women Writing Women in Contemporary Short Fiction

Kelly Cherry

Are there trends in contemporary short fiction by women? Undoubtedly. But exactly what those trends are may be almost impossible to say, or at least very difficult for a woman writer to say, the same way it is difficult for anyone to fathom, in a mirror, the visual impression her or his own face makes. You look into a mirror, and you see the person you once were, or the person you imagine others think you are, or the person you have never been but wished to be, or that person you have, always, recognized yourself as being and yet hoped against hope no one else could see. You almost never see who you are now, today, this stranger scrutinizing a reflection as if it might be, somehow, more real than the self engaged in reflecting.

One thing, however, is clear, does offer itself up to reflection:

The first thing to be said about women writers of short fiction in the United States today is that there are more of them than there were. There are many more than there were even just a short while ago. This is partly because there are more short-story writers of both sexes than there used to be. Our academic system of undergraduate English majors with a creative-writing emphasis followed by Master of Fine Arts programs utilizing the workshop method of analysis and criticism has contributed to a mushrooming (if not a flowering) of short fiction. Short stories are, after all, short; they can be read and discussed in the span of a two- or three-hour workshop as novels cannot. The short-story form may daunt the novice writer less than does the novel, which, generally at least, requires a commitment of several years and a narrative ability that seems to bear some relation, if not an absolute relation, to experience and wisdom. At the same time, the short story's traditional inclination toward epiphany, its formal belief in enlightenment and resolution, draws the young writer as irresistibly as any promise of fulfillment. The short story says to the young writer, I can be completed, I can fulfill you, happiness is within your grasp. (The older writer, of course, knows that love is fickle, even the love of an art form for an artist, and that, as with all relationships, the only fulfillment is found, oddly, in an endless giving of the self.)

So it is that, even in an era of shrinking markets, when a magazine like *Mademoiselle* ends its quite glorious heritage of 57 years of publishing serious fiction; when *Redbook,* which had published, among its pages of advice for young mothers, the work of some of the best writers, men and women, around, admits that it now prefers popular fiction; even at this time more writers are writing more short stories than ever before, publishing, if not in slick magazines, then in the academic and literary journals such as the *Georgia Review, Fiction,* the *Gettysburg Review,* a list far too long even to begin. And so it is that many of these writers of short stories are women.

I published my first book, a novel, in 1974. I had previously published four or five short stories with enough success to gratify a young writer, but my first attraction was to long forms. My very first attraction was to long poetry. The first serious poem I ever wrote—I was 16 or 17—echoed "The Waste Land," as perhaps everything written by a young poet in those days did, and sustained itself for some pages. It was titled "Heatherland," and it was naturally about a young woman—girl, we said then—named Heather: an instance of the young poet seeking to find herself in a mirror.

But my interest in long forms was honestly come by, as I had grown up with parents who were string-quartet violinists and who particularly loved the late Beethoven quartets. I had grown up loving that music myself; and there is no art more interested in problems of development than the Beethoven string quartets.

In 1974, then, when I published my first book, it was a novel, not a collection of short stories. I didn't know any other women fiction writers my own age, though I had read some of what I thought of as the older generation: Mary McCarthy, Katherine Anne Porter, Flannery O'Connor. I had read of contemporary overseas fiction writers who were women: Iris Murdoch and Muriel Spark, a few others. And I had read a young American poet named Erica Jong, whose first novel, *Fear of Flying,* had been published just a year earlier. It was difficult for a young woman writer to get published, and if she managed it she might, like Erica Jong, be praised by John Updike in the

New Yorker, but the praise would be for her "bawdiness" and, as I remember, anyway, her white teeth, which he had apparently found exceedingly mesmerizing in the jacket photograph. I hasten to add that I did not feel disinherited, exactly, by the tradition of men writers, whose works I read as or more avidly, but I did feel a need to prove something—my claim on that heritage, my worthiness—and perhaps I had been disinherited, without knowing it.

Ms. magazine started up not long before this, and while I was in full sympathy with its feminist goals of achieving equality of opportunity and pay for women, I was less enthralled with its cultural agenda, which derived, I believe, from a confusion of fiction with propaganda that still bollixes critical treatment of fiction by women. Identifying the patriarchal with the hierarchical, *Ms.*, in those early, understandably defensive days, decided to have a "review committee" rather than a book editor. The review of my first novel had come in and was so praiseful, and so firmly scheduled, that copy was sent to my publisher, who forwarded it to me. Alas, the review committee then fell to arguing about the ending of my book. In the last chapter my heroine agreed to transfer from one medical school to another in order to be near her boyfriend. Some members of the committee thought that to change schools for reasons of love was inexcusably antifeminist—though in my eyes the heroine was growing as a person by being willing to commit herself to another—and the review was killed.

Ten years later, for my fourth novel and sixth book, I did receive a lovely review from *Ms.,* though I don't know whether they were still doing things by committee. Perhaps this review represented just one voice (but I'm fond of *Ms.* and like to think an entire committee voted to return my feeling). Interestingly enough, the book, *The Lost Traveller's Dream,* was one I had intended to be a book of short stories. The stories were interlinked but only in a strange sort of way, as those in the second section were told by a narrator who was the creation of the narrator of the first section; the narrator of the third section was then revealed as the creator of the narrator of the first section. There was this ontological interlinkage, but no narrative progression tied the three sections together, and so I thought of the book as a collection of stories.

In 1984 the vogue for book collections of short stories was just beginning to pick up speed, but my editor still cleaved to the accepted publishing wisdom regarding collections of short stories; namely, that they did not sell. He tried to talk me into calling the book a novel; I balked, but I agreed to sign a contract calling the book a collection of three novellas. But I lacked the courage of my own conviction, feeling a need to achieve a wider readership, and as the editing process got underway I found myself giving in and adding material to make the book something more like a novel. The result still embarrasses me, and I hope someday to have an opportunity to revise it in the direction of my original vision.

Meanwhile, the accepted publishing wisdom, it turned out, had just gone out the window: Suddenly short-story collections were selling. A young woman named Pam Houston hit the bestseller list in the early 1990s with a first collection (and first book) of finely tuned stories titled, enchantingly, *Cowboys Are My Weakness*. The paperback rights to this book sold for a cheeringly large sum, reminding us that at least once in a while artistic virtue needn't be its own reward, or its only reward. If other collections did not sell in great numbers, they sold steadily, presumably often to other young writers. Most story writers, as we know, will continue to get two free copies of the magazine in which their work appears; my point here is not that stories are earning more money than they used to (they are not) but that more of them are being written by women.

The great triumvirate of women short-story writers in the United States today is made up of Grace Paley, Cynthia Ozick, and the late Eudora Welty; these three writers form a constellation that is a collective shining light for any woman writer of short fiction. Welty is lauded for her inimitable talent for characterization (as in her story "A Worn Path") and for her ability to render an entire world in the brief span of a story. She has created a body of work that serves as inspiration and validation for quite a few younger writers, including Lee Smith, Jill McCorkle, and Bobbie Ann Mason. Her astounding ability to unveil the soul of the Other, as in the portrait in "A Worn Path" of an elderly black woman, Phoenix Jackson, walking to the doctor's office for medicine for her grandson, proves once and for all that a woman writer is not imprisoned by self, is not confined by boundaries of biology to the subjective, the autobiographical.

Welty is also one of the major stylists of the twentieth century, although she may not be recognized as such because her use of language is never self-reflexive, never in service to an image of the author. From beautiful, clear, precise description of the natural world to stunningly decentered rhythms conveying psychological intensity, her attempt is not to prettify but to approach truth as closely as possible. Consider, too, a sentence such as this one from her story "Why I Live at the P.O.": "Papa-Daddy's Mama's papa and sulks." In my estimation, a writer who wrote that sentence would laugh all day long, and the next day, too, and have a right to. Paley's urban rhythms, her bold dislocation of structural and even grammatical convention that conveys modern speech patterns and modern life patterns so naturally that the reader forgets the formal radicalism that parallels her political radicalism, create a marvelous music. Ozick may be accurately called—she would probably dislike this shorthand, disliking any formulaic phrase, and yet the phrase will be meaningful to readers who may not yet have read her work—"the Flannery O'Connor of Jewish literature," sublimely identified by her wry and penetrating intelligence and her gift for concentrating it on thorny subjects of moral and spiritual resonance.

Born in 1928, Ozick belongs to a generation that came to the age of conscience and consciousness during World War Two, and much of her work has been dedicated to an attempt to comprehend or, if that's not possible—to comprehend the incomprehensible—at least to remember, the horror of the Holocaust. In her story "The Shawl," Rosa, a mother nursing her child, and her niece, Stella, are force-marched to a camp. Rosa's milk dries up, and the baby, Magda, sucks on Rosa's shawl, a "milk of linen." The shawl hides Magda, allowing her to be mistaken for Rosa's breasts. But then Magda learns to walk. She even laughs, though it is a silent laugh. She is life, growing and becoming itself, there in the death camp. She has survived this long—15 months—because she is, thinks Rosa, mute. But the niece, Stella, 14 years old and desperate to live too, takes the shawl away from Magda, and Magda—this is inevitable, this is circumstance, this is the inevitable circumstance that is tragedy—cries. She bursts into a huge howling. Rosa rushes to get the shawl, but she returns only in time to see Magda carried off by a guard and then hurled at the electric fence. Rosa "only stood, because if she ran they would shoot, and if she tried to pick up the sticks of Magda's body they would shoot, and if she let the wolf's screech ascending now through the ladder of her skeleton break out, they would shoot; so she took Magda's shawl and filled her own mouth with it, stuffed it in and stuffed it in, until she was swallowing up the wolf's screech and tasting the cinnamon and almond depth of Magda's saliva; and Rosa drank Magda's shawl until it dried."

Grace Paley, in a story titled "Mother" barely longer than one page, gives us the reverse lamentation, the daughter feeling the loss of her mother. The story begins: "One day I was listening to the AM radio. I heard a song: 'Oh, I Long to See My Mother in the Doorway.' By God! I said, I understand that song. I have often longed to see my mother in the doorway. As a matter of fact, she did stand frequently in various doorways looking at me." Echoing the three-times rituals of fairy tales, the narrator then recalls three times when her mother stood in the door. "She stood one day, just so, at the front door, the darkness of the hallway behind her. It was New Year's Day. She said sadly, If you come home at 4 A.M. when you're seventeen, what time will you come home when you're twenty?" The narrator's second memory is of her mother at the entrance to her daughter's room at home. "I had just issued a political manifesto attacking the family's position on the Soviet Union. She said, Go to sleep for godsakes, you damn fool, you and your Communist ideas. We saw them already, Papa and me, in 1905." And then the third memory: "At the door of the kitchen she said, You never finish your lunch. You run around senselessly. What will become of you?"

"Then," the narrator says, "she died."

Importantly, that is not a punch line. The story continues, conjuring the narrator's parents in their living room. In the middle of the mother's bid to get her husband to open up, to talk to her, the narrator admits that she wishes she could see her mother "in the doorway of the living room." But this cannot happen, and the father says he is too tired to talk.

"Then she died."

The repetition of the statement "Then she died" resonates with shock. The narrator cannot, even now, accept that her mother is gone, that so much went unsaid. It is the repetition that persuades us we are hearing more than a writer's voice, that we are hearing the voice of a narrator whose feeling is genuine and deep.

The narrator's mother dies still wanting to be talked to a little. Such a gulf that has opened up between the father and the mother! Such a sense of lost opportunities for closeness we feel reading this story, of missed humanity! And yet Paley manages to make us feel, too, the father's weariness with the dark side of life. And we feel that this man and woman know how to accommodate each other even if they do not know each other fully. But the daughter, we feel, failed to accommodate her mother when she had the chance. Perhaps the story is a way of talking to her mother a little.

The splendid African American writer Colleen J. McElroy describes a similar character in her story "Imogene," included in her book *Jesus and Fat Tuesday*, a collection that covers nearly a hundred years of black history without ever making a show of its own ambition. But Imogene is a softer character. She believes she's in love. She thinks she must be drawn to him, the man she is sure she loves, for his style, the way he walks and dresses. Or no, she thinks: "It was the touching." Or maybe, "It was the way he tilted his head." His hands, his thighs. The reader is beginning to realize that this gorgeous creature is nowhere in sight. Imogene is hunting for him in the San Francisco night. "The good looking ones run faster, she thought." She stops in a bar, the Tambourine. She'll have a drink. She decides to make it a double.

And he's there. She joins him at his table. He suggests that they go for a walk. She hesitates, then tells herself that he waited for her.

She follows him to a car. He opens the door, gives her to a "Mr. Preston." He reminds her to get fifty bucks. He says he'll be in the bar. He leaves her there.

The man in the car starts to take what he's paying for, but Imogene is thinking of the one she loves. The story closes,

> But her thoughts were clear: she remembered her man, how he had smiled and the warm feeling when his hands brushed her face just before she'd slid into the car and the door had closed. She hoped he would be in a good mood when she got back to the Tambourine. Her sweater fell open and she let her body go soft, leaning into the seat, stroking the smooth leather with her free hand.

Many of these women, one begins to think, are trapped by sex, in sex. Joyce Carol Oates's well-known story "Where Are You Going, Where Have You Been?" presents a 15-year-old, Connie, who is, we realize, trapped forever. Enormous, almost suffocating tension builds as the reader sees Connie—a girl who is only a tiny bit daring, a girl who doesn't, not really, do anything "wrong"—becoming fatally entrapped by the psychotic Arnold Friend. Her family has gone to a barbecue, leaving her at home alone. Arnold and his sidekick have been watching her and know she is alone. She knows she's in trouble; she wants to get away from it—this destiny that has abruptly manifested itself to her as hers—but there is no way she can. "We'll go out to a nice field," Arnold tells her, "out in the country here where it smells so nice and it's sunny." She is caught in an eternal darkness, on a bright summer day that cannot end.

In an essay titled "The Parable of the Cave or: In Praise of Watercolors," Mary Gordon describes how she was brought up to be "a good girl," a daughter who reflected her father's image. She still credits her father for encouraging her to write, but, she says, "now I see that I am the kind of writer I am because I am my mother's daughter. My father's tastes ran to the metaphysical. My mother taught me to listen to conversations at the dinner table; she taught me to remember jokes." She continues, "My subject as a writer has far more to do with family happiness than with the music of the spheres."

My mother, of course, loved the music of the spheres, loved it as deeply and as unsentimentally as my father did, and if she was short on other kinds of love she had that love to give me and did. I understand what Gordon is saying—that we need to attend to the quieter, less cosmic notes—and I quite agree. In two books of interconnected stories, *My Life and Dr. Joyce Brothers* and *The Society of Friends*—I attempt to call attention to those more mundane notes and even to some not previously or often sounded, the underground notes, let's say, of a woman who has had to lead much of her emotional life in secrecy. But I would not want us to cease to hear the music of the spheres, also, nor would I want us to turn over the playing of it only to the men writers. "Something sings in my heart," I wrote in an earlier story set in the Northwest, on the Pacific, a story in *The Lost Traveller's Dream*, where it appears denuded of its title;

I have a canary in my rib cage, and he sings and sings. There's salt on the air, water in my boot, and music everywhere. Sound is pure structure, the plan underlying this liberality of existential stuff, swelling. Three dark rocks rise out of the sea, wet as seals; under a gray sky, the water is as green as grass. When a wave breaks, surf forms first at the outer points and rolls down the wave's length like a prairie catching fire, white fire.... The trick is to shed your soul on the beach like a snakeskin; in that profoundly bare condition, you will be able to tread water like ground, the continental shelf will emerge to support you. Amazingly, the farther out you go, the wider your world becomes; your perspective expands, and forsaking de facto being, you achieve the infinite dimensions of the imagination. All things glow; seaweed, clouds, fish are radiant when beheld. The third eye is a tiny Christ nailed to a tiny cross on your forehead, right between the other two.

But I was, as I say, younger then, unreconciled to loss, and passionate about injustice. This is not to say that age must reconcile us to loss or make us any the less passionate about injustice; rather, it is to say that we women who have been writing awhile, not unlike the strengthening tradition itself, have entered a place that is both exotically unfamiliar and hauntingly familiar. Consider the narrator of Grace Paley's story "The Long-Distance Runner," who seizes our attention in her opening sentence by declaring, "One day, before or after forty-two, I became a long-distance runner." And she runs in the country first, and then on the boardwalk, and then to her old neighborhood, where she had grown up. She runs to the apartment she used to live in and, fantastically, moves in with the current tenants. When she goes home she tells her family of her adventures. How can she explain this? "A woman inside the steamy energy of middle age runs and runs," she says. "She finds the houses and streets where her childhood happened. She lives in them. She learns as though she was still a child what in the world is coming next."

WORKS CITED

Cherry, Kelly. *The Lost Traveller's Dream*. San Diego: Harcourt Brace Jovanovich, 1984.
———. *My Life and Dr. Joyce Brothers: A Novel in Stories*. Tuscaloosa: University of Alabama Press, 1990.
———. *The Society of Friends: Stories*. Columbia: University of Missouri Press, 1999.

Gordon, Mary. "The Parable of the Cave or: In Praise of Watercolors." *The Writer on Her World*. Ed. J. Sternburg. New York: W. W. Norton, 2000. 27–32.

Gowdy, Barbara. *We So Seldom Look On Love*. New York: Harper Collins, 1992.

Houston, Pam. *Cowboys Are My Weakness*. New York: W. W. Norton, 1992.

McElroy, Colleen J. "Imogene." *Seattle Review* (spring 1978).

Oates, Joyce Carol. "Where Are You Going, Where Have You Been?" *Where Are You Going, Where Have You Been? and Other Stories*. Ontario and New York: Ontario Review Press and W. W. Norton, 2002. 118–36.

Ozick, Cynthia. "The Shawl." *New Yorker* May 1980: 33.

Paley, Grace. "The Long-Distance Runner." *Enormous Changes at the Last Minute*. New York: Farrar, Straus & Giroux, 1974. 179–200.

———. "Mother." *Later the Same Day*. New York: Farrar, Straus & Giroux, 1985. 111.

Welty, Eudora. "Why I Live At the P.O." *A Curtain of Green*. New York: Harcourt, Brace & Jovanovich, 1941. 89–110.

———. "A Worn Path." *Atlantic Monthly* Feb. 1951: 215–19.

7

The Short Story: Process of Discovery

Tell Me a Story

Donald Anderson

I lived on nothin but dreams and train smoke …

—Tom Waits, "Pony"

I

My father could repeat from memory long sections of "Hiawatha" and "The Courtship of Miles Standish" he'd learned in school. Full texts of narrative poems like "The Village Blacksmith" and "The Cremation of Sam McGee." And he invented bedtime stories—serials about Indian boys, eagles, Eskimos, bears, gold fields, the Nez Percé, the Royal Canadian Mounted Police. There were dogs in most of his stories, as there were in my grandfather's. He—my grandfather—told me about actually mining in Alaska, concocting moonshine in Utah (which he sold to failed Mormons and Utes), humping as a sparring partner for Jack Dempsey when Dempsey was training to fight Jess Willard. In that 1919 title match, "Jack almost murdered Jess," my grandfather said. He also claimed that Dempsey fought that fight with cracked ribs and that he, James Arthur Anderson, had cracked them in training. "Willard lasted three rounds with Jack, I lasted three months," he said.

II

In 1962, I intended to quit high school to work full-time in a car wash. My best friend had dropped out to work there and, in what seemed a short time, purchased a 1947 Pontiac sport coupe. I informed my father of my plans. He informed me of his. Two years after, public high-school diploma in hand, I started college. My announced major was engineering—the degree my father would have sought had he had the reasonable fortune to skip an alcoholic father, the Depression, rheumatic fever, sleeping sickness, copper mines, a blinded eye, and an early family.

What I remember from first-year calculus is my professor, Mr. Smith— "Call me, 'Mister,' not 'Doctor.' Doctors repair worlds. They don't dismantle." He'd worked on the periphery of the Manhattan Project—knew Edward Teller, he said, Oppenheimer, Enrico Fermi. Adam Smith was a drunk. One day he arrived late for class. He selected a chalk and began a white line, waist-high across the board. When he came to the end of the board, he continued. In fact, he dragged the chalk across the windows and on around the room. At the doorway, by which he'd entered, he turned. "Even that's not infinity," he announced. He cast us a lenient but morose look, then left. After one year of college, I, too, departed. For France. I stayed three years. I did learn French, but when I returned home and to school, my new major was English.

In time, I became an English professor, until, dissatisfied in my 40s, I stopped to go back to school. I'd wearied of students' (and faculty's) Cliff's Notes versions of Beowulf, Ahab, Lear, the Brothers K, Nick Caraway, and Daisy Miller. I didn't believe I could face another essay with the phrase "Heart of Darkness" or "Sturm und Drang" in its footnotes or title, surrounded by harried prose. Then I heard myself in a department meeting: "Look. The principal feature of Shakespeare's work is hardly that he was a middle-class, middle-aged, white European male. Get a grip! Christ."

I applied to and—luck of luck—was admitted to the M.F.A. program at Cornell University. There, with bright and able children—most of them half my age—I wrote stories. I suppose I'd always wanted to. By this time, I'd negotiated divorce and a second marriage, complete with children and step-children, pets and step-pets, aging parents, and my own near death on an emergency surgical table. I admit I felt I had stories to tell.

It was during this period in my life that I discovered Andre Dubus, his essays and stories, many of which were being published in *Epoch*, Cornell's literary magazine. I responded immediately. Maybe it was because my own life and reading had caught up to the human and fictional territory Andre had for so long staked out and mined.

The day later came when Andre called to place work. As the journal's editor I accepted his story, but with an apology about the payment we could afford. I knew of an essay he'd written in which he informed he preferred to publish in literary quarterlies and journals rather than in "slicks." In this essay he recounts being published in the *New Yorker* and *Penthouse,* wherein he uncomfortably found his work amid "advertisements for things that exclude all but the rich," and in the case of *Penthouse,* "among the crotches." His essay refers to publishing in *Sewanee Review.* This story on which he'd worked 17 months, through seven drafts and 400 pages (resulting in 60), earned him 500 bucks. But the story, he wrote in his essay, no matter its worth, had been given a dignity he could see: "On those pages it lives alone, untouched by paper genitals, diamonds and gold."

When Andre called in the 1990s, I believed he believed what he'd written in his essay some 20 years before, but I also knew that since that time, he'd been maimed by a passing car that had torn off one leg and ruined the other when he'd stopped at night to assist some people in a stalled car. I knew, too, he'd suffered long hospital stays, a divorce, the loss of the custody of children, and long periods during which he could neither write nor work as a teacher. I apologized again for the sum my journal could offer. With no hint of a pitied self, he said, "That's two weeks' groceries."

After his story was published, we wrote a few times and talked on the phone. On the day before I read of his death, I'd by chance reread his essay "Into the Silence," which ends:

Short story writers simply do what human beings have always done. They write stories because they have to; because they cannot rest until they have tried as hard as they can to write the stories. They cannot rest because they are human, and all of us need to speak into the silence of mortality, to interrupt and ever so briefly stop that quiet flow, and with stories try to understand at least some of it.

III

In my own department, English and Fine Arts at the United States Air Force Academy, I troll for unprepared answers: What makes a story a story? What is it you are after when you sit down with one? What makes the best short stories just that?

"Something with a heart and soul," says Tom. "Stories are what have connected us from the first circles of men and women around fires or in caves. Stories connect us to our pasts and allow us to imagine our futures—'heart and soul' means those kinds of connections."

"If I say it's a story, then it's a story," says Bill.

"I ask myself what I am getting out of it," says Tammy. "What I don't want to say after reading a story is 'Well, there goes 20 minutes of my life I'll never get back.' That's how I felt after three hours of the movie *Ali.* There go three hours, I thought. Have you seen that movie? Do you like boxing? Maybe if you like boxing, you'd like the movie."

"Entertainment is important," Lori says. "A short story can't just be an intellectualized experience. Don't you hate that word: intellectualized?"

"When Frost was asked to explain about poems, didn't he say something like, 'A poem tells you what you knew but didn't know you knew'? That's what I think about good stories," says Stephen. "They say things I've thought, but better."

"They help you learn about your own life and they help you learn about other people's lives if you're interested in other people's lives. If you're not, you should be," says Robert. "I'm thinking of Carver," he says, "old Ray."

"The experience is intense and feels real," says Matt, the newest member of our department. "Flannery O'Conner works on some pretty serious stuff in 10 or 15 pages. You can get some living done without a huge investment of time. Small risk, big return."

"Characters bloom quickly. You meet people and that makes you somebody different," says Don.

"It happens quick and at least one element is done really well—metaphor, place, character, talk, something. It happens quick and something sticks," says Shay. "That's the deal!"

And, Peter, as if by osmosis: "A chance for something—a minimal investment that has a chance of staying."

"I like to visit the other side," says Tracy. "I like to see how it's going over there. Thom Jones and George Saunders do it for me. Kinda sounds like a cheap thrill, doesn't it?"

"No," says Jim from the next office. "There is an authentic intensity to it. No foreplay."

"Rich characters," says Niko, a former student who's now a colleague. "Characters who convey humanity, like people I know or am interested in. But it's special in some way—even if the characters are ordinary, how they get rendered is anything but. It's the previously unthought-of image or metaphor that does it. That's what makes the characters rich."

"Originality of perception?" I suggest, still a teacher.

"Yes—rich," says Niko.

Richard, who teaches our criticism course, says, "Stories grip us in a way other prose does not. They grip me, at least—the language is different. I can read academic writing and yawn. I can't read a short story and yawn. That's a difference."

I say I agree. "Russell Banks once said to me that he thought my stories were trying to be novels. 'But if you're going to write a novel,' he said, 'you'd better learn to write some bad sentences.' I guess I see what he meant."

"Yes, there's a difference," says Rich. "I remember parts of short stories in a way I don't remember parts of novels. It's like when you remember lines from poetry—the sound of words in short stories clings."

"I like stories all right," says Howard, our Classics guy, our Oxford dude, "but I guess I prefer the novel. I am drawn to history, that's true. In a novel place and time matter in a way they might not in a story. Put another way, perhaps I prefer landscape to portrait."

Glenn says, "Well, they're short, aren't they? You can read them in between things." Glenn has five kids.

One colleague, a visiting professor from the East Coast, says she doesn't have time to read fiction, because she's writing a book.

"About fiction?"

"Not exactly." The book is about Sophia Amelia Peabody of Salem, Nathaniel Hawthorne's wife.

"I see."

"But when I do have the time, I'd rather sink into a novel. Adopt a whole world. Become the character, make a series of decisions, you know?"

Howard sticks his head in: "Hey, it came to me. You ready?—if the novel is a plein-air landscape painted in oils, then the short story is a snapshot taken during the commission of a crime. Take it or leave it."

I take it.

"A series of events that ultimately has some sort of organized meaning. After language, I guess it's the meaning part we're drawn to," says Mark. "No, let me say it this way: A story is told experience, but experience given shape and order—significance."

"Art and life are different," a mentor, Alfred Kern, used to say. "If they weren't, we wouldn't need art." Another of my teachers, Edward Leuders, would quote Carlyle: "What is it all but metaphor?" Then quoting himself: "We are tricked by metaphor from cradle to grave, yet our best insights are caught in metaphors. Something curious there," he said. "Something basic, no doubt."

IV

"In the beginning was the Word, and the Word was with God, and the Word was God." This notion as much as any allows the companion notion that a word is a concept made flesh, sleekly following the Book of John: "And

the Word was made flesh, and dwelt among us ... full of grace and truth."
Perhaps like you, I've felt comfortable, accustomed to the thought of word as
concept made flesh, but why not the William Gass perception: "It's not the
word made flesh that we want in writing, in poetry and fiction, but the flesh
made word"? Gass puts it this way too:

Every loving act of definition reverses the retreat of attention to the word and returns
it to the world. The landscape which emerges from the language which has made it
is quite as lovely, vast and curious, as rich and prepossessing, as that of the deity who
broke the silence of the void with speech so perfect the word "tree" grew leaves and
the syllables of "sea lion" swallowed fish.

Or Roland Barthes:

Language is a skin: I rub my language against the other. It is as if I had words instead
of fingers, or fingers at the tip of my words. My language trembles with desire.

V

Metaphor—that old instrument of perception—is the very heart of whatever gifts a writer has to offer and whatever gifts a reader is prepared to receive.
Think of Frederick Busch's opening to "Widow Water," an opening that is
metaphor for the story itself: "What to know about pain is how little we do
to deserve it, how simple it is to give, how hard to lose. I'm a plumber. I dig
for what's wrong. I should know." Ann Beattie, in "Snow," characterizing
a failing marriage: "It was as hopeless as giving a child a matched cup and
saucer."

"That's a simile," a department member says. "That's no metaphor."

"Oh," I say, "How useful is that distinction?" Then: "They're fastballs—all
fastballs—just thrown at varying speeds."

"OK," says David, "but with fastballs, like real estate, everything is location, location, location."

We look at each other around the table. We're assembling for a meeting for
a different purpose, but someone had mentioned metaphor and I'd quoted
Busch and Beattie.

"Pitching is artful deception," says Fred, who pitched in the big leagues,
but got injured in those days before sports medicine and the logical repair of
expensive bought legs. The Philadelphia Athletics handed him his glove and
sent him home.

"The best pitchers make you believe that something you guessed was false
turns out to be true—like metaphor," Fred says.

Because part of the meeting we're assembling for is about plagiarism in freshman comp, we cite sources.

"'A promise empty as the sleeve of a one-armed boy,'" Peter says, "or something like that. It's Merwin from that collection with the word 'ladders' in the title. The one that won the Pulitzer—1970."

Tracy pipes up: "'His skin is the color of fragile boredom, or mayonnaise.' That's Tosches, Nick Tosches. His rock-and-roll book called *Country*, the twisted roots thereof." Tracy lifts the book like a chalice. This term, Tracy is teaching a course in the History of American Music, and Tosches is Tracy's guy. Tracy himself has recorded rock and roll. His *Beatle Boots of Chinese Leather*, has been released in Sweden and his *Liquor Wagon* is roaming the World Wide Web. "Neither was released under any of my bands," Tracy says. "Those two were just me."

We ask Tracy to name his bands.

"'84 Rooms,' named for a derelict hotel in San Francisco, which is now in a fairly gentrified area. At the time, it was just us and the winos." Then: "'The Cletus Butterfoam Experience.'"

"What?"

"Don't ask." Then: "'Exploding Pintos,' 'Bloody Holly,' 'The Melon Colony.' 'The Terror of Tiny Town,' 'Fear and Air,' 'Baron Wants a Facial.'"

Tracy wants to read something, and he opens *Country*. "This is about cowboy songs," he says:

In Hollywood in the 1930s was born the yodeling cowboy, one of the mightiest pop hallucinations of all time. Yodeling was not unknown among cowboys. By all accounts, it was no less common than fiddling among oceanographers or tromboning among rare-book dealers.

Fred wants back in. "My candidate is in Hamlet's 'to be or not to be' speech: 'Or to take arms against a sea of troubles, and by opposing, end them.' Taking arms against a sea is just about the most hopeless act I can imagine. Picture Hamlet raiding the armory of maces, swords, axes, dirks, spears, then wading into the North Sea and flailing away. It's hopeless—as is his situation."

"Remember Fulton J. Sheen?" Matt asks.

As soon as Matt asks, I see the archbishop's face as I'd seen it on TV, a Catholic priest joking and preening for an electronic audience. Even as a kid I understood he was selling something and selling it well. Though we only ever had a black-and-white while I lived home, I could tell part of the Bishop's suit was red. "You were born when, Matt?"

"1972."

"You know about Sheen? He was dead before you started school."

"I've read a lot of Walker Percy. He mentions him." Then: "The reason I bring it up is I'm remembering a quote from Sheen. Someone asked him what it was like to hear nuns' confessions."

"Yes?"

"He said hearing a nun's confession was like being stoned with popcorn."

For a flash, I see Fulton J. coyly eyeballing TV land.

"'Just as happy as if they had good sense,' is what my mother says," says Lori. "But you have to say it right—like this." Lori says it again. "It's a North Carolina thing—southern—I guess. When my mother says it, though, she's usually talking about my sister."

"Raymond Chandler should be an honorary member of the Metaphor Hall of Fame," says Rachel. "These may not be his best, but off the top of my head: 'Her laughter ran around the room like mice in the wainscoting'; 'The plant stems looked like the newly washed fingers of dead men.' My favorite, though, is Neruda." Rachel gives us a look, makes us wait: "'I would like to do to you what springtime does to the cherry blossoms.'"

"'Pure as the driven-over snow,'" says Betsy.

"Dorothy Parker?" someone asks. "Mae West?"

"My roommate—Antioch, 1964. God," Betsy says.

"Metaphors are little stories," I suggest.

"Well, this one was," says Betsy.

We have two Davids in our department, and the other David chimes in with a second vote for Chandler. "'Suspicion climbed all over her face, like a kitten, but not playfully.'"

I push my idea about metaphors being miniature stories. "They're all little situations, aren't they?"

We think about that. I think about André Gide, who, in coming upon stacks of Marcel Proust's notebooks after Proust's death, characterized them as "watches ticking on the wrists of dead soldiers."

As it turns out, the meeting is long. Toward the end, someone says something inane. Silly, really, and off-topic. I can hear my dead father: "Dumb as a barrel of hair."

VI

Early in my air-force career, I was stationed for a year at a radar site in Alaska—Indian Mountain, Alaska. "North of North" we called it. I panned for gold in the Indian River—thinking of my grandfather's Yukon—and found a few flecks that I stored with a pinch of black sand in an emptied prescription vial. If you shook the sand, the gold glittered through.

Morale at the site was low because our outdated equipment was nearly useless. We were to be tracking the Russian Bear in those cold-war days. Our fear was Russian bombers would overfly us to the lower 48—toward our families and homes—and we'd never know. Our equipment was so obsolete that we seldom caught our own mail plane coming in. We'd be studying our screens when someone would open the door to say the mail plane had landed, as it did each week on our unimproved, gravel runway, which sloped at an eight-degree angle, straight into the side of a mountain. In the flight pubs, it read in bold print: Successful go-around highly improbable!

During winter, Indians would motor up the frozen Indian River to our radar site to drink. The joke among us was that we never wanted to visit the Indian village if they were firing up snow machines in the Alaskan dark to head in our direction.

In any case, the Indians would whoop it up at our "club"—a designated room in our compound that we used as a bar. We had a record player, a couple of dartboards, one pool table. The camp cook would fry you a steak if the chow hall was closed and the fire crew took turns tending bar.

It was against federal law to sell bottles of booze to Indians, so we didn't. I was reminded why I'd been born in Montana: my grandfather, unsatisfied with his moonshine sales, started moving his hooch onto the Ute Reservation. The feds caught wind of that and came after him. Tipped off by a Mormon bishop, Grandfather loaded my father and his sister and my grandmother into the Model T. They ran out of gas in Butte.

We sold liquor-by-the-drink to our visitors, which was legal, no matter how many bottles it ultimately led to. Drunked up, the young Indians would kick-start their snowmobiles to drive home. Home was a fishing village on the Koyukuk—a primary northern tributary to the more famous Yukon.

There was an older Indian who, when he traveled, came by sled. When he finished drinking, he wouldn't mush home. No matter the weather, he would sleep with his dogs. At four or five in the morning, the dogs would wake the camp, yipping for food. The old Indian would toss them frozen fish, then head home. Some nights he would spend outside with his dogs, the temperatures would drop to 50 or 60 below.

In time, I asked why he didn't drive a snowmobile.

He looked at me. "What are you going to do if your engine dies, eat the carburetor?"

The summer before I left Alaska, the old Indian walked me along the river to Gold Camp, five or six miles upstream. He'd hiked in from Koyukuk to visit. He'd brought two dogs and the fish to feed them. The huskies stayed within range, like sheepdogs.

On our way to the camp, we steered clear of the banked gravel and walked on tundra, which gave with our steps and released clouds of mosquitoes and gnats. I wore long sleeves and a cap with netting. When I sprayed my hands with repellant, the old Indian closed his mouth and covered his nose.

He had pointed out the dredged banks of the Indian River. He told me about the hydraulic mining before the war. He meant, he said, "The World War: Number Two." He extended an arm to wave it across the screen of the sky. "Overdigging," he said, toeing the bleached gravel, which stretched out of sight, both banks. "Water mining strips living earth. Pollutes watersheds. Kills fish."

In Gold Camp, the dredgers were rusted, bears had ransacked the cabins, and returning soldiers had had better offers in the lower states. We found swollen cans of tomatoes bears had missed, old newspapers, and mattresses full of thin snakes and rodents. From the scat, we could see that even moose had sometimes sought shelter. The old Indian talked about gold and arsenic and spoiled water. He smelled like salmon.

Before we headed back to the radar site, we walked along the river. What I thought to be a glacier canopied the water at a bend. I asked how old the ice was.

"It'll be gone by August," he said.

The ice—blue as sky—towered above. We stood where the river tunneled through, tempted by the microclimate. Following us from the 22-hour summer sun, the mosquitoes and gnats joined black flies in the misty cool. It was as if we stood inside a cold bell.

Because I attended graduate school late in my life, I often felt as though I'd awakened to find myself surrounded by amateurs who'd purchased expensive and muscular Ski-Doos. These folk circled to talk torque and horsepower and to pretend intimacy with snow and killing weather. I felt like the old Indian who wanted privacy, safety, and to sleep with his dogs.

I once repeated his words in a graduate course where the students came each week to books—twentieth-century novels—with mine tools: excavators, dredgers, powered things.

I said, "Hydraulic mining strips living earth, pollutes watersheds, kills fish." And when no one understood: "You can ruin anything—love, art—with too much of this." Then: "Tell me you love me. Count the ways. Specify. Provide five reasons in descending order as to why you love me. Tell me more."

VII

A few years back, Andre Dubus wrote to me about a story of mine he'd chanced upon. He wanted me to know that he'd nominated it for a prize. To my great pleasure, he made a point to praise its economy. "I so much admire distillation," he said, writing in pencil on paper torn from a Big Chief tablet, the kind of tablet he would have known we'd both remember from school. True or not, I see Andre writing his stories in longhand—first in pencil on paper—the least-technological connection from his heart to his hand to the page. I see him thus armed and scribbling the small and large crimes we all commit in the name of hope and love and fear and despair and longing.

At the moment, I'm thinking of Andre's "Bastille Day," a one-page essay meditating on loss. The essay is actually less than a page, though it escorts us through a family album beginning with French ancestors storming the tower midsummer in the 1780s to Louisiana and a father's death in the 1960s on to a mother's death in the 1980s, and so on to what is now Andre's own departure.

Meantime, in a ferociously distilled work, we, with Andre, endure the loss of three wives and what he dubs the "daily and nightly living with six children," the loss of one leg and the use of the other in a random and terrible wreck, and the confinement of a vital ex-Marine to a mechanical chair.

It has taken me more than one page to maneuver about the loss I feel in Andre Dubus's absence. He has, however, in his fiction and essays, left us this: it is not the work of art to make order, but to complicate order in just such a way that it begins to resemble living.

Who are those who say that literature is no longer sacred, if not dead? What can they mean and how can it be? Whose earliest recollection doesn't figure in the request "Tell me a story"? The human race needs stories. We need all the experience we can get.

for Andre Dubus (1936–1999)

WORKS CITED

Anderson, Donald. "Tell Me a Story." *Andre Dubus: Tributes*. Ed. Donald Anderson. New Orleans: Xavier Review Press, 2001. 28–30.

Barthes, Roland. *A Lover's Discourse: Fragments*. Trans. Richard Howard. Canada: Farrar, Straus & Giroux, 2001.

Dubus, Andre. "Bastille Day." *Broken Vessels*. Boston: David Godine, 1991. 145–46.

———. "Into the Silence." *Broken Vessels*. Boston: David Godine, 1991. 90–92.

———. "Selling Stories." *Broken Vessels*. Boston: David Godine, 1991. 97–103.

Gass, William. *Habitations of the Word: Essays*. Cornell University Press, Simon & Schuster, 1997.

Tosches, Nick. "Yodeling Cowboys and Such." *Country: The Twisted Roots of Rock 'n' Roll*. New York: Dacapo Press. 109–17.

Waits, Tom. "Pony." *Mule Variations*. Compact disc. Anti, 1999.

A Story

Vijay Lakshmi Chauhan

It began as anything but a story. What shape my thoughts would take, I had no idea, not until they had run a marathon and had arrived at the finish. Then the landscape swung into view. I could see clusters of words and jumbles of images as an artist sees a knot of trees, a mass of rocks, a flock of birds, a patch of the sky. I could now arrange and rearrange till a pattern began to emerge. In the process of writing and rewriting, I discovered the form my narrative would take. Here was a story, a construct—compact yet expressive, flexible though taut. It encapsulated a myriad of emotions; in fact, a whole range of experiences—lived and imagined. No matter how it had begun—as a meditation, a confession, a monologue, a poem, or a play of the mind—it was now a shape, a form that stood as an intermediary between the self and the world that it contemplated.

Perhaps that is what all art does. It becomes a filter through which one begins to view the world. For no matter why we start painting or singing, sculpting or writing, eventually we come to confront bigger questions, the nagging questions that transform a purely subjective experience into a universal riddle, and the intensity of a throbbing moment into pulsations of boundless time.

After the initial attempt—and in the process of discovering new stories—I was to hear other voices, see other patterns besides my own. The ambience of the immediate experience and of the immediate self was to disappear into a larger vision of humanity. In writing stories about the immigrant experience, I heard echoes of the general human situation. I realized I was writing about not only my hopes or fears, not only about the dreams and nightmares of an immigrant community, but also about human hopes and fears, joys and sorrows, exclusions and inclusions. I was writing about the experience that transcends class, race, color, or gender. If in geographical space, the distance from my people and my culture had enhanced alienation and displacement on the one hand, it had, on the other hand, brought about an emotional and spiritual exhilaration. My writing was a celebration of all that we, as human beings, dread, love, and live through.

In my writing—call it immigrant fiction, diasporic literature, or the literature of the exile—I construct for the readers a new reality in the "other's" terms, employing radically fresh images and weaving together in my narrative memories of the past and visions of the present; a nostalgia for the homeland and the pains of growing up in a multicultural society; life in the leisurely small towns and life in the metropolis; search for identity within the confines of one's environs; and the search too for a place in the global community.

Estranged and isolated from their homeland as well as the host culture, and often alienated from their own selves, my characters come to exist mostly in time and memory, in the communal past of the narrators. Memory, then, becomes a tool not only to pacify some inner restlessness, but also to embark on a journey to find one's identity and roots. Born of a deep urge from which, of course, all art springs, my stories serve as Ariadne's thread to lead me out of the maze of living.

I still don't know where stories come from.

All I know is that they flutter around us, they walk beside us, they perch on tree tops, they ride the bus with us, they hide in the attic, they wait in the basement. I also know that stories don't always fly straight into our hands like pet parakeets. They dodge us, they tease us, they play with us. It's up to us to lure them into our net, to haul them out of the depths of the sea. We have to sit patiently, immersed in deep concentration, and wait for the stories to rise. Sometimes, they take the bite quickly. Sometimes, they come only to slip away. At times, they don't come at all. As a writer, I have to have faith; I have to have patience as I sit there with the line submerged, waiting for the tug before I begin to reel in the catch.

The Short Story as Process—Not What It Means

Cyril Dabydeen

The short-story form is about character; nay, a slice of life. This idea I carried around with me for quite a while, yet at the University of Rajasthan in Jaipur, India, at a conference on the short story where I was a keynote speaker, I confronted my suppositions about the short story as never before: what it means for someone like me, living in Canada and grappling with identity, and more immediate problems, such as how the story should begin (not just a dignified preamble) or what closure really means—if it must convey, for instance, the sense of the characters' lives intriguing the reader beyond the story's ending. Indeed, I became convinced that the story must reflect probability above all else as a way for the writer to reflect integrity: what someone like V. S. Naipaul, I suspect, is chiefly concerned about in the narrative form, not merely whether the novel or short story is seen as selecting and arranging incidents to "produce an artistically patterned work, a totality in which nothing is superfluous" (David Daiches).

In then British Guiana, where I grew up, I'd read the stories of Somerset Maugham and H. E. Bates, and American writers like Ernest Hemingway and Edgar Allan Poe. The stories by V. S. Naipaul and Sam Selvon I also read with zeal because they addressed who I was, my sense of self and a tropical reality—all that I was familiar with. Naipaul's "B. Wordsworth," for instance, I recently looked at again and thought of reading with my Canadian-born 12-year-old daughter in order to communicate to her the sense of pacing and character, all quintessentially the early Naipaul's. And Selvon's "Waiting for Aunty to Cough," for instance, reflecting his remarkable naturalness of style and humor, which I still cherish, in the manner of tragicomedy that permeates much of early Caribbean writing. Later, in Canada, when Selvon and I got to know each other well, he wrote to me that I was "in the vanguard of the contemporary short story writers, shuttling with equal and consummate skill from rural Guyana to metropolitan Canada." I'm not sure whether I deserve this praise.

I'd read *Kyk-over-al* and sometimes *Bim* magazines in the New Amsterdam public library (the town that both Wilson Harris and Edgar Mittelholzer came from in Guyana) in the 1960s, and one story by Martin Carter in *Kyk-over-al,* about an abandoned fetus—after an abortion—has remained with me. You see, Carter has always had this haunting effect and quality, no doubt because of the impact of his poetry, which I used to read a fair amount of. His story was overwrought, a sensibility sometimes characterizing much of the writing published around that time (as I've heard it said), though in stories by John Hearne, Clyde Hosein, and Willie Chen, there is often a difference: a delightful vigor associated with a distinctive narrative style and voice. When I began writing my own stories (I'd become a national poet early in Guyana, and became tagged with the poetry label), I was in some ways already becoming obsessed with the short-fiction form, mainly because of its tightness, and also what I saw as its potential for interiority (note: the "absolute interiority" of a poem—Carlos Fuentes) and the quality of emotion one can strive for and achieve. My first story, "A Tide at Beachhead," I got published in the *Guyana Chronicle* in 1970; but I had also won a prize in 1968 in a national short-story competition based on human rights (A. J. Seymour was one of the judges). This story, "Pillon's Corner," about a Chinese family eking out a living as a shop owner with hostile forces around, was uppermost in my mind at the time (unfortunately this story is now lost).

In a sense, I suppose my vision was already becoming dystopian, nothing overly romantic in me; and in Guyana I'd also been reading other writers like Virginia Woolf (imbued as I was with her sense of reality as "the luminous halo, a semi-transparent envelope"), D. H. Lawrence, and even a Victorian writer like W. H. Hudson—his *Green Mansions* enabling me to see how the "spirit of the place" is presented by "outsiders." Other Caribbean writers like Lamming, Mittelholzer, Carew, Harris, Roger Mais, and Sylvia Winters I also kept reading.

When I came to Canada, I immediately began reading stories by writers such as G. D. Roberts (an early short-story writer with distinct animal and nature themes), Hugh Garner, Margaret Atwood, Alice Munro, Mavis Gallant, and Norman Levine (from Lowertown, Ottawa). Their perspective was sometimes unique, for me, not entirely dissimilar to the Caribbean short-story writers I kept reading. American short-story writers like Bernard Malamud also came to me—maybe mainly because Bharati Mukherjee was reading him (I'd become acquainted with her in Canada)—as I kept evaluating scene and situation, and noted each writer's sensibility and "integrity" at work.

Plot, not just characters, I began looking at critically, expecting everything to be presented with a "terrifying honesty." By now I'd begun seeing myself as a transplanted writer grappling with my ingrained West Indian consciousness, sustained by unique rhythms and close acquaintance with immigrant people's lives around me, and in me; and would character alone determine unity and consistency in the narrative form and structure as I continued to strive for aesthetic expression? The Barbadian-born Austin Clarke's stories and novels I also read around this time: the way Clarke captures the verisimilitude of Caribbean immigrants' existence in Toronto with his genuinely authentic voice and dialectal energy, unmatched by any other "Canadian" writer. Clarke I would also listen to speak at a "Black Writers in the Canadian Milieu" conference at McGill University about an inchoate patronizing attitude meted out to him by some other Canadian writers who deigned to give him "advice," because he was black or his having come from the "colonies."

The literary magazines began to become my staple reading material, as I took in the "new writing," all of place and experience in the Great White North and my making subliminal comparisons with who I was, my sugar-plantation self juxtaposed with anticolonial instincts. Indeed, I kept evaluating how stories came to be "located" and "problematized," with intuitive elements or intimations of postmodernism, all that I was becoming increasingly aware of. But above all, it was the sense of the imagination and its infinite possibilities expressed through narrative form, voice, and point of view that I kept contending with. Now too I had begun publishing my own stories in Canadian literary magazines such as the *Fiddlehead* (University of New Brunswick), the *Dalhousie Review* (Dalhousie University), and the *Antigonish Review* (St. Francis Xavier University) on the Maritime coast. My stories also began appearing in other parts of Canada, for example, in the *Canadian Author and Bookman, Grain, Wascana Review, Quarry,* and *Canadian Fiction Magazine.* A few of my stories also started gradually appearing in the United States, the United Kingdom and Europe, and even in Malaysia.

The evolution of the story as narrative process began to take stronger hold of me, especially the sense of the "I-witness"—to write, not to tell others what to do, according to Margaret Atwood—or, in one apprehending the omniscient narrator's voice, evoking "meaning" essentially through states of feelings. Cadence, rhythm, and dialogue became integrated with my West Indian consciousness no less, but in my also becoming a "Canadian" writer as part of the aesthetic experience and in my wanting to establish "connections" (Atwood). I was now writing about Canada beyond being a mere "tourist."

I also began to view narrative as self-exploration as my own ideas of the Great White North grew, and I would rethink "plot," associating it with the "ubiquitous unconscious" (Proust) and the idea that life is full of plots or no plots at all, or with Chekhov: "Plot is what makes people bang the door. What comes after," which I cogitated on, my yet being bent on capturing what Dorothy Parker calls "the silent artillery of the heart."

Irish and European short-story writers I also began reading, not least Joyce, Chekhov, and Maupassant (the latter two in translation). And inevitably it has always been my tendency or aesthetic impulse to evoke memory as the "mother of the muses," the same tied to the Jungian notion that anything psychic is "Janus-faced," always looking forward and backward. I kept becoming convinced too that the short-story form combined the poet's sense of style and the novelist's sense of drama (by now I had published two short novels, *Dark Swirl* and *The Wizard Swami,* in the United Kingdom), and I was aptly suited to write the short story (if nothing else). Thus, with Gabriel García Márquez, I would also be imbued with the idea that "the best fiction has a suggestive power, an ability to evoke presences not specifically described."

My ingrained tropical self and formative experiences were helping me to strive toward developing a distinctive voice, I figured, bearing in mind the sense that tropical peoples tend to be more "oral," or "highly contexted" (as anthropologist Edward Hall describes it): their being given to nuances of speech intonations and rhythms, while acting out varied or hybrid influences that others in staid temperate climes may not always be inclined to want to "dramatize." Ironically, around this time I started detecting a kind of ambivalence in some magazine editors who would reject my stories: they would have problems with my stories' place or setting, and ideas about how the narrative should evolve within an accustomed convention. One vaunted magazine editor in the United States, for instance, questioned the structure of one of my stories: she couldn't figure out why children (characters) in the story were surprised at seeing a "naked man." People of the tropics, she wrote to me, are accustomed to seeing naked people running around. Outdated images of Tahiti? Borneo? Tobago? Victorian landscapes of brown and black forms, half-clad, all with "a different complexion or slightly flatter noses than ourselves"?

I recall also a book publisher retuning my manuscript and striking out the word *tabla* (Indian drum) throughout and writing "table" as a correction. Bah!

As a form of compensation I would remind myself that the imagination is all (Joyce's view that "memory is the imagination" and Elie Wiesel's "the kingdom of the imagination" I now often quoted). And indeed, for me, the short story is process, a form not always with a finite end, as I kept grappling with narrative technique, voice and point of view more than anything else. This process also involves what I conceive as John Metcalf's (an English-born writer in Ottawa) timely warning that "too many stories have littleness of scope and ambition, a littleness of technical ability and caring, a littleness of emotional depth and impact." I often bear this in mind each time I write and/or read a new story.

Traditional notions as to whether the short story must concern itself with a character facing great odds (à la *Moby Dick*), or with man quarrelling with himself and others, as in Hemingway's *Old Man and the Sea*—the epic struggle—I also contend with. And the verities of time, place, and action are all subliminally in my consciousness when I sit before the blank page or computer screen and try to create a mood or situation, or a certain voice, as the creative instinct akin to frisson takes over.

Flashback/memory/splicing all come together, I believe, in my quest for an epiphany (of sorts) without my trying to be belletristic or striving to develop a story within a story, in the manner of the subplot, though I would ask whether the average reader cares for such artifice (not just magazine editors who, on occasion, may want a straightforward anecdotal story). The "luminous halo, a semi-transparent envelope" is what it all boils down to, as I would think back on Virginia Woolf, or read someone like Jamaica Kincaid in her *New Yorker*-published stories.

The short story is "a bird in a cage, not a man in house," I would contemplate. It is a window to look out on the outside world, also. In contrast, the novel has many windows to look out on, but the short story's unique form enables it to achieve its particular effects through what Katherine Mansfield calls the "artifice of a bird singing."

"Show not tell" is time-worn, yet Wayne C. Booth's maxim lingers; and the emotional energy I expected results in achieving heightened imagery in the attempt to particularize everything and simultaneously whittling away at abstract or generalized language. With Isaac Bashevis Singer, the impulse is always to make it more local, and ergo everything becomes universal. The overall aim, more than anything else, is in trying to capture the quality of experience while striving for a quiet intensity in style and manner (if nothing else).

Over the years I might have unconsciously tried writing metafiction also, as I reflect on South American/Amazonian contexts as integral to my background, with the view that the story doesn't necessarily have to begin at the beginning (as Mavis Gallant once said, though she isn't a metafictional writer). I've believed too that narrative technique can lead one anywhere, even to surrealism à la John Cheever ("Where kings in golden suits ride elephants").

I have also been tempted to write postcard fiction over the years, and tried teaching it in Ottawa as a distinctly Canadian form, though it isn't my forte. I prefer room for dialogue and interiorization, bent on achieving fluidity in style. John Gardner's sense of the story, "we step into a vivid and continuous dream," I also bear in mind, while I may consciously try something new technically in order to reveal the dark secrets of one's self as part of the whole. Invariably in dramatizing the "other," the story is still fundamentally a process—a work-in-progress—as I keep trying to discover who I am now living in the cold white north of Canada.

A poet I will keep being too, and maybe with a D. M. Thomas try to write stories more and more "as a relief from the poem's intensity." At the conference in Jaipur, India, I might have come full circle as I reflected on where my forebears came from and ended up in Guyana and the Caribbean—and my now being in Canada—all as the source of memory and sustained experience stirring the sense of immediacy in me, though in my never failing to see the short-story writer's job as showing the reader "a world completely absorbed and possessed by the human mind" (Northrop Frye), while hoping to achieve a "suggestive magic" (Baudelaire), and expressing at the same time the object and subject, "the world outside the artist and the artist himself."

Deaths

Frederick Busch

I am a professional writer of serious fiction, which means that I don't always earn quite enough to be able to avoid trying to teach people who may have talent, but who surely have the desire, they think, to write fiction that someone of a sophisticated range and taste might wish to read. When I do this fiction coaching, as I sometimes think of it, I am met with sullen or even outraged questioning. It occurs after I have indicated, on a commentary written in response to student work, that I do not choose to read stories about electric elves from a far-off solar system who have come to earth to either suck our blood, give us free dope, or teach us a lesson about cherishing peace. Nor, I tell my students, will I read a story about waking up, greasy and hungover, in a fraternity house, after having had unprotected sex with someone—the narrator now notices—whose species is in doubt.

"What's good enough for you?" they say, although sometimes with a tone of what might pass as respect.

"Serious fiction," I say. "Something plausible, in American English, with something actual-feeling at stake. Bad news, in other words," I say.

Now, what I do best and most, whether I teach or not, and whether that work always meets with your approval, is write. I am not by inclination or training a theorist. Yet you have made the mistake of inviting me to expatiate on the nature of short fiction, and, flattered away from sensible behavior, I have made the mistake of accepting your invitation. With this understanding—that all parties have got themselves in trouble, and with my prejudices clearly in mind—let me tell you a story.

We are in a church in upstate New York, and a lot of us have turned out
for the funeral of a 14-month-old child who suddenly became ill and who,
too quickly, grew sicker and then died. A lot of people take turns at talking
to those assembled there, and what they say makes little difference—to the
parents of the child, I suspect, and to his grandparents, one of whom does his
best to speak for the stricken family, and to the rest of us who listen, for we are
heartsore and discouraged. Several clerics are there, and what they say seems
at best irrelevant, at least to me, because throughout—among the flowers and
among the musical chords and among the people who come to the lectern
and the people who leave, near those who weep and near those who almost
do not weep—always, to the left and at roughly shoulder height, slanted on
its bier—there is the baby's coffin.

It is painted white and is very, very small. It is fastened to white poles or
rods that extend before it and behind it. And it is tilted, as if to show us that
which is inside. But the coffin is sealed. But we know what it contains. And it
looms larger and larger through the talk, the necessary and maybe lifesaving
but also maybe useless and even, some of it, empty talk that some of the living
might require in order to believe that they can fashion ways of surviving what
the coffin, silent, of course, in the music and the needful talk, does say.

And then, as if they have been speaking to forestall what they next must
do, but now cannot help but do, the survivors fall still. The music, too, has
stilled. The church is so quiet, you would think we all had agreed to hush
our breathing; or, you would think, the small white box—growing larger
as we stare at it—had silenced us. And then six large men, with reluctance,
approach the box, as if knowing that what is in it—death, after all—will hurt
them, and as if knowing that, when they do as they must, they will signify
for all of us, agree on behalf of everyone there and, in fact, of everyone here
as well as anyplace else, that this baby disappears, now, into the ground, and
that death grins in triumph.

They do their duty. They shuffle the box. They are awkward, perhaps
because of its size: how do six large men get a grip on something so small?
They lift it by the rods, of course, the two in front and the two in back; the
two in the middle get their shoulders under the box containing the baby, and
everyone takes the weight.

Here is what happens. Their knees buckle. I can see them go weak. They
are lifting a very small weight, and their legs are failing beneath them. We
know why, of course. The weight is immense. It is of an actual child who has
died, and who remains real in the church and in the tiny coffin, but who also,
in that doleful instant, has become a metaphor; the death, the ceremony, the
needs of the mind in its agonies, have transformed a life existing only in words

back into real substance. And strong men thinking of the baby, instructing themselves Don't *drop* it!, telling themselves how to get down the steps while holding the box and not stumbling—these men feel a terrible weight that the box does and of course does not contain.

Now, I did not think of writing that agony. I did not think that there was a sage little lesson for me and my friends and associates in the small boy's death. But I believe, now, that there was, and that the agony of which I partook is a way of thinking about what we do—which had better deal with matters of life and death, or we are liars in a lying trade.

I believe that we are responsible for finding and communicating in plausible ways the immensity those dutiful men felt down from their hands and shoulders to their knees. I believe that we must write of matters no less important than that immensity. And I believe that when we do so in the short story, we are dealing with a form that is about the matters I have been trying to describe: the victory against which we thrash by calling it death.

I suggest that the short story is informed by death.

I suggest that the short story exists to end.

I suggest that its crucial line is the last, and its breathing body, composed of early and middle sentences and scenes, no matter how vital, is dedicated to the achievement of its dying close.

When he was 26, William Saroyan published his brilliant, idiosyncratic collection of stories *The Daring Young Man on the Flying Trapeze.* He not only dared, for example, to write a story about a story writer who died for his art; he even, as if he had something to tell the world, wrote a preface. Furthermore, in the preface he dared to tell us about literary style:

A writer can have, ultimately, one of two styles [Saroyan said]: he can write in a manner that implies that death is inevitable, or he can write in a manner that implies that death is not inevitable. Every style ever employed by a writer has been influenced by one or another of these attitudes toward death.

That is a mouthful for a kid to know, or believe he knows, and it is true. If Raymond Carver had wanted to deny our haunting by death, and if he had believed that short stories were about anything else—failing small businesses, say, or tough luck, or the sad state of medicine—he would not have reworked his story from "The Bath" through its final state as "A Small, Good Thing" by finding on its fringe an angry baker who earns some of his small income by commemorating time with birthday cakes; Carver makes him, by the end of the final draft, a kind of secular priest, he gives bread to the bereaved parents not because he has any claim to the powers of transubstantiation, but because, like them—I steal and alter a line from Lawrence's "The Odor of Chrysanthemums"—he cowers, as we do, before death, his master.

In Carver's story, the shortness of the finally fairly long story resides in the shortness of the life of the child he calls "the birthday boy." In my anecdote about the funeral, the brevity of that story is 14 months—the infant's life span. In all the stories we write, in the stories we need to reread, the shortness of the life that we, the readers, are allotted, as well as the metaphoric life of the character, measured against the infiniteness of time. As a short story closes down, holding to a cynosure—maybe best exemplified by that trademark freeze-frame at the end of an Ann Beattie story—the moment teased away from, treasured out of, time is what we covet; it is part of our acknowledgment, even while we resist it, that time will have us.

Philip Lopate, in a 1997 essay in *Zoetrope* called "Always Be Closing," with his gift for finding the grain of communal experience and going against it, tells why he dislikes stories, complaining that "for the short story to work, it has to be about one thing. Not only that, but that one thing must be felt to be hastening toward its conclusion with every woven effect."

He's right, of course. Every line in "Indian Camp" is about the fear of death, especially the earliest lines, cut by Hemingway—preserved in the fragment "Three Shots"—because, by the time he concluded the story, he knew that the opening language about the terror of dying was implied, and more powerful because not said directly, in the body of the story. It is not a story about learning, although learning goes on. It is not about initiation, although it creates a *rite de passage*. It is about how death triumphs; and about how little the boy, at the end, has learned from moments that have taught us, his elders; and how he has reenacted our initiation. The irony of Nick Adams's certainty that he will never die is given its tone by the older Nick, the sayer of the story, who has learned, now—from war, from the world's violence, from seeing and hearing and smelling death after death—what his younger self didn't know. He knows, and we know—and Nick almost knows but doesn't yet want to—that death is always, of course, triumphant.

And the story is not only about death. It is shaped by death. The inner movement of the short story, its every element bending toward the same conclusion, is achieved by nothing less than death. That is the conclusion stories reflect. A novel is many lives and much life and instant after instant; the story is generally only one, and the writer tries to stall, to stop, time and to hold back a life or scene or a feeling against time's—against death's—flood. The closing of the story reflects the closing-down of life. The story is a desperately, maybe a sorrowfully, maybe a bravely held breath.

And then there is breath that is stopped. "The Shawl" is Cynthia Ozick's 10-page scream on behalf of Rosa, a Jewish mother whose 15-month-old daughter, Magda, dies in a prison camp, in "the coldness of hell." To prevent herself from uttering "the wolf's screech" that rises in her throat in response to her child's murder, Rosa pushes her shawl into her mouth—"stuffed it in and stuffed it in"—and shuts herself up with the shawl her baby loved and with which she tried to protect her. The shawl is the source of the story's title. It is the metaphor for love that fails, for courage that falters, for odds too huge, for brutality that triumphs; it says that the war against the Jews, here against women and children, is won by those who hate them unto death. It says that death triumphs. And then it tries to vanquish death. The story itself is the screech that Rosa must not utter because, if she did, "they," the guards, "would shoot." Ozick screams for Rosa. The final line of the story, then, responds to the silence suffered by Rosa, by those who did not speak against the killers, by those who, immune from them, did not speak on behalf of those who were not. History itself—the lives and deaths of the victims—rides on the language with which the story concludes.

Ozick writes that Rosa "took Magda's shawl and filled her own mouth with it, stuffed it in and stuffed it in, until she was swallowing up the wolf's screech and tasting the cinnamon and almond depth of Magda's saliva; and Rosa drank Magda's shawl until it dried." That language commemorates the baby's impertinence and the mother's inability to save her. It celebrates the beauty of the 15-month-old and announces the horror of her murder. It strives for exquisiteness, but not for Magda's experience. The moment becomes Ozick's, for it is she who screams here, for Magda's and Rosa's sake, and for her own. The dying rhythm of "until it dried" is less an enactment of the living death than it is the writer's need to make the moment about impermanence permanently memorable. The final clause, following a semicolon—"and Rosa drank Magda's shawl until it dried"—rhymes, finally, with "died," and suggests that Rosa, in drinking the baby's saliva, is drinking the baby's life to save her own. It is a terrible and realistic conclusion, but not any longer a realistic story; the dreadful and gorgeous final clause renders the story an evaluation and a condemnation and maybe an act of pardon, and perhaps a sign of the author's compassion, and surely an attempt to cause the matter of the story, through the fiction's own death just before the last sentence, to permanently scar the reader and therefore live beyond the 15 months permitted to Magda.

Grace Paley's "A Subject of Childhood" is about moments in the midst of a full and difficult life, when a little boy announces to his mother, "I'm never gonna go away. I'm gonna stay right next to you forever. . . . " His mother, the narrator, holds him and cradles him; he is the essence of what's temporary, aimed at growing enough to depart, and he is what Dickens called a different infant, "an item of mortality": nobody gets forever. Then, as he thinks eternity while his mother knows brief instants, "the sun in its course [Paley writes] emerged from among the water towers of downtown office buildings and suddenly shone white and bright on me. Then through the short fat fingers of my son, interred forever, like a black and white barred king in Alcatraz, my heart lit up in stripes." The heart is buried "forever" in its prison of flesh; the boy's love is promised "forever"; the remarkably imprisoned heart does, because preserved in the amber of good metaphor, last forever—although, outside of the language, of course, it cannot. The image is not about mother love, or the love of a baby boy. It is about how time wins, and the story closes on the instant the story points to as crucial; it is what the story has labored to bear us—the prayer against death that cannot come true unless the story that carried the prayer is sufficiently memorable. The combat with time is about the story itself, then, as well as about the moments it seeks to celebrate. Stories, I suggest, are about the act and art of telling. It is that telling that is a matter of life and death, no less than the lives and imminence of death, which occur within them.

Thus, when Bernard Malamud writes his wonderful story "Angel Levine," he gives us a tailor whose life becomes a simulacrum of the Book of Job. All is ashes, and his wife, Fanny, sickens, and it seems that she will die. Like a loving child who does not wish to complain, but who of course very much does wish to complain, Manischevitz—the story of dreadful trials takes on the tone of a Jewish joke—Manischevitz prays, "My dear God, sweetheart, did I deserve that this should happen to me?"

As if sent by God in response to his prayers, a black "bona fide angel of God, within prescribed limitations," as he describes himself, named Alexander Levine, appears in the small, besieged apartment of the tailor and his dying wife.

He asks Levine, "So if God sends me an angel, why a black? Why not a white that there are so many of them?" "'It was my time to go next,' Levine explained."

After trying hard not to believe, Manischevitz, at last, says, "'I think you are an angel from God,' [thinking, as Malamud writes] "If you believed it you must say it. If you believed, you believed." In response, Levine departs for heaven after miraculously curing Fanny. The tailor says to her, "A wonderful thing, Fanny.... Believe me, there are Jews everywhere." It is a shopworn parochialism out of the old neighborhoods that are now gone forever. It is a playing on Jewish bigotries, which assert themselves with the same remarkable stupidity found in African American or various white and Christian bigotries. The story works as a declamation against death, a wish to live through heavenly protection, because it is told like—because it sounds just like—a Jewish joke: that form which is dangerous with its truths to the teller, as it is provocative to its auditors; that form which gave us the self-parodying self-celebrations and its Yiddish intonations we are so happy to discover in Isaac Bashevis Singer, Saul Bellow, Herbert Gold, Philip Roth, and Woody Allen. It is the railing against death, and it is the immensity of a cruel universe, and here it is delivered with the force of news, of sorts, because the form and statement are aligned, and they deal with the same high stakes.

Surely, William Faulkner's "A Rose for Emily" is not a Jewish joke. But it is a kind of parody—while also a kind of celebration—on the collective memory, and the collective inquisitiveness, of a small southern town. The "we" who investigate and pass along the salacious details of Miss Emily's long *affaire de coeur* with death enjoy the triumph of death as much as they do the investigation of its journey to her bed. The story evokes a shudder, but also not a terribly benign smile. She was aimed for a kind of death all along, "we" think, and the placement of the grinning skull on her pillow celebrates, for us, her momentary victory, and its final and appropriate reversal: death was meant to have us on its terms, the very like-minded, rectitudinous townsfolk think, and the story takes its final form the way a skull's jaws click into place. It's a cruelty to Miss Emily that the town can stand beside her bed and read her secret history. And it's a pleasure to them that they do. The form of a story—its mixture of high rhetoric ("the profound and flashness grin," "the patient and abiding dust") and low gossip—is that of death's jape and convention's last laugh. And in that respect it is not unlike the low chuckle you can hear in Flannery O'Connor's voice in "Good Country People," and we watch Hulga, the high-minded rural philosopher, seduced of her wooden leg and abandoned in her disgrace by a weasel-like traveling salesman of Bibles. Did you ever hear the one about death and the one-legged maiden?

Albert Murray's *Train Whistle Guitar* (1974) is a cycle of stories about growing up black in the deep South between the two world wars. It explores Murray's idea of the omni-American hero—part slave, park Yankee backwoodsman, part Native American—and it celebrates the American character with a language that can, at times, be sung. Murray recalls how children sit under the table or on a grown-up's lap when the afternoon or evening turns to storytelling, and how the child knows to listen and not speak, and how the child, who will become an artist, learns the way in which stories are told. "Sometimes," Murray writes, "it would be obvious enough that they were only telling the tallest tales and the most outrageous lies they could either remember or fabricate, and sometimes you could be every bit as certain that their primary purpose was to spell out as precisely as possible the incontest-able facts and most reliable figures.... " The student knows that his job is to become informed. He learns a heroic episode in the lives of African Ameri-cans that night, as filtered through their own version of what was then taught as largely white American history. Uncle Jerome stands before the narrator and says, "This boy is worth more than one hundred shares of gilt-edged pre-ferred, and the good part about it is we all going to be drawing down interest on him. Then he handed me a five dollar bill ... and told me to buy myself a fountain pen.... " The narrator becomes the future, and the death of the peo-ple is denied as he is sent forward, on their behalf, to preserve them with his pen. Uncle Jerome then begins to speak, and the narrator knows that Uncle Jerome is going to "preach a whole sermon with me in it that night. And so did everybody else, and they were looking at me as if I really had become the Lamb or something. So I looked at the mantelpiece, and I heard the Mother Goose clock.... " The child is the Lamb: he must live forever on their behalf, he must be their American history; but he hears the clock and reminds his narrative to toll time for us, and we know that one person is the Lamb, as much as he may represent that sacrifice and achievement to his people. Death chimes louder than Uncle Jerome's version of eternal life.

In a similar fashion, Robert Stone, in his great story "Miserere," has Mary Urquhart stand beside the stolen fetuses of aborted children as a corrupted priest blesses them for burial. The prayer to the Lamb goes up, Stone writes, "in the crack-house flicker of the hideous, consecrated half-darkness"; she offers, "It is due, by old command," and salvation is only a word, and death has entire dominion, while the protagonist, in her agony, begs God, who is not love, to "Have mercy on us."

The story lives for death—for a death of sorts—in the way it preserves a vast moment from time, death's tireless henchman, while taking its shape from the work death does. Stories are, then, in a sense, about ending and about endings, and of course they are also the heartfelt prayer, the valiant promise, that what we have loved might live forever.

WORKS CITED

Ozick, Cynthia. "The Shawl." *New Yorker* May 1980: 33. 33–42.

Paley, Grace. "A Subject of Childhood." *The Little Disturbances of Man.* New York: Penguin, 1985.135–46.

Saroyan, William. Preface. *The Daring Young Man on the Flying Trapeze and Other Stories.* New York: New Directions, 1997. 9–16.

Stone, Robert. "Miserere." *Bear and His Daughter.* Boston: Houghton Mifflin, 1998. 1–24.

8

The Short Story: Why We Write

Telling Stories in My Head

Chris Offutt

Despite having written more than 100 short stories and publishing two collections, I don't consider myself a writer. The writing is secondary and always has been. What I am is a storyteller.

I am not attempting to draw cultural distinctions about my role in society, casting myself as contemporary shaman, soothsayer, court jester, or mythomaniac. I am content with my job description. I have always strung words into sentences on paper, but today the world calls me a writer due solely to having published. Before that, people considered me a restaurant worker who was not living up to his potential. I was pretty smart for a hillbilly, pretty well read for a dishwasher, pretty talented for a waiter.

What mattered was publication. Without such a claim, I was someone with a pencil and a part-time job. I was the scruffy guy scribbling on a park bench that you might shake your head over, wondering idly what he found so fascinating that he could publicly wall himself off from a gorgeous June day, oblivious to strolling women, a singing busker, the flight of birds, and sunlight sparkling on a pond. Even though I wrote several hours a day for a decade, I would never be regarded as a writer until a magazine printed a story. This didn't happen until I was age 31 for the simple reason that it didn't occur to me to send stories out.

After publication transformed me into someone worthy of interviews (as if I was a different person from the day before) I was suddenly thrust into the position of commenting about something that I had never talked about. I told journalists that I wrote to keep terror and despair at bay. It felt true and sounded enigmatic. There was the suggestion of darkness and volatility, exactly how I thought writers were supposed to be—such as Poe and Dickinson, Strindberg, Melville, Rhys, Keats, Shelly, Woolf, and Rimbaud. Those people were real writers. I was just a guy who increased the intensity of life by telling myself stories. Writing them down was a way of eliminating that particular sequence surging through my head.

Two weeks ago I was telling myself a story about what might ensure during the rest of my life. With luck I've got another 40 years to go, and a variety of scenarios presented themselves as plausible and attractive. They were all good, I have to admit, full of fame and money and exotic vacations and good health for my family. What glorious stories I told myself! Each future was an attempt to avoid the reality of staring at small black marks on white paper, with my back and neck slowly becoming more and more tense.

I suddenly realized that the enormous number of hours I spend actually writing has very little to do with the process of telling a story. In fact, they are at odds with each other. Producing prose is a self-conscious high-wire act in which one has to remain aware of arbitrary concerns such as spelling and punctuation, subject-verb agreement, capitalization, tense, and grammar. None of these so-called rules has anything to do with telling a story. They are mere conventions undergoing gradual change. The artist learns them, uses them, dispenses with them.

The stories I tell myself are only loosely grounded in language. Many of them move rapidly through my mind in the form of imagery and jarring memory. They are an attempt to understand the world as well as depict it, to fight the tedium of existence while seeking my own place within life.

Publishing my stories jarred me so much that I lost track of who I was. (In fact, publication has less to do with storytelling than writing does.) Eight years ago, I was wrong about my reasons for telling stories. They don't keep emotions at bay, but the opposite is true. I feel terror because I tell myself scary stories—such as a plane crash, drowning, or train wreck. Despair is a result of telling myself stories of losing my wife and children. I become angry when the stories involve injustice, sad when they involve suffering, and paranoid when they are about running into someone from the past I'd prefer to forget.

My stories are a way of clothing emotion. If I feel bad about myself, I tell a story in my head to encapsulate the sensation. When I feel good, I invent circumstances to suit the emotions. (Perhaps the reason I prefer writing stories to novels is that my moods change rapidly.) As a person moving through life in a highly charged emotional state, narrative is the central tenet of my existence. Assigning story to what I feel gives me a context for living.

As a child I told myself elaborate stories about the death of my parents and my eventual adoption by a favorite teacher. Others included saving the grade school from armed attack, preventing my family from economic ruin, and hitting a home run to win the county championship. At puberty, my stories soared into previously unimaginable ranges of detail and imagery. In most of them, a catastrophe set off a series of events that placed me in a situation where people suddenly liked me. The cool guys decided to seek my company. The cheerleaders desired my kiss. My parents and teachers considered me worthy of attention.

These silent stories of childhood were designed to transform myself into someone that other people wanted for a friend. I was always afraid that the more you got to know me, the more you'd find to dislike. Most of my stories were a way of concealing that fear. Telling them began as a defense, settled into a habit, and is now a livelihood. This progression has taken me to the distinctly American pinnacle of success as a storyteller—I teach fiction writing to college students.

The truth is, I'm a guy from an odd place—the Appalachian foothills of eastern Kentucky—who just didn't fit in at home. Leaving showed me that I fit in even less with the rest of the country. I cannot lay claim to being from an oral culture. Where I grew up, no one talked more than me, which was nonstop. It was only natural that when I was alone my brain shifted to silent narration.

Telling stories in childhood supplied me with escape and a sense of well-being. As an adult I have not devoted myself to writing, but merely continued the odd practice of inventing interesting events in my mind. I firmly believe that my best writing never reaches the page. I am a good writer on paper, but a great writer in my head. The process of writing is very slow. There are all those formal concerns. Making sentences doesn't hold a candle to the lightning flow of synaptic energy firing electricity through my mind, taking me in a nanosecond from inception to end.

My working technique is to write stories that reflect my life simply because the stories I tell myself always have. It's not an aesthetic decision. Frankly, it's not a decision at all. It's just how I've lived for 42 years. Nowadays I have to pay more attention to structure, description, dialogue, action, insight, and above all—characterization.

I choose a person I'm interested in writing about and pick a crucial point in his or her life. Then I throw a bunch of obstacles in the way and watch how the person responds. In many ways this has been my own history, although thankfully, due to telling stories, the obstacles have lessened. My life has grown more complicated with marriage and children and coaching tee-ball and teaching college. Each success in life has increased my ambition. My life is better due to the stories I tell myself. Writing them has made me a better father, husband, citizen.

Here's a true story. In 1986 my wife and I were living on my home hill in eastern Kentucky. We were newlyweds who owned a small house with no plumbing, no heat, and no insulation. We heated with wood and slept on a couch bed in what was essentially a failed construction site. We cooked with a hotplate and a small toaster oven. When the weather turned cold, we were miserable. When the money got tight, we were in despair. The only skill I had was writing. (Carpentry and plumbing were clearly not working out.) My wife suggested I apply to graduate school for creative writing and I reluctantly agreed. I wrote three stories and put them in the mail, something I'd never done before.

This required an act of will that I could only find by inventing a scenario of the future. I told a complex story to myself that began by getting into an M.F.A. program—with financial aid. As a student I would write stories about life in the hills of Kentucky, not the popular stereotypes of the region. The stories would evolve into a book that would be published by Vintage Contemporaries, a new imprint with a snazzy design. I would be cool and worthy of attention. Eventually I could give my wife a house with a bathroom and what she wanted most of all—children.

In the ensuing four years, all of that occurred, right down to the publisher, the plumbing, and the kids. It may sound preposterous to tell the story of an unemployed hillbilly imagining a comprehensive series of linked events, and that it came true; nevertheless, my wife can verify. I became a published writer by telling myself the story of my success.

As a result I believe with great ferocity in the power of telling myself stories as an aid to life. And that is why I try only to tell myself good stories now. As a kid, telling stories kept me alive. Today they give me hope. Narrative is sustenance.

(I might add that I thought about this essay for a couple of weeks before beginning to write. I told it to myself often. At times it was quite brilliant. Unfortunately, the best parts never quite reached the page.)

Glory Be

Susan Rochette-Crawley

I was eight years old the year I realized I "wanted" to be a writer, and that was also the year that my mother gave me a subscription to the Nancy Drew Book Club. This was 1961 and every girl who loved writing and reading fantasized about becoming a titian-haired sleuth with two best friends and a rumble seat. The first story I wrote after reading several of the Drew mysteries was entirely centered on how the revealing evidence was found. No motive, no crime, no criminals, just the deductive reasoning one uses to "find the evidence." The only readers I had for that story were my parents. My father just said, "Umph!" My mother, who was only slightly more interested, said, "Who is the main character?" Full of feelings of failure and chagrin, I put my story away and became hell-bent on reading rather than writing, which was a talent that, my mother told me, would certainly develop as I grew older and began to understand more about "character." Though neither my mother nor I realized it, I was already gathering experience in character through two main influences that were in apparent contradiction to each other: the saints' legends I was reading in my prayer book, and the less than saintly nuns at Immaculate Conception Grammar School.

For instance, Sister Mary St. Agnes was, in character, nothing like the Virgin and Martyr under whose auspices she was teaching. And though our religion teacher was called Sister Mary St. John the Baptist, no one ever saw her eating locusts, and no matter how much many of us may have prayed, she still came to class each day with her head solidly on her shoulders. In short, I was learning not only about character but also about irony, obsession, pity, remorse, miracles, character flaws, good, evil, and miserable, tragic endings.

For all my Catholic education gave me, I only regret that I haven't repaid in full the number of stories I owe the Church for the amount of experience to which it exposed me.

The saints' legends and my clumsy attempt to "find the evidence," for who knows what notwithstanding, taught me two valuable lessons as a young writer. The legends taught me that the essence of a life and one's work can be fitted into a very small space, can be summed up in an economy of carefully chosen words. From the legends I learned to love the small, the brief and concise vignette. Re-creating the process of "finding the evidence" taught me to stay my course, to include nothing in a story that was not vital to its unraveling. I was learning, unbeknownst to me, what Flannery O'Connor calls "mystery," the essential quality that all short stories have in common. It was up to me to find out how I understood the sacred qualities of a story—their "mystery"—regardless of whether it was the mystery the Nancy Drew stories flourished under or the mystery of life, the stuff of which legends are made.

As a result, when I write fiction today, I choose most often to write short stories, and the stories I write usually center around the contradictions life hands us, the ironies we seek to explain and understand. Always, though, in order to begin a short story, I must hear a strong voice, see a vivid image, inside me. If I am to write that story I must understand how the "voice" or image, usually so insistent I can't resist putting it down on the page, differs from what I know about myself, and how the differences between my life and the life of the story either overlap or completely depart from one another. I've started many stories that I've had to put aside for a while because what I was hearing and seeing internally did not reflect the mystery of the story itself, but rather became forced pieces of dialogue or inadequately rendered portraits of complex character. One must learn to be very patient and quiet in order to become a writer.

But all the stories I set aside for the time being have, if they are worth their salt and I have the luck and determination, one thing in common—they don't get "lost." In other words, they persist in my imagination and eventually find a home on the written page. I attribute this to a quality I am beginning to understand as a gift, though haunting and obsessive as it may seem. In the interim between writing stories, I've found that much of my time is spent in reading and writing nonfiction, in writing essays about what some may call, in its archaic meaning, the "complaints" of writing. Before I address how reading is essential to the art of writing, I'd like to say a few words about its lesser-known sister, the writing of criticism and theory, and how that informs my writing of fiction.

A writing teacher I once had told me, as I'm sure many writing teachers have told others, that if I find myself "blocked" from writing a piece of fiction I had been working on, to turn the block around I should simply keep at writing by writing through the block itself. By being willing to write such things as "I'm having a terrible time writing this story but I will conquer these stumblings by writing about the stumblings themselves." While I still think this is good advice to students, especially students who are faced with the dread of writing in general and those writing for a class in particular, with me such writing quickly turns into something closer to an anxiety-ridden session with a therapist who is trying to help with a deep-seated fear of spiders, housework, or social gatherings. For instance, such attempts to write myself out of stumbling blocks always contained a lot of "Oh, my's!" "Drat's!" and "By my faith's!" In short, writing about not being able to write waxed melodramatic, hypersensitive, and sometimes even downright solipsistic. But from that advice and the lessons I learned in trying to apply it, I found that not only was it pleasurable, it was frankly soul-searching and eventually healing to write nonfiction essays about something wonderful, dreadful, embarrassing, or revelatory, with little or no thought about myself or how I might write if I were not "blocked."

About the same time, in my mid-20s, I found the essays of Montaigne to be enormously instructive. Here, it seemed to me, was a fiction writer who was totally and permanently "blocked." Most of his essays were "on" one thing or another but often "about" nothing in particular. The modern founder of the nonfiction critical essay, Montaigne's essays showed me how to turn intimate drivel into public instruction. From his essays I learned the silence and existential experience needed to objectively yet straightforwardly organize thoughts, turns of phrases, plots, and empirical evidence into something more than quaint personal reflection.

After an ungodly number of years in graduate school and with the help of Montaigne, I learned the differences between personal reflection, melodrama, and "explication." I learned what a thesis was, how to apply it to a mystery, and what to do in order to "find the evidence" needed to critique anything from a classic to a Chinese dinner. And just when I was getting the hang of it, along came this terrifying entity loosely regarded as Theory.

What dogma was to the Counter-Reformation, theory had become to the academic community. Though I'm only guessing, I wonder if the current division between theory and creativity doesn't originate in the artificial separation that has been established by those who divide knowledge and hence writing into the "scientific" versus the "creative." Take, for example, Darwin's *On the Origin of Species* or Einstein's special theory of relativity. Are these works taught anywhere in the field of creative writing as examples of solid pieces of fiction that have only lately been accepted as works of some degree of fact? I suspect not. And yet one of the great creative geniuses of the last century, James Joyce, incorporated many so-called noncreative writings into his writing of *Ulysses* and, especially, *Finnegans Wake.* It seems no accident to me that this is the writer whose "theory" of the epiphany has dominated the form of the short story and continues to do so even today.

Though no nonfiction I write pretends to the status of Einstein and Darwin, or even James Joyce, I have found that formulating theses and theorizing about fiction and narrative has given me more directions to turn in as a fiction writer, has enlightened me a bit about why writers of fiction make the choices they do. Above all, writing speculative bits and snatches of theory has shown me what still may be accomplished by fiction writers. Writing nonfiction, especially in those dry spells when a story bucks and snorts but refuses to take forward steps, often clears the air, removes a fog of ideas I have that, though important in themselves, have nothing to do with the story underway.

Theory, good theory, is just as creative as good fiction. In my readings I've found that Derrida's emphasis on "absence" in writing is not dissimilar to emphasis, in fiction, on the idea of chiaroscuro, originally borrowed from theories of painting and rendering but particularly important to the "iceberg" theory of minimalist writing from Hemingway to Raymond Carver. In the fictional world, especially of the short story, what is absent from the writing itself is essential to understanding the story in its depth. One thinks here of "Hills Like White Elephants" and the precursor to Carver's award-winning story "A Small, Good Thing," found in its skeletal form as "The Bath." And of course, Wayne Booth's very early theoretical work *The Rhetoric of Fiction* has been used as a handbook for fiction writers over the years, particularly in its detailed study of the role of the narrator and discourse. Frank Kermode's theoretical work, for instance, is also very useful to the study of writing fiction. Before Kermode's book *The Sense of an Ending,* the concept of "closure" (or the lack thereof) was not widely discussed, either by fiction writers or critics for, that matter. Works such as Julia Kristeva's *Stabat Mater;* Christina Snead's *Stories, Theories, Things;* and Eudora Welty's book of essays *The Eye of the Story* are all works that depend in some measure on a willingness to see how fiction is theory and theory is most often fictional. Though the list of comparison between "theorists" and "fiction writers" could go on, this appears to me to be the moment to turn to the importance and significance of reading to the development of fiction writing.

One of the major differences, it seems, between fictionists and theorists is the former's obligation to read any and everything possible. Fiction writers can't afford to be afraid of theory, nor can they shun reading everything from the dictionary to the menu at their favorite restaurant. While theorists of the snobbish sort eschew reading the popular, the trashy, and the poorly written, fiction writers are expected to have promiscuous reading tastes. There is a TV commercial circulating these days that puts two twins divided at birth at odds with each other. One is adopted into a family that reads fishing catalogs and magazines; the other is raised to read the *Wall Street Journal.* Naturally, it is the *Wall Street Journal* child who grows up to be "successful." While success in this case is measured by (what else?) money and self-sufficiency, it wouldn't surprise me one bit that, if put to the test, the child who read fishing magazines wasn't the better writer. This is because that child has grown up with a greater familiarity with detail, has learned the importance of the precise name of things and, as the TV commercial goes, the patronage—a room of one's own, if you will—of his family into adulthood.

After a time I stopped reading the Drew mysteries. But those books lead me to such better writers as Agatha Christie, Georges Simenon, Edgar Allan Poe, and Nathaniel Hawthorne. Nancy Drew, in my age of innocence, was responsible for shaping future tastes. In the latency of my development as a writer, I read novels, short stories, *Sports Illustrated, Popular Mechanics, The Imitation of Christ,* Turgenev, Chekhov, Flannery O'Connor, *Ingenue, Seventeen, Cosmopolitan, Elle, America,* the *National Catholic Reporter,* the *Georgia Review.* I still make it a practice to read the dictionary—*Webster's, American Heritage,* the *Oxford English Dictionary,* it doesn't matter. My favorite "quiet" writers to read still include Mary Stewart, Alice Munro, and *The Joy of Cooking* cookbook. I like to listen to almost all kinds of music, but lately I've been transfixed by the wealth of good storytelling in such singers as Sheryl Crow, Melissa Etheridge, Iris Dement, Kate Bush, Allanah Myles, Joan Osborne, Joan Jones, Sinead Lohean, and Loreena McKennitt. I read maps as closely as if I were a general planning to charge the nearest intersection.

What I hope you see is that I read anything and everything I can. Some of it finds its way into stories directly, but most of it informs the narrators I eventually find myself up against. The one thing I'm afraid of being is a writer who doesn't know which voices and images know more than I consciously do.

A Short Story

Richard Ford

Here's how you write one.

First, enough of all this hoo-ey (as my father used to say) about the short-story form. The form is this: I write it; I call it a short story; it is one. End of argument—though it doesn't have to be all that short. I just have to want to call it a "short story." There's no police involved in this business.

Second, what you need to do is read a lot of all kinds of short stories. This could be viewed as a controversial suggestion by people who fear influence and believe your creativity gets tainted by what you read. For me, though, I first read a short story ("A Worn Path," by Eudora Welty) long before I ever thought about writing one, and so I never had the chance to write one without knowing that others already existed. You could say that my chance to invent the short story was lost right there, and with it a measure of choice and literary originality. I have therefore had to be consoled that although I couldn't dream up the very first short story, there is perhaps something to be gained—when I sit down to write one—in knowing that there's a precedent for what I'm doing, and that I'm setting off for "short," not just into the clueless blue, and that I can begin at a very early moment in my cogitations to think about matters of scale, proportion, length, complications of formal features, temporal structure, and the other crucial issues related to, well ... the short-ness of things.

Anyway, the impulse to "write short" is probably in the genomes, whether we know there are stories or not. What's inherited is the appetite we develop for pleasure obtainable from all kinds of brevity: pleasure derived from emphasis, from intensity, from abstraction, from self-imposed restraint, from stopping, from the anticipation of all these things, and more, including the general "less is more" rule, mostly invoked by us in painful conversations with our friends.

Reading will not only show you what's already been done and therefore need not be done again, it will also show you what's been done in ways you don't like and might want to avoid, or that you don't like but want to improve on. It will also admit you to the multitudinous ways stories can vary in their representation of life's essential mystery and density, thereby conferring upon you the freedom of your own vision—if you have one. And reading will give you vicarious experience of what it's like to read what you yourself may write. I mean, if you don't want to read short stories yourself, the urge to write them seems pretty blunted—not that a good story or two hasn't been written by a blunted sensibility. Remember Hemingway and John O'Hara. But I'd guess most people who write stories and have no interest in reading them aren't the best at it. My overriding premise is you write something chiefly so somebody else will read it. And for this reason it seems good to put yourself into a reader's, so to speak, shoes.

Moving along—third, if you like. Once I think I'm going to write something that will be a short story, I begin pretty specifically to size down my thinking and anticipations—this, whether I have anything in mind to write or not. Sometimes I do—which is always nice—but sometimes I'm pretty sure I don't and am only responding to the appeal of shortness, and consequently end up going around looking for something suitable to "write short" with.

But whichever it is, when I start thinking about what my short story might be, I begin thinking short: limiting the number of possible characters, the number of incidents, the fictive time the story will take up, imagining what an ideal length might be (this last is usually exceeded, often to my dismay). Of course I realize that this thinking short defines my personal version of what a short story is (a narrative with few characters, few incidents, short span of time, etc., etc.). And even as I write this down I think about wonderful stories by other people (Alice Munro, for instance, and her luminous story called "Nettles"), stories that completely defy and make mockery of my ideas, leaving them seeming barren and hidebound and ultimately the source of my mediocrity. But Henry James wrote once that the terrible, whole of art is free selection, and I know I'm free (whether I act that way or not) to define stories any way I want to, and that in defining them this way I'm entering the "terror" of not choosing a hundred other possible wonderful ways. Oh my, you can't win. Maybe I'll have to "open up" more next time and then I'll finally be on the road to being as good as Ms. Munro, or almost as good.

And not "to beat a dead horse to death" (as my father also used to say), but by doing this scaling down and limiting and proportioning, I necessarily start a short story with the understanding that I'm going to write a short story. Not a novella; and not something of an uncertain character that might just as well (if I were really lucky) turn into a novel. This latter sort of spontaneous hybridizing happens naturally to writers all the time. They, of course, often lie about it or at least don't readily admit to the fortuity, wanting to seem always in control. It once happened to me; an intended short story "became" a short novel called *Wildlife*. I don't remember how now, but it did, and even though it doesn't seem like me. But still, it occurs to me that getting matters straight early on could make your important decisions surer; could encourage you to think ahead about what you'll be doing (never a completely bad idea) and what you won't be doing—identify blind alleys and other mistakes of writing on the fly and in that way cut down on the number of "haulings back." This attitude may mean I'm just a control maniac. Most writers are (I thought about becoming a highway patrolman when I got out of college, but chose writing books as a not-dissimilar alternative). And again, in this way, everything that's overstudied, unspontaneous, droning, predictable, and lacking of brio about my stories is traceable to my ... call it "aesthetic."

Yet I will say on redirect that one of the pleasures readers obtain from entering a story (I'm sure the reverse is occasionally true) is the pleasure of committing themselves to the judgment of the writer, of letting themselves submit to the writer's authorizations (this comes after that; we start here, we end there; this pause is needed). Stories of course don't just get written front to back; eventually they get written back to front and from the middle out; they get added onto, rigged around, shortened, characters' names and genders get changed. You can call this development, or something like that. It's unpredictable and opportunistic, but it's as much a part of the creative process as the high excitation before the first words get put down. Writerly "judgment," in other word, isn't always exercised the way a road builder builds a road. But in my experience, the earlier I think I know what I'm doing the better. Chaos may rule in my head, and I may like that. The single stroke that makes a story snap together may come apparently from nowhere. But, the longer I have to think about what I'm writing—before I write it—the better I do it.

Limiting, again. Call it point number four. Those sensors of mine that respond to the generic "short story" signal—assuming I don't have a story already in mind, as I often don't—those sensors begin sorting around through the world, or rather through my notebooks, in search of material that might become part of a story I might write. It's tiresome to talk about what anybody writes in a notebook. It's tantamount to your old girlfriend telling you her

dreams. Not all writers keep notebooks, and all of us who do keep one probably do it differently. In a general (and I hope not boring) way, I'll just say
I write things that interest me in mine: snatches of overheard conversation;
partially figged-out story scenarios, names I might assign to characters I might
write (Joe Markham, Carter Knott, Joe Brinson); jokes; odd occupations I get
out of the newspapers (director of a child's grief-management clinic); little,
usually pretentious philosophical disquisitions I go off on; quotations from
books I'm reading; dogs' names (Barkley). You see my method. There really
isn't one.

But these I scour in the belief that because I put something down once, I
was at least mildly interested in it. And if I see it again and am still interested
in it—enough to copy it out on a sheet of paper with other listed gleanings—
then maybe I'm more than a little interested in it. My notebook becomes
a disordered record of things I've thought about or noticed or wanted to
remember. A story made up of many of these things will have a chance
of being at least of actual moment to me because the process of repeated
appraisal guarantees that the note and what it represents, and what it can be
cross-bred with to become something different, are basically important—to
me. The story will testify to how and how much.

Any of these things might somehow fit into a story. A dog named Barkley
means there will have to be a dog. The name "Marbeeta" means there will have
to be a woman, or at least a transvestite. A child's grief-management clinic
will mean, I guess, that someone will have to work there, or have worked
there, or have a girlfriend named Marbeeta who works there, or wants to.

But chief among what I'm looking for in my notebook is a dramatic
event or situation, something that can form the center of a story: a man and
woman, along with the man's daughter, taking the woman's ex-boyfriend to
jail, where the boyfriend is to begin a term of incarceration; a man spies his
former lover's husband in the concourse of Grand Central at Christmas and
elects to go talk to him; a woman goes on a Christmas ski holiday with her
mother, her two nieces, and her sister's estranged evil husband; a man escorts
a woman he barely knows to a noisy American election-night party in the
Ritz Bar in Paris. To me—though perhaps not to you—these situations are
interesting, provoking. They impress me as situations I can address language
to, and along the way bring to bear the other materials I've noted out. With
all of these I can try to make up something new: imagine a consequence or
consequences to this basic dramatic setup; find out what my own facility for
language can come up with. A story, after all (a novel, too, and a poem, and
an essay) can be thought of as simply occasions for the employment of well-
chosen language, occasions for which the reader becomes the beneficiary.

Not of course that any of these notebook entries—including the main one—need ever to have happened. Maybe some will have happened on the earth, maybe not. Maybe I'll have done some of them myself, or only have heard of them, or just have made them up in a fun "what-if" kind of way. Writers are notorious for not respecting (or even knowing) the difference between what did occur and what they wrote as having occurred. Many writers believe that the distinctions between these two classes of event are—at day's end—rather overly tidy distinctions, and never as interesting as what gets made of each. It is also true that some things that actually do happen often prove difficult to work with, become refractory to the writer's process of development through change. My Grandpa Ben did not kill a man in a hotel lobby in Kansas City. But "my Grandpa Ned," who bears a striking resemblance to another man, needs to do it for my story to find its climax, only I have a hard time feeling convinced about it. Often the real events, the actual people, cling to their factuality in ways that can make them unbalance a story, even ruin it. Fiction, after all, needn't be a news report on life. Life's just where the trip begins, and of course where it ends. But in the middle, in the story, we depart from life as we please in order to think of what might happen, and what difference it would make.

I'm not ready to leave the situation back at the party yet, I mean the party in Paris, on the night of the American election. Consider this point number five. As I write this essay I have not yet written this story, although I think I will. Something about the Ritz Bar (a place I've been); a brassy-lit roomful of hard-drinking, loudly declaiming Americans, mostly men, mostly Republican stockbrokers with their tweed jackets off and their bright suspenders catching light off the chandeliers. They confidently think the Republicans will win. There's the usual thick, bluish overhead haze of cigarette and cigar smoke, the clink and pop of champagne bottles, several TVs are noisily on up behind the bar, broadcasting the American news six hours early. And then somehow there'd be movement—out into the cold, November Paris nighttime; a drive through the city back to where I don't know, but definitely down the rue d'Amsterdam, on to the Place de la Concorde and across the river into the Sixth. Who the man and woman are, I don't know, but I'll decide before I start. What their relationship is, I also don't know. But I think (and here's where my limitations lurch into play) that they will attend the party together and somehow (I don't know how) something will occur there that will cause them to leave the party, also together, and that significant changes of some sort will eventuate when they do—changes in their feelings for each other, for their view of the world, for their view of their futures. Do they end up making love or fighting? I don't know. Whose interior do I conjure? I don't know.

Does the woman have a child? I don't know. Do they ever see each other again? Ditto. Does this story remind you of a scene out of *The Sun Also Rises?* Probably. Would I have ever even thought of it if I hadn't read that novel? I don't know. I have been to Paris, though. And some of these things I've certainly seen. But would I have even gone to Paris if I hadn't read Fitzgerald and Hemingway and Faulkner, or my uncle Ford Madox Ford? Maybe, maybe not. Maybe I have nothing new to say. Or else, maybe I should just write it and see if I do. The thought of getting to write that scene in the Ritz Bar, with those American stockbrokers in their optimistic suspenders and their big Montecristos, hoping the election will go their way and that they'll go on getting fatter and richer far from home—all that appeals to me. Plus the way that a story can isolate that scene, abstract it, emphasize this or that, rig it into a provocation for something else I can write—all that's pretty appealing to me, too. Maybe I'll start it in a taxi on the way to the party. Or else inside the woman's flat (not apartment) in Vincennes as she prepares to leave, saying good-bye to her (crippled? disapproving? sleeping? brain-dead? mulatto?) daughter. Maybe the woman's English. And then there's that line out of my notes that I definitely want to use: "Pity the poor planet." Can somebody really say that? And what would someone say in reply? Maybe it can be the title? And then there's this image of an Arab man standing beside a truckful of lawn mowers at dawn. Can I use that, or is it too absurd? Do they have even lawn mowers in France? Does it slightly alter the story's tone? Maybe it'll be slightly absurd. Definitely it'll be more than I know it to be now.

So who cares, really, where the first urge comes from? Let Professor Bloom fret about it. To me, it's wonderful just to get to imagine any of this, to make up what they'll say, to use the words they'll use; to make whatever I know or can dream up and jam together of life into something consequential for a reader.

All of this is making me feel uncomfortable now. I feel like I'm trying unwittingly to codify something that can't and shouldn't be codified; putting lightning back in the bottle. (What was lightning doing in the bottle, again?) In my view, I've just been trying to say what I do when I write, or rather when I get ready to write, a short story. And—again, in my view—I've only said these things in a folksy way to give consolation to my younger colleagues (with whom I identify), and to give cold amusement to my older, jaded ones.

My discomfort arises from a just-felt fear that I might soon get a call from *Writer's Digest*; or because I've been perceived to want to make the esoteric creative process into something like a Lego Eiffel Tower, a textbook publisher in Texas will now want me to write a handbook that will make me more money than all the real books I've written multiplied by 10. I'm not sure I can refuse.

Plus the whole business makes me feel old—as though I'd reached a point of looking back and will soon discover that I've been wearing the same sleeveless purple cardigan for three weeks and spending too much time at the cantaloupe bin at the Whole Foods. That I've lost my edge. Did Henry Miller feel this, I wonder. Did he ever write a little essay like this? I hope someone sends me a postcard and tells me he did, on both counts.

Enough, then. I've told too much. I said I'd tell all about how to write short stories, but I'm not going to. Don DeLillo once said in an interview that writing is a concentrated form of thinking, and that is my point of leaving—the point prior to writing when one has to think about things, given that certain crucial materials have been congregated: think about the arc a story might describe; think about what a good first line might be—a line that will lead into a scene you can actually write and which might then lead to another one; think about where a story might actually end—what room, what hour, in whose company, after what has happened.

All that's left is the actual putting on and taking off of words from pages. And to say anything about that seems indelicate, a bit like those terrible touching manuals in which two people named Nikko and Bobbie try to teach you how to make love to your spouse. Not that plenty of people don't need to know how to do that; it just doesn't seem likely that if you need it you're ever going to get very good at it. In any event, at some point instruction has to stop and you take the plunge we all take by ourselves.

If what I've said here makes anybody feel more comfortable with his or her own beginning processes and habits and uncertainties, then good. Probably nothing I could say would cause anybody to be a good story writer. Most people aren't very good story writers. And every time I read one who is, I'm shocked by how free she or he is from the press of life's conventions and from other people's pervasive and wearing ways of thinking and believing and doing things. Sometimes it seems great writers are right on the brink of being completely crazy precisely because they're both in touch with what I, the reader, ordinarily and mundanely think about as I muse along, yet also are so thrillingly, novelly immune to it that they can tell me something of life that's completely unexpected and essential. The line separating these two realms is, I suppose, as good a representation of art's slender domain as anything. And trying to make great literature, with its homey protocols and strict residence in language, offers a use and a solace for what might otherwise be a pointless if not in fact slightly threatening view of the world.

Here is the great Miss Welty, putting on display the very point I'm trying to end this with, and doing it better than I could in a hundred years of describing. It is her classic New Orleans story "No Place for You, My Love." Two refugees from love's wars have lurched together, or almost together, on a sweltering summer-Sunday's drive to the end of the earth, where everything and nothing seem to matter in equal proportions.

They moved on into an open plot beyond, of violent-green grass, spread before the green-and-white frame church with worked flower bed around it, flowerless poinsettias growing up to the windowsills. Beyond was a house, and left on the doorstep of the house a fresh-caught catfish the size of a baby—a fish wearing whiskers and bleeding. On a clothesline in the yard, a priest's black gown on a hanger hung airing, swaying at man's height, in a vague trainlike, ladylike sweep along an evening breath that might otherwise have seemed imaginary from the unseen, unfelt river.

With the motor cut off, with the raging of insects about them, they sat looking out at the green and white and black and red and pink as they leaned against the sides of the car.

"What is your wife like?" she asked. His right hand came up and spread—iron, wooden, manicured. She lifted her eyes to his face. He looked at her like that hand.

Then he lit a cigarette, and the portrait, and the right-hand testimonial it made, were blown away. She smiled, herself as unaffected as by some stage performance; and he was annoyed in the cemetery. They did not risk going on to her husband—if she had one.

Under the supporting posts of the priest's house, where a boat was, solid ground ended and palmettos and water hyacinths could not wait to begin; suddenly the rays of the sun, from behind the car, reached that lowness and struck the flowers. The priest came out onto the porch in his underwear, stared at the car a moment as if he wondered what time it was, then collected his robe off the line and his fish off the doorstep and returned inside. Vespers was next, for him.

WORKS CITED

Munro, Alice. "Nettles." *Hateship, Friendship, Courtship, Loveship, Marriage: Stories.* New York: Alfred A. Knopf, 2001. 156–87.
Welty, Eudora. "A Worn Path." *Atlantic Monthly* Feb. 1941: 215–19.

9

The Short Story: Form

Harvesting *Blackberries, Blackberries:* A Black Woman's Publishing Tale

Crystal E. Wilkinson

I was 14 years old in 1976, the first time I remember being published. The book was a romantic teenage story that I bound myself with my grandmother's Singer sewing machine—a book of 14 pages with one crooked seam along the red line that snaked down the left side of the blue-lined paper. My block lettering was large and leaning and I carefully placed on the cover "MY DREAM COME TRUE by Crystal Elaine Wilkinson."

There was only one hand-stitched, hand-lettered copy, and I was never concerned with selling it. Never concerned about reaching my audience.

What I remember most about these stories is not their substance but the process of writing them and how closely I garnered them once completed. How good it felt to run my fingers over the words I had made and how important it was to me to have them all together, one page on top of the other as a bound volume.

My grandmother guarded this first work of mine. She watched me from behind the screen door, my body cradled in the overgrown roots of a poplar tree, going about writing like killing snakes. Her call for me to come to supper fell on deaf ears. She found me down by the creek or out by the edge of the woods at dusk in a scribbling fury. She respected my shut doors and witnessed my silence while I worked on that first book.

I don't know, perhaps my grandmother knew those words would be important to me one day, or maybe it was important to her to save the musings of the would-be writer granddaughter she had nurtured. When she died in

1994, I found that rare one-of-a-kind book tucked safely away in a box of papers with my name on it, the book nestled in its own folder among the bad rhyming poems and choppy fairy tales that made up my early writings. Even then my tales were centered around brown womanish girls with country ways.

If a writer's work is defined by what she knows, then my stories have always been black and country like me. I am someone who has walked hills and knobs. Someone who was grandparent-raised. Someone who knows the value of sorghum and pinto beans, rhubarb pie and bread on the table. Who knows of outhouses and one-room churches. Who knows a black woman's heartache and pain, rituals and celebrations. What I didn't know then was how far away from my work the act of trying to become published would push me if I let it. I was told over and over again that short stories don't sell. I was also told that perhaps my black, country stories weren't mainstream enough, not urban enough to sell to a wide audience.

The truth be told, it was the love of writing and the love and affirmation of black folks, country folks, and those few urban souls who could identify with my stories that kept me writing. They helped secure my hand on the words and not the "business" of publishing. There was nothing better than my Monday-night meetings with the Affrilachian Poets, gathered in a writing circle sharing our southern-centered poems and stories.

When I think back to the earliest of times when I was barely a teenager, I realize I am remembering one of the purest times of my writing life. I didn't know or care then that it would be more than 20 years before I would have the pleasure of cradling a newborn volume of my own "officially" published words in my chubby brown hands. I was 37 years old when Toby Press (London) released *Blackberries, Blackberries,* my first collection of stories.

"Why did you have to go all the way to England to get your stories out?" a woman asked me at the release party for the collection. Why, indeed, especially now, when there is so much talk about black fiction writers. The word in the world is that black fiction is *en vogue.* That there is a field day to be had if you are a black writer. All the major publishers are now scurrying to upstart black imprints. What I found when I began this publishing journey was that what most publishers seem to want from black writers is some cardboard cutout of what they think black writing is. So I settled on just concentrating on writing more, not publishing. I didn't have a teaching position at a university in which my job hung in the balance on how many books I published. My teaching job was secure.

I decided I would not join the ranks of the factory wordsmiths who got paid high sums to crank out formula fiction. And furthermore, I love the short story, and although I am working on a novel now, I was not concerned (at the time) with expanding any of the stories into a novel. I wanted them to remain whole and to continue to be a reflection of "what I know."

In 1996, I attended the Zora Neale Hurston/Richard Wright writing conference at Virginia Commonwealth University, my first national conference outside Kentucky. There I met my agent, Marie Brown. Marie came with a kindness, an understanding and love for black literature, and more than 20 years in the publishing business. After the conference and interacting with its founder, Marita Golden, I began to think about publishing more seriously.

Marie and one of her assistants, Leslie-Ann, spent the next several years asking me to make changes in the stories and sending them out. What we got in return was mostly what I call love letters:

" … I love the voice, but we've had a tough time with stories, unless they follow a novel … "

" … while the writing is spirited we've decided to pass … "

" … despite great writing and humanity of her work, it is extremely difficult to break out a new author based solely on a short story collection … "

These responses I understood, and I was even flattered by many of them. They are the "good" rejection letters that every writer hopes for if it has to be a rejection. On the other hand were more troubling responses that when summed said that country, black characters in contemporary settings weren't believable.

I found myself questioning my work not in an editorial way but in its core—its black, country, womanish content. Up until this time writing had always been like breathing to me. Something I did to stay alive and nurture my spirit. There was nothing more consoling after a hard day's work as a public-relations officer and a teacher than to find a nook or cranny to squeeze myself into with a pen and journal. To put the kids to bed and release myself to my characters and their worlds. One reason I guess that I hadn't written a novel was that I didn't have time to be married to characters for 200 pages. I worked full-time, was an active member of my community, and tried to get to all the Girl Scout events, basketball games, and after-school activities I could. Writing stories to completion and releasing the characters within 30 pages is part of what I need from writing stories that no other genre gives me.

The business of publishing had made me question my value as a writer. Maybe they (the publishers) were right. Maybe I had nothing to offer the world at large in my stories. But even more than getting my book in the hand of the masses, I longed to be published to just have a book in my hands. Just like the 14-year-old me had longed for. The problem was that I was allowing the freedom to be sucked out of the process. My grandmother was no longer there to guard my sacred time or my work. It was up to me to stand up and fight for the words myself. So I stopped focusing on publishing at all.

The Christmas before *Blackberries, Blackberries* was published, I received an e-mail from Matthew Miller, owner of Toby Press. I had sent him a story from an advertisement I had seen. I had sent the story out of one of those late-night surfing-the-Web experiences. Matthew expressed a strong interest in my work, but I initially dismissed him. Whether I was conscious of it completely or not, what I now believe is that I had returned to being just a writer and had completely removed myself from the business of it all that had made me so unhappy. I also had never heard of Toby Press. But one e-mail followed another until I had a book deal on my hands. It wasn't until then that I began to notice full-page Toby Press ads in the *New Yorker,* the *Atlantic Monthly,* and other literary magazines and began to notice articles about the new publishing house.

As my agent negotiated the contract, I grew closer and closer to being published, but I remember my response as being cool. My friends and coworkers couldn't believe my calm, but all of this was foreign to me. People began to whisper about me publishing a book that had a "large" advance. In reality my job continued and still continues to pay the bills, and there was no large advance. I allowed some of my students to follow me through the publishing process, and they were shocked at how little money there was overall. But it was never about money for me. There were no parts of this publishing process that made me jump up and down or act a fool. Don't get me wrong, I was happy, but it was a quiet happiness. A feeling that never touched the rush I felt when writing or the feel-good feeling that came over me when a story was completed.

My publisher was in England. Even though he is an American citizen, he lives and works in London, and for some reason for me that made it all less real. To make things even stranger, my editor was in Scotland and she didn't understand any of my rural Kentucky colloquialisms. I stood up and fought. We went round after round. I stood firm on protecting the heart of my work, but praised her for correcting my editorial glitches. We eventually crossed the cultural divide and came to an agreement on the manuscript.

By the time the proofs came by express mail, I was exhausted from the process and growing more anxious, but still not quite feeling how I thought I would be feeling. It was summer when "the box" arrived. I had just returned from three weeks of teaching fiction to high-school students. The box was there in my living room. I knew it contained 10 books, and I circled the box for a long time. My daughters were still at school, but my 19-year-old son was home. "Mama open it," he said.

"Open it," he repeated over and over, surely thinking his mother had lost her natural mind. I finally stuck my finger around the edge of the box and ripped it open. I pulled one of the slick perfect-bound books from the box and held it close to my heart. This was the feeling I had been looking for. I returned to the girl writer who loved the idea of her words compiled, spread out in one book. I sat down with it. Kissed it. Touched it. I wasn't worried about sales, about carrying books from reading to reading on my back. All that would come later. At that moment I wasn't concerned with reviews or interviews or who would and wouldn't read it. My thoughts were of my grandmother, whose wide and watchful eye had set the writer in me free. I closed my eyes and flipped the pages through my fingers close enough to my face that I could feel the wind from them. I pictured my grandmother at that screen door watching me write myself a future that reached far beyond the bounds of our clapboard house, our gravel roads, and our outdoor toilet. I sat crying and amazed that these hickory-nut, water-from-the-well, jam-cake stories were about to be put out into the world. Touching *Blackberries, Blackberries* in my hands, knowing that my grandmother was proud, made that moment so, so sweet.

WORK CITED

Wilkinson, Crystal E. *Blackberries, Blackberries.* London: Toby Press, 2000.

FETCH! "Solid Objects," *A Dog of Flanders,* and the Short Story

Charlotte Zoë Walker

If a writing life begins in childhood—why wouldn't a writer's muse come bounding in on four legs, tail wagging, ears flapping, fetching something marvelous from that far meadow?

CHILDHOOD AND *A DOG OF FLANDERS*

A child in World War II during a blackout at a navy base in California sits on a doorstep beside her mother and baby brother, waiting in the darkness of that summer night until the sirens tell them it is all clear, and the lights can go on again. There is a song, "When the lights go on again, all over the world," that the child hums to herself. She has heard that some children have dolls that glow in the dark to comfort them during blackouts, and she imagines that the doll in her arms can glow in the dark. But it does not. And years later, when she asks her mother if she ever did get a glow-in-the-dark doll for blackouts, her mother insists that no such thing existed. "They would have given off light, and then it wouldn't have been a blackout," her mother says.

But the girl-now-a-woman reminds her mother that once, just after the war, they visited Knott's Berry Farm, where she was allowed to purchase a glow-in-the-dark Jesus. She loved being in her bedroom with the glowing green Jesus looking kindly at her after the lights were out. Was it the fluorescent Jesus that inspired her to ask a Sunday School teacher the unacceptable question? If Jesus had been born on Mars, would he look like a Martian? The question was rebuffed, but thinking about it might have been one of the influences that later made her a writer. In any case, she found answers of sorts, in later years, in the Periodic Table of Atoms, in Eastern gods with elephant heads or many arms, in trees and waterfalls. No religion worked for her, but there was always some kind of spirituality or mysticism. And it began with that radioactive mysticism—not entirely safe, perhaps—glowing in the postwar dark.

They moved during those war years to Hayward, California, to a pleasant little stucco house on Haven Street, when she didn't even know what "haven" meant. Her father was usually "at sea," and the little girl felt solemn and responsible about a poster she saw that showed a ship going down in dark waters. "Loose Lips Sink Ships," it read. She asked her mother what it meant, and her mother explained that one might accidentally give away important information to the enemy, and that could cause a ship to be sunk—maybe even the ship their own dear father was on. And so she was very careful not to talk too much, and thought often about whether she would be able to withstand torture in order to keep her father's ship from being sunk.

She loved the sea, because her father was on it. She loved ships, because her father sailed on one. She loved dolphins and flying fishes, signal flags and bosun's pipes, because when her father was home he would tell her stories about them. She also loved the songs her mother sang—like "Don't Sit under the Apple Tree," and "Mares Eat Oats and Does Eat Oats." ("Marezydoats and doazydoats," her mother would sing quickly in her warm, cheerful voice, making the girl and her brother laugh.) She loved the Victory Garden that she and her brother helped their mother to plant. The vegetables grew huge in that garden. Her mother planted a little grove of fruit trees too, and watched them grow for a few more years. When the war was over, and her husband safely home, her joy and relief were mingled with only one regret: that they were forced to move just when the trees were big enough to bear fruit. The girl, no matter how old she grew or how much she aged, always longed to go back to the house on Haven Street and pick a peach or an apple, a plum or a pear, from one of the trees, and bring it to her mother. It would be a mythical fruit and give her mother eternal youth.

During the war years, when she was only in second grade, the little girl had to walk a mile and a half to school; because of gas rationing, there was no school bus to her neighborhood. School was strange and often unpleasant, and she had few friends there. But the long, country road was filled with beauty and fascination, and she enjoyed the solitude of the walk home in the afternoons. Two perilous adventures occurred to her on that road. For a long distance, she walked next to a deep wood, and one afternoon a heavy, old-seeming man with a stubbly face stood at the edge of the woods with a large burlap bag over his shoulder. The bag looked strange to the girl, and she imagined that there was a child inside it. The man spoke to her in a rough voice, saying, "Why don't you come here?" She stood and gazed at him. Why would she go there? It seemed a stupid idea. But she gazed, wondering what was in the burlap bag. Should she try to rescue the child inside it? But she knew he would put her in the burlap bag, there would be room for her in there too. She stood for another horrible instant, considering. Then she bolted, and ran and ran the rest of the way home.

The second perilous adventure occurred for the sake of beauty. She had a glass mayonnaise jar that she was trying to fill with bits of colored glass. She once had found some ruby-colored glass from a broken taillight. There were bits of light-green coke bottle, and the blue shards of an Evening in Paris perfume bottle that her mother had used up, and some dark green from a wine bottle. As she walked along the road, she would keep an eye open for any bits of broken glass that might go in her collection, which was growing higher and brighter and could already catch sunlight from the window sill. One day, near the same woods where the man with the burlap bag had been, she saw a broken milk-of-magnesia bottle—more than half of it intact! What a glorious treasure! She already imagined how the blue would sparkle along with the other colors in her collection. She picked up the bottle, and lifted her arm to dash it to the ground—so that she'd be able to pick up the smaller pieces and carry them home in the tiny pocket of her cotton dress. But as her arm swept the broken bottle downward, it cut a great gash in her left hand before her fingers could let go. Instantly huge gouts of blood rushed from her hand, and she began to run, screaming, the full half mile that was left on the way home. Her poor mother looked out the window to see her screaming, bleeding child running to her—and marveled ever after that not one soul had stopped to help her child. The child regretted that she had not had the presence of mind to bring the beautiful blue glass along with her as she ran home. But, in any case, the glass collection was forbidden for a long time—whether by her mother or herself, she could never remember. But she carried a scar on the web between her left thumb and forefinger—a badge proclaiming that once in her life, she had almost died for art and beauty.

She began to find a different kind of beauty in books. Her mother would take the little girl and her brother to the library, and because she had learned to read so young and so fast, the little girl would have the books finished by the time they got home from the library. Because of gas rationing, they could not go back for two weeks, so her mother convinced the librarian to let her take 20 books instead of 5, and bigger and thicker books sometimes, so that they would last a few days longer. This was a wonderful thing that her mother accomplished for her! In later years, when the rebellious (or at least eccentric) daughter felt her mother didn't understand her, didn't understand her passion for books—she would forget that it was her mother who had given her that sea of words to swim in, that feeling of abundance, the great pile of books, more than others were allowed, a great, toppling, freely chosen pile she couldn't even carry by herself.

One of the books was *A Dog of Flanders;* it was the first story she ever read with a tragic ending. She was completely lost in the world of the boy and his dog, and the boy's passion for art, his longing to be a painter. Though there were no books about girls and their dogs in those days, she loved the dog especially—that brave and constant companion! She identified too with the boy's passion for art, his longing to be a painter. But what horror!—to come to the wintry end of the story and find them both dead of cold and hunger, in front of the painting by Rubens the outcast boy had struggled through freezing weather to see; cuddled together, yes—but dead! And no more words on the page to save them!

She wept with sadness and anger for her friends who had died at the end of the book.

It's only a story, her mother comforted. Don't worry, it's only a story, it's not real.

But why did they die in the story? the girl demanded.

Because that's the way the author wrote it, her mother said.

Author? That was the first time she realized that there were actually people who made the books she had thought as natural as pears or apples, who "wrote" the stories that she loved. But what sort of author would kill a child and a dog? Furious at the author of *A Dog of Flanders,* she made a promise to herself: When she grew up, she would be an author too, and she would not write stories whose endings were betrayals. She would not make children and dogs die, or readers cry. It was a sacred vow, a resolution.

FETCH!

In these early memories, I seem to find my poetics of the short story. There is menace: the man in the woods with the burlap bag. There is mythic adventure: a father at sea amid flying fish and dolphins. There is war, and an unknown time when courage may be required, when even a child's strength may be measured. There is a brave mother, singing cheerful songs and planting gardens. There is the perilous quest for beauty: those beautiful broken bits of glass and the too-eager hand that cuts itself on luminous color. And there is the sudden shock of learning what writing is, what a writer is: one who has that power to kill a boy and a dog for the sake of a story—and to betray a trusting reader, make a child cry. How does one exercise that power correctly—that is, in service of life, of art, or of truth, rather than the marketplace? Perhaps it was not the best way to begin a life of writing—trying to undo a wrong, bring a boy and a dog back to life.

The author of *A Dog of Flanders* was a woman with the pen name Ouida, whose sentimental fiction was immensely popular in her day. Recently I rented the video of a stiff and sentimental, rather miserable children's movie based on the story. Astonished to find the old story resuscitated, I was curious to see whether the filmmakers would have preserved Ouida's tragic ending. Yes! There at the end, the boy and his dog lie dead of hunger and exposure, in front of the huge painting in a cold, gray church. No! Angels intervene, the scene rolls backward, the boy and dog get up, and those who had rejected them lift them up, and lead them home in a joyful procession back to safety, love, and community.

Did the filmmakers fulfill my vow, then, by rescuing the boy and the dog? Clearly not. For me, their ending was more false than Ouida's. Is such a rescue doomed, then, to sentimentality as horrid as this film displayed? Is there no hope for hope? I think the answer must be hidden in the words and the spaces between the words that have woven themselves into a story. My own stories have sometimes been rejected for being "too forgiving," "too optimistic," or flat-out "sentimental," when I thought that I simply saw a different truth—a less violent, more hopeful one than is the fashion—and wrote it with the best words I could find. Is it possible to write well with such a vision?

I find this issue of sentimentality versus hope an interesting one. Sometimes the most "sentimental" ending is actually the tearjerker, as in Ouida's story, or to take an example from modern film, *Terms of Endearment.* The reader or viewer is manipulated to tears for the sake of a commercial or political agenda. Completely opposite to this is the tragic vision of a writer or artist who bears witness to cruelty and injustice. Such work is essential, is powerful because of its truth telling, and performs one of the greatest functions of literature. In our own time, however, I am convinced that many of the cruelties in fiction are not so much bearing witness as serving a marketplace. When my students end a story by killing off the main character in a way that seems unjustified by the story, I ask them why, and they often reply, "Because it was the only thing I could think of." I ask them to pardon their characters for one more draft, and stretch themselves to think of the complexities of character, of other possibilities, of more interesting resolutions.

There may be as much truth in a vision that doesn't fit today's markets as there is in what is most highly promoted and praised. But if one's vision is different, the best and the worst of one's work may be equally ignored, making it hard to judge one's own successes and failures. In these circumstances, it takes great endurance to keep challenging oneself to get it right. There is a constant dialogue between the self and the work.

Occasionally, there is another writer or an editor who helps—as when John Gardner met with me one sunny afternoon not long before his death, tossing an apple to his dog Esmé, and speaking the words of encouragement that my writer's soul needed; when Alice Walker called one glorious night to tell me that she had accepted my novel for her Wild Trees Press; and when Stanley Lindberg, the great, now sadly missed editor of the *Georgia Review,* published a 16-times rejected story of mine that later was chosen for the O. Henry Awards. The award was all the more precious to me because of Stan's vote of confidence after so many rejections; and equally as cherished is my memory of a conversation with Stan over the copyedited manuscript—his insightful and critical attention to each phrase, each word. Such moments have been rare for me, as I know they are for many other equally dedicated writers, and I sometimes wonder if we might come closer to what we long to write if they came more often. But those of us who love writing don't stop at that lament; we continue writing, continue seeking the right words, the right silences, the right structures for our stories.

Still, I must ask the question—has the dog of Flanders been a poor muse? When I toss him a solid object, something luminous, glowing, plucked from the sea or the earth, and he catches it in midair, eagerly fetches it back to me—is the story doomed? Yet I still toss the ball into the air, and my old friend still goes leaping after it.

"SOLID OBJECTS"

Virginia Woolf wrote a story called "Solid Objects," in which a man gives up his political career because he becomes fascinated with oddly shaped, sometimes luminous, sometimes opaque "solid objects." The first object is discovered by his hand as it idly digs in sand at the beach and brings up an ocean-polished lump of glass. "The green thinned and thickened slightly as it was held against the sky or against the body. It pleased him; it puzzled him; it was so hard, so concentrated, so definite an object compared with the vague sea and the hazy shore" (91). Isn't this one way of describing what a successful work of art or literature does, in relation to the haziness of life in general? I have always assumed that this is what Virginia Woolf was speaking of.

In Woolf's story, the man's fascination with a strange piece of glass from the sea leads him to a habit of being on the lookout for other "solid objects," until he has gathered several. "Anything, so long as it was an object of some kind, more or less round, perhaps with a dying flame deep sunk in its mass, anything—china, glass, amber, rock, marble—even the smooth oval egg of a prehistoric bird would do" (103). At first he tries to give these fascinating things a use by placing them on the mantelpiece as paperweights for his official papers. But eventually there are more objects than papers to be weighed down, and he gives up any pretense of giving the objects a function outside their own being and his fascination with them.

I suppose it's not surprising that these solid objects of Virginia Woolf's story—and those that appear in her diaries too, when she struggles to express what her writing is about—remind me of the colored bits of glass I collected and was wounded by as a child. To my amazement, I find that other writers, too, speak of their art in this way. In *Speak, Memory,* Nabokov describes the peculiar quality of translucency that he loved in childhood, and recalls licking his bedsheets and pulling the fabric tight about colored-glass objects, to see them glow. Nabokov's story "Signs and Symbols" ends with an old man gazing at the small, variously colored jars of jelly that he and his wife had purchased as a gift for their son, hospitalized with a wryly named disease that surely affects writers above all others: "referential mania." And when I conversed about writing with Frederick Busch (in an interview published in *Poets and Writers*), I was delighted to hear him characterize the short story in a more liquid, but equally translucent way, as he spoke of "the completeness that we like to find in a short story, that sense of a shimmering drop of life" (34). As our conversation about the short story continued, Fred Busch went on to mention Ann Beattie's story "Janus," in which a simple bowl takes on a presence not unlike Woolf's or Nabokov's solid objects, and as he put it, "becomes in a sense the hero of the story" (34).

This is what a story is for me: a distillation or condensation of life into a work of art, made so perfectly of words that it is indeed a "solid object." For me, it is better than a poem because it doesn't announce itself as "a poem," yet it has that concentrated impact that we think of poetry as having. It seems as if the short story is going to be opaque; it seems as if it is going to be merely a "story," realistic or fantastic, absurd or loving or comic, or fiercely bearing witness—and yet through the rightness of its words, the craftsmanship of its shaping, the illumination of its being, it comes round on itself soon enough that you can see its shape, feel its heft—can hold it in your hand. Here it is, this piece of life cradled in your hand, and yet you can plunge into it, lose yourself in its experience, its language, its "poetry" perhaps—and then emerge again, the object still held in your hand, your eyes still gazing at its unique shape, its translucence, its color.

This is why I love to write stories, and why I love to read them. A real story is like one of Virginia Woolf's varied solid objects—not one like another, but each something different, unique. If stories are turned out as if by a factory, like bricks—they are, paradoxically, not solid objects; they are perhaps building blocks of some kind, but what they build is not art, and there is no joy in discovering or making them. But the great stories are something different: finding them in the work of other writers is indeed like finding a piece of glass in the sand, or a strange, star-shaped piece of china, or a darkly gleaming meteorite.

WORKS CITED

Nabokov, Vladimir. "Signs and Symbols." *The Stories of Vladimir Nabokov.* Lincolnshire, England: Vintage, 1996. 598–604.

———. *Speak, Memory.* New York: Harper & Brothers, 1981.

Ouida. *A Dog of Flanders.* Mineola, N. Y.: Dover, 1992.

Walker, Charlotte Zöe. "Practitioner of a Dangerous Profession: A Conversation with Frederick Busch." *Poets and Writers* 4.3 (May–June 1999): 33–35.

Woolf, Virginia. "Solid Objects." *The Complete Shorter Fiction of Virginia Woolf.* Ed. Susan Dick. Fort Washington, Pa.: Harvest Books, 1989. 102–7.

Mercury Blobs

Sylvia Petter

In my high-school chemistry class in Australia, I was fascinated by mercury. I would hold a blob of it in my hand and watch the substance I had been told was inert develop a life of its own as it tried to escape my cupped palm. Once it did. It fell on the lab floor and smaller and smaller bloblets rolled off in all directions. I was scolded. Mercury was a poison. I was told to leave it alone.

After dreams of becoming a veterinarian faded—delivering calves would be hard to reconcile with an innate wanderlust—I didn't know what to "become" and so studied German and French. Years later I became trilingual and lost any semblance of "mother tongue." The bloblets were rolling all over the place, and I became a translator. *Traduttore. Trattore.*

I was living near Geneva in a French-speaking environment. I had studied German and French literature, but my knowledge of English literature was restricted to poetry devoured as an adolescent (to make sense of heartbreak and idealistic stirrings) and pre-exam recitations of *Julius Caesar* while standing on the kitchen table. Later followed a diet of airport novels, albeit the big themes of Uris and Michener. One day at London's Victoria station I picked up a writing magazine and saw the announcement of a short-story contest. At 42 years of age, I started to write my first piece of fiction. I could not stop. I wanted to find out how it would end. The story did not win a prize, but I was hooked on a sense of magic.

Yet I had to believe in my right to write fiction. Monthly, a writers' group met in Geneva. I joined in and soon claimed my right. Once a month, though, was not enough. There was so much to learn, and then I went online.

Almost 30 years after my chemistry class, the sergeant of an online writing group called Boot Camp (to which I stayed faithful for three whole years) nicknamed me Merc. Mercury Blobs. "You're all over the place. A blob of mercury on a lab floor. You must find structure!" Those words and six more—"write, write, write, submit, submit, submit"—led to my first collection of short stories, *The Past Present*. But there was something else: our Boot Camp sergeant had imposed a reading list worthy of any degree in creative writing. Read. Read. Read.

Today, I still am looking for structure, but the bloblets need their space to explore. I write every day, sometimes on paper, sometimes in my head. I like to feel the connection between hand and pen. I must learn to touch-type and not break the connection. I must learn to rewrite. Rewrite. Rewrite. Each day I try to harness the bloblets. Sometimes I succeed. Then there is story.

10

The Art of the Short Story

The Short Story—A Surviving Species

Aleksandar Hemon

In a recent review of several short-story collections in the *New York Review of Books,* ominously entitled "An Endangered Species," Joyce Carol Oates asserts that the short story is a minor art form that, in the hands of a very few practitioners, becomes major art. Its effect is rarely isolated or singular, but accumulative: a distinguished story collection is one that is greater than the mere sum of its disparate parts. In isolation, striking and original as individual stories might be, it's likely that they would quickly fade from literary memory ...

Well, I write short stories for a living, and it is hard to face up to the fact that I am forever sentenced to the indignities of "a minor art form," particularly since it is extremely unlikely that I'll ever belong to the coterie of "a very few practitioners," to which J. C. Oates apparently has unlimited access. Having read since I could see, and having spent interminable years in graduate school, I still do not know how exactly you can measure art. Where is the border between the minor and the major? (The first Billy Wilder movie was *The Major and the Minor,* in which the [impostor] minor was Ginger Rogers, but I don't think that's what we are talking about here.) J. C. Oates is hardly original when she employs the phrase "a minor art form" talking about the short story, with the implication that the art form majoring over the short story is the novel. The offhand disparaging is less annoying than the persistence of the phrase in describing the short story, and I want to make a humble contribution to its inevitable demise.

It has become hard to dispute that the novel as a genre had its heyday in the nineteenth century, the time of the rise of the nation-state. Timothy Brennan notes that

It was the novel that historically accompanied the rise of nations by objectifying the "one, yet many" of national life, and by mimicking the structure of the nation, a clearly bordered jumble of languages and styles. (49)

The novel became necessary for creating national narratives, taking the shape of an accessible epic describing the birth and the struggles and the rise of a nation, often through the medium of an individualized subject representative of the nation (one, yet many)—think of *War and Peace,* or any Balzac novel. There are many novels, of course, that do not follow the simple pattern of birth, struggle, and rise, but the structural analogy between the nation and the novel goes well beyond that. As Benedict Anderson shows:

The idea of a sociological organism moving through homogenous, empty time [i.e., a hero advancing through a novel] is a precise analogue of the idea of the nation, which also is conceived as solid community moving steadily down (or up) history. (26)

Think, if you wish, of *Moby Dick,* or Gogol's *Dead Souls.* What we see in novels like that is "the 'national imagination' at work in the movement of a solitary hero through a sociological landscape of a fixity that fuses the world inside the novel with the world outside" (Anderson 30). This is why, I think, the novel was and still is a privileged genre: it is conducive to the ideological operations of imagining a nation through a solitary hero who progresses through "empty" time, thereby filling it with national presence. The nineteenth-century short story, conveying a fragment of life and dealing with "one thing" as opposed to "many things," is less conducive to establishing the narrative progression that echoes the national progress. In a sense, the short story in the nineteenth century—and it is on the nineteenth-century stories that most of the genre theorists base their studies—did things that the novel couldn't and didn't want to do. The short story was fed with the national-narrative leftovers, while the novel was the foundation of the national literature, the pillar of the national culture and therefore the nation. Moreover, the novel has been the critics' darling since the last century because literature has been studied and written about in a discipline "with roots in a philological tradition first formulated with the idea of nations in mind, in the very period when modern nation-states were being first formed" (Brennan 44). But there is a slight, and immensely important, complication in all this. The vehicle for the rise of the nineteenth-century novel was the press—almost all (if not all) "great" novels, and minor ones too, were published in installments in newspapers and magazines. Newspapers and magazines, incidentally, were also the vehicles for daily, continuous imagining of the nation, which, Anderson notes, took place in an extraordinary mass ceremony:

the almost precisely simultaneous consumption ("imagining") of the newspaper-as-fiction.... The significance of this mass ceremony—Hegel observed that newspapers serve modern man as a substitute for the morning prayers—is paradoxical. It is performed in silent privacy, in the lair of the skull. Yet each communicant is well aware that the ceremony he performs is being replicated simultaneously by thousands (or millions) of others whose existence he is confident, yet of whose identity he has not the slightest notion.... At the same time, the newspaper reader, observing exact replicas of his own paper being consumed by his subway, barbershop, or residential neighbor, is continually reassured that the imagined world is visibly rooted in everyday life.... Fiction seeps quietly and continuously into reality, creating that remarkable confidence of community in anonymity which is the hallmark of modern nations. (36)

One can easily imagine citizens reading regularly, weekly or even daily, the installments of a novel describing a hero on a quest akin to the national quest, and then exchanging thoughts and ideas on the street, at work, at parties, collectively involved in connecting and constructing the narrative, belonging to a community inaccessible to citizens of other countries speaking other languages and reading other novels, or for that matter the "noncitizens" of their own country.

But here is the complication: the same newspapers and magazines published short stories as well. In other words, the novel and the short story had an even start in the press, yet the novel became the major national art form, and the story was relegated to the minors. Clearly, the successive narration of a novel had advantage over the "momentary impression" of a short story. But I also think that the novel took off and ran far ahead of the story in the field of national literature the moment the novel moved on to become solely a book. I cannot pinpoint the period in which the complete transfer of the novel from the press to the book took place—I hope there is a graduate student somewhere writing a thesis about that. It seems to me, however, that it happened at the time when, on the one hand, nation-states (at least in the West) became relatively firmly established, which meant that the national cultures and literatures were neatly sorted out and organized, with all the founding literary fathers in their rightful place—at the time when something like "American Library" or "German Masterpieces" editions first become possible; and, on the other hand, at the time when the middle class, the heart of any modern nation-building project, begins to believe that a book (and the novel in it) is a cultural commodity and a sign of a relative privilege, marking literacy, literariness, and sound citizenship. It happened at the time that would, I am convinced, coincide with advances in printing technology that made books affordable to middle-class readers.

In the meantime, the short story as a genre is stuck in the press, available and accessible to a large number of people and incidental in the press (that is, few readers would buy the paper solely for the story in it), thereby more populist and less a part of "elite" culture that the middle class ever dreams of belonging to. The short story thus becomes a minor art form, evanescent in the daily consumption of flimsy news stories, which still, however, bond the nation. The short story becomes legitimate in a national literature system only in a collection, and its presence in the press is just a mark of its inferiority, the symptom of which is its ever-present readiness to fade from readers' unkind memory. Paradoxically, it is precisely the-short-story-in-the-press that establishes the rules of the form. The short story was not established as a form by "the few practitioners," but by countless anonymous reproducers of patterns (*repetireurs*), writing stories that make the rules (strong opening; a solitary voice; fragment of life; the moral, punch line, or epiphany, whatever you wish) seem natural, self-evidently necessary, and inherent in the form. The short story as an "art form" is shaped by writers who repeat and reproduce models, by editors who bless those models and claim they know what the readers want, and finally by the readers who consume the short story as a thing-in-itself, as an already completed, indeed organic, form. In short, the short story becomes standardized and recognizable as a particular commodity, with specific channels of distribution. The story becomes an "art form" through a continuous practice of writers, editors, publishers, and readers. The short story has changed and will change again, and to study the form out of its material, historical context is a grave mistake.

The operational modes of standardizing the short story are still in place. Ask anyone who published a story in the *New Yorker* (like me), and they will tell you that the *New Yorker* editors do not leave it alone—they torture it and maim it (or cuddle it until it purrs, it depends on your attitude) until it becomes an example of what they think a short story is and should be. The illusion created is that the *New Yorker* editors choose good stories out of the bottomless pool of stories, all written with the natural form in mind, and that the good stories most closely approaches the self-evident ideal of "what a good story should be," on top of which they are "well written" (also miraculously self-evident). Then they kindly share it with the reading public. But what really happens is that the literary authorities approve a particular brand of the short story (the *New Yorker* is the FDA of American literature) and then standardize it by repetition, until the form becomes naturalized and its "qualities" self-evident. And somehow most of the good, "well-written" stories take place in the magic triangle of sex, marriage, and divorce, unless they are "ethnic" and thereby "real," in which case all kinds of strange things could happen in them.

Furthermore, the naturalization taking place does not just provide general standards (though it pretends to so) but American standards. The *New Yorker* efforts in establishing what American fiction is are more than conspicuous—recall the issue on "The Future of American Fiction." The stories shaped by being published in the *New Yorker* are not just shaped to meet the formal standards, but to meet standards of Americanness, whatever that may be. Curiously, but not surprisingly, the *New Yorker* seems to be deliberately invested in practices of imagining the American community, as described by Benedict Anderson. The good stories about the American life written by Americans for Americans in all their colorful diversity, meeting high American standards of storytelling, published in the *New Yorker* and similar magazines, work to imagine a community, and not just a literary one, but a national one.

I do not mean to berate the *New Yorker,* for they are just at the forefront of the press standardization. One can argue that smaller magazines are also complicit in the formal cowardice that sets back the contemporary short story but perpetuates "American" literature. Particularly since smaller magazines are the main outlet for a large number of creative-writing-workshop graduates. I would argue—at the peril of affronting a few people in this business—that the creative-writing workshops are an important part of the standardizing machinery. Not only because they teach "what a good story should be" and how to make it "well written," but also because a lot of them promise to enable you to write a publishable story—they teach the standard that would enable you to enter "the market," which, naturally, is American. Of course, a lot of people can go beyond that, and a standard story doesn't have to be bad. Nevertheless, creative-writing programs provide training for writing labor, as it were, and cheap labor at that.

But what is wrong, one might reasonably ask, with another story about a 50-year-old white American man going through a divorce or a routine affair, until he reaches an epiphany; or with a wistful story about a Midwestern (thereby as American as it can be) childhood spent listening to a train whistling, hunting with the remote Dad, or dealing with Mom's erratic boyfriends, until that tragic night; or with a satire about a spiritually hollow America populated by physically maimed idiots who live in malls and amusement parks? What is wrong with stories like that? Nothing really, apart from excruciating boredom. And the fact that they largely fail to respond to a changing world (including the United States)—the world marked by disappearing borders and the global expansion of capital; the world of refugees and immigrants and spectacular economic disparity; the world of unprecedented technological advances; the world in which national identities and cultures break down, transform, and merge; the world, finally, to which national literatures based on phantom essences (Americanness, Serbianness, Whateverness) are simply and sadly and fundamentally unable to respond.

But therein lies the hope for the short story. As the novel is the darling of national literatures, it is liable to go down with them, or at least go through a painful transformation that national cultures are going through. The short story is readier to respond to a new world precisely because of its alleged inferiority. The short story is less dependant on the validation of the institutions of national literatures. Being inherently dependant on the press, which is always quicker to adjust than the book, the short story can respond to the readers and their rapidly changing world with an immediacy inaccessible to a novel. Furthermore, as the conditions of reading are changing with the mind-numbing expansion of the computer industry and the transformations incurred by the internet, the short story slips into the new medium almost effortlessly, while the novel will have a hell of a time adjusting—the progress of a sociological organism is a whole different story in a borderless, nonchronological cyberspace. The hypertext experiments, some of which (Michael Joyce, for example) are at the forefront of a fiction revolution, are entirely dependant on the short story. And it is a question of time before every Web magazine includes a short story, or many of them—conceivably, every Webmag could have its own anthology. The cyberspace is theoretically endless, providing a lot of space for the demoralized, and almost demobilized, creative-writing-program armies, who can provide plenty of content. And one can imagine a large number of writers from around the world posting their stories on the Web, without waiting to be admitted to national canons. This might or might not be good, and maybe it is just wishful thinking, for it is all at the beginning and nobody has lived and written through times like this before. Nevertheless, it seems to me that the change is inevitable—the short story may be playing in the minors, but it is ready for the new rules of the game. We can begin to pine for the past (always a symptom of conservative pathology), or we can simply get ready for the future, indeed shape it.

An endangered species? Only if you live in the previous century.

WORKS CITED

Anderson, Benedict. *Imagined Communities: Reflections on the Origin and Spread of Nationalism.* Rev. ed. London and New York: Verso, 1991.

Brennan, Timothy. "The National Longing for Form." *Nation and Narration.* Ed. Homi K. Bhabha. London and New York: Routledge, 1990. 41–70.

Bufford, Bill. "Comment." *New Yorker* 21 and 28 June 1999 ("The Future of American Fiction Issue"). 65.

Oates, Joyce Carol. "An Endangered Species." *New York Review of Books* 29 June 2000. 38–41.

Migration and Stasis in the Art of Short Fiction (Or, Some Words as Experiment)

Diane Glancy

The short story is a migration to a destination. It is conflict and more conflict that moves to crisis and resolution, which is the destination of the short story. There is a necessary tension between the vehicle and its cargo, between the vehicle and the road that follows in its wake. The passengers are character change. Their luggage is the epiphany.

In a short story about a granddaughter and grandmother, for example, the conflict is evident from the first sentence of the story: They had quarreled all morning, squalled all summer. Several pages later, the resolution is apparent in the last sentence: The girl walked close behind her, exactly where she walked, matching her pace, matching her stride, close enough to touch her granny's back where the faded voile was clinging damp, the merest gauze between their wounds.

This part is easy.

To get you there.

Fiction is a nomad. A pilgrim through the reformations of faith it takes to get through the overall ride-of-life which the art-of-the-short-story is.

You see the *variablenesses* already.

But the structure of a short story is its stableness (stasis). The four unchanging elements of the short story seem to be conflict that leads to character change that leads to resolution that leads to the epiphany.

For instance (continuing with the granddaughter/grandmother story):

A girl goes to stay with her grandmother for the summer. The father writes, *Turn in your plane ticket for school clothes.* The girl is mad ... *she fled. Just headed away blind. It didn't matter, this time, how far she went.* The girl finds two bikers. They ride to grandma's. Ride off again. The grandma gets in her truck (with the dog, who has been yipping all through the story). She chases them down. *Give her back.* The girl gets in the truck. The grandma takes her to the cemetery to weed. The bikers show up. The grandma knows these boys mean business. She, the girl, the dog, get past them in the truck. Outrun them for a while. The truck gets stuck in the mud on an old dirt road. The grandma, girl, and dog run. They hide under a dock. The bikers come. The dog is yipping (we know he won't be still). The grandmother holds the dog underwater. Drowns it. The bikers can't find them. They leave. The women came out from under the dock carrying the *freight* (not weight) of the dog. They are now friends.

That's Mary Hood's "How Far She Went" (a short story that follows the designated route of named roads and numbered highways [though the same are sometimes both] and is a direct journey to the short-story structure). You (easily) see how the vehicle arrives at its destination. The conflicts that escalate between the grandmother and the granddaughter cause character change (the grandmother decides the granddaughter is worth more than her beloved dog) and the granddaughter sees, for the first time, that she is valued by someone. The resolution is the acceptance of the intrusion of the other into each of their lives. All this provides (carries as luggage carries) the epiphany, which on a basic level is something like: *estrangement isn't always permanent.*

Thus, the short story is a mode of transformation. A way to get from one place to another, hopefully a place the characters need to get to, or if they didn't, it is a place that follows logically and naturally the lineup of events.

There are the necessary curves and turns (impediments) in a short story. At one point in "How Far She Went," the grandmother remembers the unwanted birth of her own daughter, the girl's mother. She remembers saying, *Tie her to the fence and give her a bale of hay,* making it harder for the grandmother to accept this unwanted child of an unwanted child. Yet, through the circumstances of the story, the grandmother is able to sacrifice her beloved dog for the granddaughter. And the granddaughter, who hated her grandmother, now gets in line behind her.

With their baptism in water under the dock, the granddaughter and grandmother are reborn into new life, which is a new relationship with one another. The *doggedly* life was dead (though didn't the grandmother love it?). Thus, the epiphany is the delivery of something arrived—*life from death,* which is central to the hope of man.

There are other elements to a short story: the action of plot. Tone. Speed (pacing). The tightness of the elements moving to a common end. The common end itself (toward which elements move) which open to needed answers. There are, after all, many possibilities in a piece of luggage (different versions or interpretations of a theme, which also can provide different epiphanies for different readers).

There also is the element of spirit, or the spirit-of-being, in a short story. Or the redefinition (I hope) of the story as *something living* or *something-that-lives*. An agency that the vehicle of the short story is.

The art of the short story is the generative force of storytelling, a need that is everywhere like air. An old word for breath is the voice as it *tells story*.

The story is a process of an unresolvable need to *tell*, unresolvable other than in the telling and telling of stories.

Stories are old gatherers collecting twigs for cave fires. They ignite from one another. They burn many ways.

For instance, I was reading a paper a colleague, Roy Kay, had written on Chinua Achebe's *Things Fall Apart*, when I came across one of the Igbo stories. Soon, I felt the shaking of story into stories, or possibilities, or ideas for further stories. I felt the generative force that story is.

The Igbo story is a long story about a Tortoise, but to make it short, a turtle asked some birds if he could fly with them to their feast in the sky. The birds agreed, loaning him some of their feathers, from which he made wings. When they got to the feast, the turtle said that there was a custom of taking new names for a feast. The birds had never heard of this, but they agree. The turtle named himself *All of you.* When they sat down to eat, the turtle asked the hosts, for whom is the feast prepared? The hosts answered, *for all of you.* The turtle then eats all the food. The birds, angry, take back the feathers, and the turtle falls from the sky. The birds tell the turtle's wife that he is coming. Set out some things on the ground for him, they say. When the turtle falls, he crashes into the things, and his shell shatters into many pieces.

This story of the turtle itself shatters into any number of explanation tales: Why the turtle's shell looked *cracked*. Why is it *half* of a ball? Because at one time the turtle wanted to fly (this was when the turtle was still round as a ball). He asked the birds for some feathers, which they loaned him. But the turtle didn't fly as he should. He bumped into the birds. Took up too much room. Didn't look where he was going. The birds took back their feathers, and the turtle fell from the sky. His ball (orb) (sphere) broke in half when he hit the ground (that's also why the turtle's shell looks cracked).

The turtle story also could be one of pride: The round turtle, proud of his roundness, presented himself to the Maker as a moon, or planet, or star—

something far beyond that which he was. Since he wasn't as capable of being as clerical as he thought, he fell back to earth.

In Igbo's story, the *things* on the ground the turtle falls against could also be the complications the characters must *fall* against in a short story. (Not only an unwanted daughter, but an unwanted granddaughter who begins the same lifestyle that got her mother into trouble [we assume]. But now the grandmother has a chance to do something about it.)

Further suggestions for other combinations of stories embedded in the turtle story continue to emerge from Igbo's story of the Tortoise. The art of writing the short story is, in part, a conversation with other stories. From one story, other stories are constructed:

At one time, the turtle was not round at all, but flat. But he wanted to be round (as the moon). He asked and asked and never quit asking the Maker to make him round. The Maker agreed, but the turtle wouldn't be quiet. He kept pestering the Maker until the Maker made him round as the moon, but it was only the half-moon the turtle looked like, because he was so impatient. The turtle wanted to be like the moon, but he wouldn't wait until the sun covered the whole surface. So the turtle became the darker half.

The turtle or Tortoise shows up in countless folk stories. Sometimes a story circles back and picks up older stories, or fragments of an older story, at the same time it travels forward. In a Native American creation myth (Cherokee as well as other tribes), mud was brought from the floor of the ocean and placed on the surface to dry (which cracked as it dried). The dried mud became the turtle's back, which became our continent. America is called *Turtle Island* by the Native Americans. It is the basis of our foundation. (Was not dry ground found in the water in "How Far She Went"?)

Thus, the parts of a story interact, show up at various times in various places, according to where they are needed (called by circumstances).

The purpose of a short story often is the explication of our human condition. (Maybe the origin of all short stories is the beginning of Genesis: *Let there be light.*) It is the reason short stories break into ideas for further stories that can be twisted and applied to various destinations. From big ideas, little ideas begin to form, which themselves grow large and break again. That is the part of the short story that is the *something-that-lives.*

A voyage then, is the vernacular of the short story. (A nomad, as I said). Sometimes containing a story about story (within story). Meaning embedded in its reason for being.

A clumping of marks on a turtle's back. A writing that *makes story.* The vehicle that carries the cargo of meaning (both freight and weight). So a turtle could say a number of things. (However many things are needed to be said.)

The props of language are often in its *resonations*.

In New York, in 1999, I saw a play called *The Weir*. It's a story of four patrons in an Irish pub telling four ghost stories: Little people knocking on the door. The ghost of a woman on the stairs. The ghost of a man in a cemetery. A daughter calling on the phone after she is dead. And I wondered, where was the basic *whereness* (the plot-drive, the conflict/resolution, the mix of the elements together)? Now, this was a play, not a short story, but a story nonetheless in script form. Each character met his/her limitations and found they had to continue with them, or there were small changes and/or epiphanies for each.

But I thought, maybe the story was in language. Maybe the story was in the concept of the weir: A weir is a dam built across a river to regulate the flow of water, to raise the level upstream for farmers. A weir is also an enclosure of stakes set in a stream to catch fish.

The weir could be the bar (the setting) itself where stories are caught in the imagination. The weir also is the stories themselves.

It is the carrier as well as the carried. Maybe the story is in the way the weir acts as vehicle, as well as content (cargo), of its own cause, in the way language has to be used to talk about language. A generator of a big bang on a small-bang level in the intrinsic rumbling of the creative process.

A short story is a combustion through written language, those sticks of words rubbed together. Language is an agreed-upon event. A carrier of meaning in sound or the silence of black flecks of writing on the page, the fish caught in a cage.

In this (con)text, our first cries are ourselves answering ourselves. Yes. A story answers the "outness" (what is out there), but mainly the "inness" in the vastness of our being. It turns to an infiniteness that opens when the variables resonate and get us linked to others. That's the art of the short story.

The grammar (sentence structure) = the fish-catching enclosure of stakes in a stream.

After the play, I went to the Metropolitan Museum in New York, and there was an actual fish cage in a "Native Paths" exhibit. A rattle trap through which the stream runs, letting fish in, but not out. The way a story is picked up by the real (when all the story elements run through a story). There's an old magic of speaking *into being*. When you get it right, the story enters real life.

In the looseness and rigorousness of language, David Abram, in *The Spell of the Sensuous,* quoting the literary theorist Merleau-Ponty, quoting another theorist, Saussure, mentions the *weblike* nature of language, a construct built by construct, an interdependency, a living, changing field of action. Which the short story is, reverberating in all directions as a stone (stasis) dropped into a (migrating) stream.

Nature writes with the return of the season. The clouds in various formations, sometimes even absence of formation, and all the storms that come from it. The scrawl of leaves, the fall and return of them. The same pattern in *change-a-bell-ness.*

At the core of writing is the road map for the movement of travel.

A bell ringing.

The short story is an uncovering. (Because the larger mind, the one that understands this art-made-to-look-like-life, can get to the metonymy of being that art is.)

The art of the short story takes the rock off the mouth of the well (when all the sheep are gathered). (*We cannot roll the stone from the well's mouth, until all the flocks are gathered together* [Genesis 29:8], though Jacob did.)

Jacob was at the well in the desert when he saw Rachel coming. He opened the rock from the mouth of the well so that she could water her sheep. Jacob wanted to marry Rachel, but Laban, her father, tricked him. Jacob agreed to work seven years for Rachel, but when Jacob unwrapped his bride, he found Leah, Rachel's older sister. He had married the other daughter first. He had to work another seven years for Rachel, the desired one (Genesis 29).

A short story is regulated by a speed limit to hold you in it.

A short story is a life-giving force. The passing of a vital survival force before your eyes.

Depending on the resourcefulness of the position of the hearer to survival.

A metaphor of our thinking is what writing is.

The exactness of story line to critical inquiry.

A migration of the imagination. A subversion of learning the art of short fiction by after-thought (the process of *rewriting the already written*).

You know these old questions a story has to answer (the stasis):

What does the character want? (Jacob wants Rachel). What keeps the character from getting it before he gets it (or doesn't)? (Jacob discovers Leah instead of Rachel the morning after the wedding.) (But what is Leah but a preliminary draft of the final version?)

In my own work, I sometimes rely on experimentation in the writing process, and on the redefinition of the short story as a *being.* (In Native American literature, the landscape, or setting, is often cast as a living being, a character, paralleling what is happening in the story. It's the reason I often go to a *place* for the *story* I'm writing.) When a story is defined as *being,* there are possibilities of transformations in its elements—the possibility of one thing becoming another. It has its roots in native stories of animal transformations and conjurer's magic.

In *Firesticks,* my second collection of stories, I place short stories and creative nonfiction between different sections of a novella, which the title piece is. I intentionally break up the structure of the longer piece, shuffling not only shorter pieces, but pieces of different genres between its sections. In *The Voice That Was in Travel,* my fourth collection, one of the stories, "Jupter," is one page in length; another, "Blast," is half a page; another, "The Birds with the Breeze of their Wings," is a fourth. How else could 21 stories fit in 116 pages? In another story in the collection, "A Later Game of Marbles," I also experiment with "dot" writing from a "dot" painting I bought in Australia. In "America's First Parade," I rely on numbered sections.

My other two collections, *Trigger Dance* and *Monkey Secret,* also contain moving variables because I felt the world move as I tried to write on it. But destabilizing a story is not a reaction, but a relationship between the reliability of the unchanging elements and the movability (migration) of the webbing of language and its meaning.

It gets back to the concept of a weir. A metonymy of water to a cage (water is not a direct part of the cage, but the cage is not a cage-in-action without the water).

Writing is a theoretical looking-for-a-garage for the vehicle of transportation that a short story is.

WORKS CITED

Abram, David. *The Spell of the Sensuous.* New York: Pantheon Books, 1996.

Glancy, Diane. *Firesticks: A Collection of Stories.* Norman: University of Oklahoma, 1993.

———. *Monkey Secret.* Evanston, Ill.: Triquarterly Books, 1995.

———. *Trigger Dance.* Chicago: Fiction Collective, 1991.

———. *The Voice That Was in Travel.* Norman: University of Oklahoma Press, 1999.

Hood, Mary. *How Far She Went.* Athens: University of Georgia Press, 1984.

The Justice-Dealing Machine

Clark Blaise

Passionate readers of short stories, if that is not a redundancy, should have no trouble agreeing to a few stipulations. First, the short story and its related subgenera—the sudden fictions, the story-byte, the flash, or even its stately auntie, the novella (but not the novel)—are the hot literary forms of our intermillennial age. The energy and furious activity sucks us in. So much friction, so many collisions, inside a confined space. A related stipulation: word-count considerations aside, stories are the expansive literary form of our age; novels the condensed. Stories say the most about a very few moments. The novel says the least about a great many more. When filmmakers "adapt" a novel for the screen, they're really turning a novel into a short story. A third stipulation: Every story should end (and every great story does end) on the curtain-dropping note, the intent (or the shadow of the intent), struck by Frank O'Connor at the close of "Guests of the Nation": "And anything that happened to me afterwards, I never felt the same about again." If not those words (and who would dare be so bold to state them now, although John Updike echoes them at the close of "A & P": "… and my stomach kind of fell as I felt how hard the world was going to be to me hereafter"), they leave us with the feeling that something profound has been attempted, and often achieved. This is the reader-writer short-story contract: I will never feel the same way again (about whatever), after reading this story. Why begin reading a story (or writing one), if not for the expectation that perfection is achievable, and that this one might just blow the reader's (or the writer's) socks off? The same note is sounded at the close of Flannery O'Connor's "A Good Man Is Hard to Find" ("She would of been a good woman," The

Misfit said, "if it had been somebody there to shoot her every minute of her life"), which recapitulates Chekhov's "Gooseberries" ("the rain rapped on the window-panes all night") and Joyce's "The Dead" and "Araby" ("Gazing up into the darkness I saw myself as a creature driven and derided by vanity; and my eyes burned with anguish and anger") and ironically in Mann's "Disorder and Early Sorrow" as the narrator gazes upon the ruin of his culture, and his family: "Heaven be praised for that!" In fact, there's not a successful story I can think of that does not rephrase, or adapt, the same Frank O'Connor sentence. Either the central character, the narrator, or the reader will be moved, literally, and never returned to the space he or she had been inhabiting. He or she will be lifted up and transported and set down in a different place by whatever the author shows them. And I'd suggest a forth stipulation, which is the one I want to linger over in the next few pages. Stories trace a fundamental "change of heart" (emphasis on *fundamental*), a change that is so deep that it transcends the normal, rather sentimental association of the word *heart*. It shakes the pillars of consciousness ("nothing would ever be the same"). It stops, temporarily, the stars in their courses. The question is, how does a story do that?

In the summer of 1961, I was blessed to study with Bernard Malamud, whose description of a "story" (one day in class) was "the dramatization of the multifarious adventures of the human heart." On its most engaging level, Malamud's "The Jewbird" is touching and moving. It can be read as a tall tale, a comic whimsy. It can also be seen as a version of the eternal conflict between social duty and the awakening of personal responsibility. The short-story contract promises that the final product will blow our socks off and earn a line like Frank O'Connor's. In Malamud's working: "Who did this, Mister Schwartz?" asks the child, looking at the talking, tortured, expelled crow, now dying. "Anti-Semites," the Jewbird answers. How do we explore, fundamentally, the human heart in 10 pages or less?

Flannery O'Connor once quoted from Catholic theology: "the roots of the eye are in the heart." That's a beginning (and was there ever a clearer eye than Flannery O'Connor's?); the heart does inform our speech, our seeing and hearing. But how to get to the heart; can the senses alone deliver us there? Clearly, there's a place for plot and setting and character, for concrete details; pertinent, overheard dialogue; and all the other devices learned in workshops, but even when all the techniques and senses are developed perfectly, will we get to those "multifarious adventures," or to Frank O'Connor's moment of conversation? Not without a deeper commitment.

I'm suggesting a fifth stipulation. Short fiction is a justice-dealing machine. The extra level of intuition that lifts a story to greatness is its deployment of "justice," not in its legal, but in its literary sense. And what is the enemy of justice? For lack of an obvious word, I'd say "morality." Justice dares to challenge the difference between morality, which represents the "proper" and the popular, and the lonely, unwelcome discovery that we are truly alone, separated from society, religion, family, or any other code to sustain us. All the burdens fall on our flesh, unprotected. In other words, it is a special understanding of the meaning of justice that delivers us to the Frank O'Connor moment.

Literary justice derives in myth from the story of the baby Achilles, dipped in the river that provides him immortality. He has only one vulnerability, the heel by which he'd been held. Any testing of Achilles must involve the exposure of his hidden vulnerability. The character of Achilles can be read, apart form his heroism, in his need to hide that same vulnerability. Any story concerning Achilles is incomplete until (however indirectly and improbably) an arrow finds his heel. Let that moment stand, then, for everything we want to hide, every weakness we've spent a lifetime disguising, and for every indirection and sophisticated technique of short-story writing. The short story is the straightest line to the best-hidden secret. Relentlessly, short fiction drives to the stripping away of all defenses, the exposure of the one thing we had always repressed.

Literary justice has nothing to do with ethics or morals or public standards of right and wrong (and, especially, not with "correctness"). Patricia Highsmith, author of *The Talented Mr. Ripley* and a number of other morally complicated, justice-dealing novels, wrote in *Plotting and Writing Suspense Fiction* that "the public passion for justice [is] quite boring and artificial, for neither life nor nature cares if justice is ever done or not." ("Public justice" is what I'm calling "morality.") "Justice" is quite properly terrifying; God is just, Allah is just, and Thomas Jefferson feared God's justice for the young republic's embrace of slavery. The reason that morality is boring and artificial is that morality is merely the approved collective behavior and beliefs of a majority at any given time and place. Morality is poll-driven, V-chipped, and has nothing more than a gossipy interest in revealing flaws and secrets.

In "Guests of the Nation," morality, in the form of IRA honor, demands the execution of British prisoners, but justice declares it cold-blooded murder. In "The Jewbird," justice confers no special degree of righteousness to a family of poor Jews who use and then expel the ghost of their cultural past, the unwelcome, unkempt, feathered visitor. In "A & P," an act of righteous defiance gains neither advantage nor gratitude. The mass-killer Misfit of "A Good Man Is Hard to Find" is out there, and your car will pop a tire just a few feet from wherever he's hiding. The Misfit represents blind and pitiless justice. The family, with its clichés, its Bible, its innocent grandmother and children, is moral to its core.

When I was beginning my career as a literature professor, I was invited to testify for bookstores and publishers against the city of Milwaukee's ban on the open sale of Terry Southern's *Candy*, as well as *Tropic of Cancer* and *Lady Chatterley's Lover*. In preparing for trial, it was necessary to decide what the claim of moral values (i.e., "community standards") versus artistic freedom might be. Morality is nothing more profound than the beliefs of the majority, as interpreted by the police and D.A., and, if it comes to that, a jury of our peers. The designated enforcers of social values knew that the majority, anywhere in the country, could be counted on to suppress "obscene" works, and they knew obscenity when they saw it. I was reading my D. H. Lawrence, George Bernard Shaw, and Wayland Young (*Eros Denied*), all of whom drew vivid distinctions between changing standards of "morality" and what has endured from antiquity as "justice" in the literary pantheon.

As societies evolve, they grow more accepting of "obscene" images and excluded (usually sexual) minorities. That plasticity is the proof that morality has nothing to do with the immutable canons of justice. Fortunately, it was 1964, one of those moments in cultural history when moral standards were molting. The times were a-changin', and the city attorneys understood that as well, and dropped the case before trial. It would have been impossible for me, as a 24-year-old, to say then what was on my mind, namely that justice is the enemy of morality. Moralities are social contracts that reflect the collective beliefs of a given society at a particular stage of its development. Stoning adulterers is moral, clitorectomies are moral, capital punishment is moral. In "Guests of the Nation," it is the moral imperative of war (an eye for an eye) to execute enemy prisoners, even if justice tells us that killing men we've gotten to know and even to like is premeditated murder. In "A & P" it is moral to make a sexual goddess ashamed of her beauty, to banish her from the store and force her to dress according to company standards so as not to discomfit the submanager's sense of propriety, or cause a reassessment of his own repressed sexuality.

The problem that Highsmith addressed is how to understand the uncomfortable complexity of justice. The career of her special Misfit, Mr. Ripley, slices through the layers of morality. Because of her special relationship to justice, and contempt for high-minded public morality, Highsmith's Ripley (like Flannery O'Conner's Misfit) remains mythically disturbing. If I were asked to testify in a case similar to Milwaukee's today, I might try to suggest that justice is inherent in form, not in content. Great writers cannot rest until they have performed the arrow's duty, flying through unprotected flesh to expose the core of justice that generates any valid conflict. Without the writer's understanding that every character has an Achilles' heel, there is no story. Without the demonstration that a character is somehow and somewhere vulnerable (but only in a way, and in a place, that a story can discover), the story is unfinished, or unsatisfying. Not to show any disrespect for my great teacher, perhaps I could say, whimsically, that stories explore the multifarious adventures of the human heel.

WORKS CITED

Highsmith, Patricia. *Plotting and Writing Suspense Fiction.* New York: St. Martin's Press, 1993.

———. *The Talented Mr. Ripley.* New York: Vintage Crime/Black Lizard, 1992.

O'Connor, Flannery. "A Good Man Is Hard to Find." *A Good Man Is Hard to Find and Other Stories.* Orlando, Fla.: Harcourt Brace, 1983. 1–22.

About the Contributors

DONALD ANDERSON is editor of *War, Literature, and the Arts: An International Journal of the Humanities*. He is editor also of *Aftermath: An Anthology of Post-Vietnam Fiction* and *Andre Dubus: Tributes*. His collection *Fire Road* won Iowa's John Simmons Short Fiction Award. He lives in Colorado.

AMIRI BARAKA is an American poet, playwright, and political activist. Born as LeRoi Jones, Baraka studied at Rutgers and Howard Universities, receiving his B.A. in 1954. He gained notoriety in 1964 when four of his plays—*Dutchman, The Toilet, The Baptism,* and *The Slave*—were produced off-Broadway in New York City. A provocative political analyst, he has written many works that express a strident anger toward the racism of mainstream white American society. Working with his second wife, Amina Baraka, he edited *Confirmation: An Anthology of African-American Women* (1983). His collected fiction was published in 2000.

ALFRED BIRNEY (not to be confused with the Canadian poet Earle Alfred Birney) is a multicultural writer from the Netherlands, although most of his works cross literary borders drawn by critics and academics. His father is Eurasian, his mother Dutch. He was born in The Hague in 1951 and raised in different parts of the country. He was a musician until he was 30 years old. While he published articles and books in this field, he also started to write his first fictional stories. However, music stayed paramount. An injury to his left hand while practicing martial arts prevented him from pursuing his musical career and tipped the scales towards literature.

CLARK BLAISE is the child of expatriate Canadians who roamed the United States in search of better employment. Blaise has written, "As a native-born American with foreign parents, and as a child who attended an average of two schools a year in 25 different cities, I grew up with an outsider's view of America and a romanticized exile's view of French Canada.... My interest is in 'tribalism' on the American continent, and in all groups who refuse amalgamation and prefer codes and taboos of their own." *Southern Stories* (2000), Blaise's most recent story collection, deals with his feelings of displacement as a fat, lethargic Canadian American boy living in various rural areas of central Florida. Another book by Blaise, *Time Lord: Sir Sanford Fleming and the Creation of Standard Time,* appeared in 2001. The book recounts the remarkable life of the Scotch Canadian who, with the invention of time zones, succeeded in imposing order on the world's methods of measuring time. Critics are searching for clues as to why Blaise, given his past obsessions with identity and alienation, has applied himself to a study of the creation of standard time. The *Ottawa Citizen* believes it knows the answer: "Clark Blaise never stays in one spot for too long. No wonder he wrote a book about time zones. Really, he's been writing it all his life."

MARION BLOEM was born in Arnhem in the Netherlands in 1952. In the early 1950s her parents (Eurasians, mixtures of Asian and European people, of Dutch nationality) migrated from Indonesia to Holland. After high school she studied clinical psychology at the State University of Utrecht. During her study she wrote her first children's books, and soon she started to write, direct, and produce short feature films. Bloem publishes short stories in Dutch magazines, and some of her short stories are published as compilations. Her first novel (*Not Just a Common Indonesian Girl,* 1983), an autobiographical story about her Eurasian background, was for half a year at the top of the best-seller list. Her work has been translated into English, German, Persian, Japanese, and Hungarian. She is frequently invited in the Netherlands, Germany, Austria, and Belgium to read from her work and to lecture.

WANDA BOEKE is a professional translator who has worked with a variety of writers and filmmakers in the Netherlands, France, Belgium, and Spain. Her translations, published in the Netherlands, Great Britain, and the United States, include contributions to *Cimarron Review, Exchanges, Dutch Crossing, Poetry International,* the *Greenfield Review,* and *Callaloo.* Recent publication of *Unnatural Mothers* and *The Cockatoo's Lie* introduced Dutch novelists Renate Dorrestein and Marion Bloem to American readers. Wanda Boeke now lives in Connecticut.

FREDERICK BUSCH has published 21 books of fiction, beginning in 1971 with *I Wanted a Year without Fall* and including *The Mutual Friend* (about Charles Dickens), *Girls, The Night Inspector* (his novel of Herman Melville),

Don't Tell Anyone, and his most recent novel, *A Memory of War.* Until recently, he taught undergraduates creative writing at Colgate University. Frederick Busch lives in upstate New York with his wife, Judy, and his aging Labradors. He is finishing up his next novel, *North;* working on a story cycle; and dreaming of a house on the coast of Maine.

VIJAY LAKSHMI CHAUHAN writes about the immigrant experience, which she takes as a metaphor for the condition of exile. In "Pomegranate Dreams," the title novella in *Pomegranate Dreams and Other Stories* (2002), she explores this subject from a young South Asian girl's point of view. Her short stories—published in *Wasafiri, Orbis, Amelia, South Asian Review,* and the *Paris Transcontinental*—have been translated into Chinese and French. A Ph.D. in English, a former Fulbright Fellow, and the author of a book on Virginia Woolf and several scholarly articles, Vijay Lakshmi teaches creative writing and world literature at the Community College of Philadelphia. Mother of a son and a daughter, she lives with her husband in Glenside, Pennsylvania.

KELLY CHERRY is a poet, fiction writer, essayist, and translator. Her most recent books include *Augusta Played* (1998), *Death and Transfiguration* (1997), and *Writing the World,* (1995) a collection of essays and criticisms. She is the Eudora Welty Professor of English and Evjue-Bascom Professor in the Humanities at the University of Wisconsin in Madison. Her translation of Sophocles' *Antigone* will be published later this fall. She lives with fiction writer Burke Davis III in Madison, Wisconsin.

CYRIL DABYDEEN is an acclaimed poet and short-story writer. He has written eight books of poetry, five books of stories, and three novels. He has also edited two key anthologies: *A Shapely Fire: Changing the Literary Landscape* and *Another Way to Dance: Contemporary Asian Poetry in Canada and the U.S.* He has appeared in about 60 literary magazines and anthologies in Canada, the United States, the United Kingdom, Australia, Asia, and the Caribbean. He was recently a finalist from the University of Ottawa (where he teaches) for the National Capital Educators Award of teaching excellence. A former poet laureate of Ottawa, his latest books of fiction are *My Brahmin Days* and *North of the Equator.*

LUCY FERRISS is a novelist and scholar whose five books include *Sleeping with the Boss: Female Subjectivity and Narrative Pattern in Robert Penn Warren.* She has published extensively on feminist approaches to Warren, and most notably in the *Mississippi Review, Double Dealer Redux,* and *To Love So Well the World: A Festschrift in Honor of Robert Penn Warren* (1992). Recent honors include a Fulbright fellowship, a Yaddo Fellowship, the Pirate's Alley Faulkner

Award in the Novel, and a National Endowment for the Arts Fellowship in fiction. She teaches literature and creative writing at Hamilton College and lives in Clinton, New York, with her husband and two sons.

RICHARD FORD, a Mississippi writer who in 1996 won the Pulitzer Prize for Literature for *Independence Day,* was born in Jackson, Mississippi, on February 16, 1944. While growing up, he went to Davis Elementary, the same elementary school Eudora Welty attended, then went on to get his B.A. from Michigan State University and his M.F.A. from the University of California. Ford wrote short stories for *Esquire,* the *Paris Review,* and the *New Yorker* before completing his first novel, *A Piece of My Heart,* in 1976. He has written many more novels, such as *The Ultimate Good Luck, Wildlife,* and *Independence Day.* Ford has won many awards and is a member of the Writers Guild. His awards include a Guggenheim Fellowship, a National Endowment for the Arts Fellowship, the PEN/Faulkner citation for fiction for *The Sportswriter,* as well as the PEN/Faulkner Award and the Pulitzer for Literature for his novel *Independence Day.*

MERRILL JOAN GERBER is a prizewinning novelist and short-story writer who has published seven novels—among them *King of the World,* which won the Pushcart Press Editor's Book Award for an "important and unusual book of literary distinction," and *The Kingdom of Brooklyn,* winner of the Ribalow Award from *Hadassah Magazine* for "the best English-language book of fiction on a Jewish theme"—as well as five volumes of short stories, nine young-adult novels, and three books of nonfiction. Her short stories have appeared in the *New Yorker,* the *Atlantic, Mademoiselle, Redbook,* and many other magazines, as well as in literary journals such as the *Sewanee Review, Prairie Schooner,* and the *Virginia Quarterly Review.* Her story "I Don't Believe This" won an O. Henry Prize Award in 1986. She earned her M.A. in English from Brandeis University and was awarded a Wallace Stegner Fiction Fellowship to Stanford University. She presently teaches fiction writing at the California Institute of Technology in Pasadena, California.

DIANE GLANCY teaches Native American literature and creative writing at Macalester College in St. Paul, Minnesota. She published five books in 1999: *Fuller Man, The Closets of Heaven, (Ado)ration, Visit Teepee Town, Native Writings after the Detours,* and *The Voice That Was in Travel.* Glancy won the 1999 McKnight Artist Fellowship/Loft Award of Distinction in Creative Prose.

ALEKSANDAR HEMON is the author of the collection of short stories *The Question of Bruno.* Born and raised in Sarajevo, Bosnia-Herzegovina, he has lived in Chicago since 1992. His short fiction has been published in the *New*

Yorker, TriQuarterly, Esquire, the *Baffler, Ploughshares, Chicago Review,* and *Best American Short Stories 1999* and *2000.*

JANETTE TURNER HOSPITAL was born Janette Turner in Melbourne, Australia, in 1942. Her family moved to Queensland in 1950, where she undertook her education at Queensland University and Kelvin Grove Teachers College with a B.A. in 1965. She later taught in country Queensland and Brisbane, married Clifford Hospital in 1965, and moved with him to Boston and then on to Kingston, Ontario. Her first piece of fiction, a short story titled "Waiting," was published in the *Atlantic Monthly* in 1978 and received an Atlantic First citation. Janette Turner Hospital has held writer-in-residence positions at the Massachusetts Institute of Technology in Boston, the University of Sydney, and La Trobe University in Melbourne. She divides her time between Canada, the United States, and Queensland.

JANET KIEFFER's short stories have garnered awards from the H. G. Roberts Foundation and BBC Radio, as well as finalist status in the Iowa/John Simmons Writing Awards from the University of Iowa. They have appeared in various publications, including *Bomb Magazine,* the *Atlanta Review, Mississippi Review Online,* and *Short Story Journal,* and are forthcoming in the *Bark* (Berkeley, California) and *Grain Magazine* (Saskatchewan Writers' Guild, Canada). She studied fiction writing in the undergraduate fiction workshop at the University of Iowa in the late 1970s, earned an M.A. from Webster University in St. Louis, and is currently finishing an M.A. in creative writing at the University of Colorado at Boulder.

KAREN KING-ARIBISALA was born in Guyana. She has traveled widely, having been educated there and in Barbados, Italy, Nigeria, and England. Her first collection of stories, *Our Wife and Other Stories,* was the regional winner for Best First Book (Africa Region) in the Commonwealth Writers' Prize 1990–91. Karen King-Aribisala currently resides in Lagos, Nigeria, where she is a senior lecturer in the Department of English of the University of Lagos. She is married with one son.

MAURICE A. LEE is Dean of the College of Liberal Arts and Professor of English at the University of Central Arkansas. He is also the founder and Chief Editor of the Journal of Caribbean Literatures (JCLs), which he founded in 1999. Maurice received his B.A. and M.A at Oklahoma State University in Stillwater, Oklahoma, and his Ph.D. at the University of Wisconsin, Madison. While a graduate student at Madison, he worked with the late Darwin T. Turner in developing the African American Studies Program there in 1969. He also was one of the primary researchers for the on-going Dictionary of

American Regional English, the monumental research project founded by the late Dr. Frederick Cassidy. He has taught at Temple University, the University of Northern Iowa, and Haverford, Vassar, Bard, and Antioch Colleges. While at Temple, he worked with the late Dr. Alex Haley as a researcher on the "Kinte" project funded by the Carnegie Institute. He currently serves as the permanent director of the International Conference on the Short Story in English which meets every two years. Dr. Lee has given Masters classes on American Literature in several countries. He is married and has six grown children and one granddaughter.

ALECIA McKENZIE was born in Kingston, Jamaica. After attending Troy State and Columbia universities in the United States, she worked for several media organizations, including the *New York Times* Regional Newspaper Group, the *Wall Street Journal* Europe, and InterPress Service. In 1992, her first book of short stories, *Satellite City,* was published, and it won the regional Commonwealth Writers Prize for Best First Book the following year. Since then it has been translated into several languages. Alecia's stories have appeared in anthologies such as *The Oxford Book of Caribbean Short Stories, The Penguin Book of Caribbean Short Stories,* and *Caribbean New Voices,* as well as in literary magazines, including the *Journal of Caribbean Literatures.* Her forthcoming collection is titled *Diaspora Dance* and will first appear in the Italian translation as *Racconti Giamaicani* (Jamaican Stories).

ANDRÁS NAGY, born in 1956 in Budapest, is working as a writer and as an academic. He published several books (including fiction, stories, essays, and collections of dramas) and has taught in various universities both in Hungary and abroad. He published his first collection of short stories 25 years ago, while still a student at the Budapest University; later he also focused on playwriting, and many of his plays were performed. He won several awards for his works and received grants to write both in Hungary and abroad. He taught courses about the short story, and when spending a semester at the International Writing Program at the University of Iowa he became very attracted to the American way of storytelling (particularly by Raymond Carver, Richard Ford, and Deborah Eisenberg). Besides his artistic activity, Nagy has a Ph.D. in philosophy and a genuine interest in Kierkegaard (he established a "Kierkegaard Cabinet" in Budapest). Currently he is teaching at the Theater Department of the University of Veszprém and is involved in a major research focusing on the Hungarian 1956 revolution. He also works for films and regularly writes essays and studies. Nagy leaves in Leányfalu (a small village north of Budapest), and speaks English, French, and Italian.

CHRIS OFFUTT earned his B.A. at Morehead State University in Kentucky. He then obtained his M.F.A. in creative writing from the University of Iowa. Offutt is the author of *The Good Brother*, a novel, and two short-story collections, *Kentucky Straight* and *Out of the Woods*. He has also published a memoir called *The Same River Twice*. Offutt's work has appeared in collections such as *Best American Short Stories 1994*. He has been named "Best Young American Writer" by *Granta*. Offutt has also been the recipient of a Guggenheim Fellowship and an NEA Fellowship. Offutt is adjunct faculty at the Iowa Writers Workshop in Iowa City, Iowa.

SYLVIA PETTER is Australian and was born on March 30, 1949, in Vienna, Austria. In 1951 she migrated to Australia with her parents. She does not hold dual nationality. She attended primary school at Loreto Convent, Kiribilli, and Normanhurst, and high school at Hornsby Girls' High School, Hornsby. She studied French, German, and psychology at the University of New South Wales in Sydney and graduated with a B.A. in 1969. In 1977, she returned to Geneva to work for the International Telecommunication Union (ITU) where she is still employed. Her work has also appeared in the U.K. anthology *Woman to Woman*, the *Europress* (France) anthology *Moments in Time*, and more recently in *Valentine's Day—Revenge Stories: Women against Men*, which was published by Duck Editions, edited by Alice Thomas Ellis, and includes stories by Alice Munro, Joyce Carol Oates, Carol Shields, Fay Weldon, and others. Sylvia lives in France and visits her home in Sydney, where her mother still lives, as often as possible. She is married and has one daughter, who will be coming to Sydney this year to take up university studies.

JAYNE ANNE PHILLIPS was born and raised in West Virginia. Her first book of stories, *Black Tickets*, published in 1979 when she was 26, won the prestigious Sue Kaufman Prize for First Fiction awarded by the American Academy and Institute of Arts and Letters. Featured in *Newsweek*, *Black Tickets* was pronounced "stories unlike any in our literature ... a crooked beauty" by Raymond Carver and established Phillips as a writer "in love with the American language." Phillips was praised by Nadine Gordimer as "the best short story writer since Eudora Welty." *Black Tickets* has since become a classic of the short-story genre. Jayne Anne Phillips's works have been translated and published in 12 foreign languages. She is the recipient of a Guggenheim Fellowship, two National Endowment for the Arts Fellowships, and a Bunting Fellowship from the Bunting Institute of Radcliffe College. Her work has appeared most recently in *Harper's*, *Granta*, *Doubletake*, and the *Norton Anthology of Contemporary Fiction*. She has taught at Harvard University, Williams College, and Boston University, and is currently writer-in-residence at Brandeis University.

VELMA POLLARD is one of the Caribbean's foremost poets. She was formerly a senior lecturer in language education at the University of the West Indies at Mona, where her areas of expertise included the Creole languages of the Anglophone Caribbean, the language of Caribbean literature, and Caribbean women's writing. She is the author of *From Jamaican Creole to Standard English: A Handbook for Teachers*, *Dread Talk: The Language of Rastafari*, *Considering Woman*, and *Shame Trees Don't Grow Here*.

SUSAN ROCHETTE-CRAWLEY is an assistant professor of English at the College of Humanities and Fine Arts and holds a Ph.D. in English from the University of Wisconsin–Madison. Dr. Rochette-Crawley's professional interest is in narrative theory, particularly short-story theory and the conjunctions between narrative and gender. Her recent work has focused on theories of marginality, gender, and genre criticism. She also writes fiction and teaches fiction writing. Her current research interest focuses on a reevaluation of Virginia Woolf's concept of "spots of time" as a possible rejoinder to the emphasis on "epiphany" in short-story criticism.

MINOLI SALGADO is a poet and short-story writer who teaches English at the University of Sussex, England. Her creative writing is closely allied to her academic interests in post-colonial literature and migrant identity. Her literary and critical writings have been published widely in books and journals in the United Kingdom, Europe, and the United States, including: *Wasafiri*, *Short Story*, *Journal of Commonwealth Literature*, and *Journal of Modern Literature*. She is currently completing a critical study of Sri Lankan literature in English, *Writing Sri Lanka: Literature, Resistance and the Politics of Place*, due to be published by Routledge, and is the author of *Broken Jaw*, a collection of short stories, which is currently in search of a good home.

OLIVE SENIOR was born and brought up in Jamaica. She was educated in Jamaica (Montego Bay High School) and Canada (Carleton University) and at the Thomson Foundation in the United Kingdom. In Jamaica, Senior has been editor of two of the Caribbean's leading Journals—*Social and Economic Studies* at the University of the West Indies and *Jamaica Journal*, published by Institute of Jamaica Publications, of which she was also managing director. In recent years she has spent much of her time abroad, and since 1993 has been based in Toronto, Canada. The Caribbean nevertheless remains the focus of her work, starting with her prizewinning collection of stories *Summer Lightning* (1986), which won the Commonwealth Writers Prize in 1987, followed by *Arrival of the Snake-Woman* (1989) and *Discerner of Hearts* (1995). Her poetry books are *Gardening in the Tropics* (1994) and *Talking of Trees* (1986). Nonfiction works on Caribbean culture include the *A–Z of Jamaican Heritage* (1984) and *Working Miracles: Women's Lives in the English-Speaking Caribbean* (1991). Senior's work is taught at universities internationally. Senior has been writer-in-residence in Canada at the University of Alberta, the Banff International Writing Studio, and the University of the West Indies in Jamaica and Trinidad. She has been an Arts Council of England Visiting International Writer, a Hawthornden Fellow, and Dana Distinguished International Writer at St. Lawrence University.

KIRPAL SINGH began writing at the age of seven when his first little poem, made of eight lines and dedicated to his teacher, was read aloud in class. From an early age his passion for reading and writing manifested itself in the fact that he'd always rather stay home and read or write than go to movies, sporting games, and so on. Over the years the initial passion for reading and writing has remained, although, he now assures us, his socializing tendencies sometimes have to be curbed by his wife! After finishing his first and Master's degrees at the then University of Singapore (1973, 1976) he was awarded a Colombo Plan Scholarship to pursue his Ph.D. in English at the University of Adelaide, Australia. He became the first Asian to do so and obtained his doctoral degree in 1980, finishing a highly accomplished thesis on Aldous Huxley—a seminal influence in all his own later thinking, writing, and outlook. Kirpal published his first books while still very young and at school: *Singapore Pot-Pourri,* a collection of poems, plays, stories, and essays by several hands, which came out in 1970, while *Articulations,* an anthology of poems by seven poets, appeared in 1972. His first major book, *Twenty Poems,* was published in 1978 by P. Lal of the well-known Calcutta Writers Workshop. Since then Kirpal has published numerous books—among them we may cite *Palm Readings* (1986), *Jaspal* (1997), and *Monologue* (2001). His best-known collection of poems—*Catwalking and the Games We Play*—appeared in 1998, and in 2001 he helped edit *The Merlion and the Hibiscus,* a Penguin anthology of stories from Singapore and Malaysia. A highly sought-after keynote speaker and performer, Kirpal does a lot of traveling and enjoys the stimulating company of fellow writers and scholars. He has been given several major research awards by universities all over the world, and in 2002 was given the Pewter Award for services to education by the Singapore government.

VICENTE SOTO (born in Valencia, 1919) left his native Spain for London in 1954. The Francoist dictatorship, while excluded from the Marshall Plan, had just been granted the definitive seal of approval as an anticommunist bulwark by the emergent Western superpower, the United States, in the form of the 1953 bases treaty. Franco, then, was here to stay. Bad news for a hounded Republican who had fought on the wrong side of the bloody Spanish Civil War. "I could still live in Spain on the condition of not being able to live," Soto has frequently confessed. Already wrenched from his birth city, Valencia, to Madrid, Soto was uprooted again, this time further away. Temporal and physical displacement, nostalgia, and exile are central to his writing. Soto's first published work—*Vidas humildes, cuentos humildes* (Humble Lives, Humble Stories, 1948)—bears witness to a primary fascination with short fiction. Since then, he has alternated long with short narrative forms, winning the prestigious Premio Nadal for his novel *La Zancada* (The Stride, 1966). He returned to short fiction with the collection *Casicuentos de Londres* (Not-Quite-Stories from London), for which he won the 1973 edition of the Premio Novelas y Cuentos, followed two years later by the Premio Hucha de Oro for the story "El Girasol" (The Sunflower). The collections *Cuentos del tiempo de nunca acabar* (Stories of Time Never-Ending, 1977), *Pasos de nadie* (Nobody's Footsteps, 1991), and *Cuentos de Aquí y Allá* (Stories from Here and There, 2000) confirm the enduring appeal of the short story for Soto. His novel *Mambrú no volverá* (Mambrú Isn't Coming Back) won the 2001 Premio de las Artes y las Ciencias de la Comunidad Valenciana, and the Premio de la Crítica Valenciana (2002). In 2002 he was awarded the Premio Lluís Guarner for lifelong achievement in literature. Soto continues to live and write—in Spanish, always in Spanish—in London.

BILLIE TRAVALINI, with degrees in English and creative writing and a 20-year career as a journalist, says writing poetry is not a stretch. What she learned as a professional writer was "the tremendous discipline, the education about people and the need to be clear and concise in your writing." Says Travalini, "I love poetry because every word has to be there for a reason. Because of the shortness of the genre, you can't have a word just because of the sound; it has to have meaning. While journalism deals with day-to-day living, creative writing has a universality that teaches lessons in life that never go out of style." Travalini has completed a book of poems, *Healing Myself: One Woman's Story of an Abusive Childhood and Recovery,* and her unpublished novel was recently selected as one of the 15 finalists in a Middlebury College fellowship program. A writing teacher, she currently serves as fiction editor for the *Journal of Caribbean Literature* and is director of the Delaware Literary Connection, whose forthcoming Delaware anthology she is editing.

KATHERINE VAZ is a Briggs-Copeland Lecturer in the Department of English at Harvard University. She earned her B.A. in 1977 from the University of

California–Santa Barbara and her M.F.A. in 1991 from the University of California–Irvine. Her research interests include fiction writing and Portuguese and Luso-American literature. Professor Vaz's recent publications include *Mariana* (1998), *Fado and Other Stories* (1997), and *Saudade* (1994).

CHARLOTTE ZOË WALKER is a professor of English at the State University of New York College at Oneonta, where she teaches fiction writing and environmental literature. Her novel *Condor and Hummingbird* was published by Alice Walker's Wild Trees Press (1986) and in England by the Women's Press (1987). Her short stories have been anthologized in *Prize Stories 1991: The O. Henry Awards* (1991), *Intimate Nature: The Bond Between Women and Animals* (1998), and elsewhere. She is the editor of *Sharp Eyes: John Burroughs and American Nature Writing* (2000).

CRYSTAL E. WILKINSON, who describes herself as a "black, country girl," grew up in rural Kentucky. She currently teaches creative writing and serves as assistant director at the *Carnegie Center for Literacy and Learning* in Lexington, and chairs the creative writing department for the Kentucky Governor's School for the Arts. She is a charter member of the Affrilachian Poets, a group of performing African American poets from the South. Her work has appeared in various magazines and journals. *Blackberries, Blackberries* is her first published collection. She has worked in journalism, marketing, and public relations, and was interim director of the Blue Grass Black Arts Consortium. Her poetry and short fiction has appeared in *Obsidian II: Black Literature in Review; Now and Then: The Appalachian Magazine; Calyx; Collage and Bricolage; The Briar Cliff Review;* and *Southern Exposure.* She has received fellowships from Indiana's Mary Anderson Center for the Arts and the Kentucky Arts Council, and participated in the Zora Neale Hurston/Richard Wright Writers Week at Virginia Commonwealth University.

IVAN WOLFERS, born in Amersfoort (The Netherlands) in 1948, studied medicine and graduated at the University of Utrecht in 1975. He received his PhD in Cultural Anthropology for his work on "Changing traditions in Asian Health" at the Leiden University in 1987, and was appointed as professor in Health Care in Developing Countries at the VU University in Amsterdam in 1989. He has published professionally on development, culture, and sexuality (especially HIV/AIDS) and has been writing fiction since high school. His first novel was published in 1980. It had a strong autobiographic theme: growing up after World War II as the son of a Jewish father and a Christian mother, and being an outsider at a Christian school. Since then most of his novels have been located in Asia, where his characters are Caucasian men who try to find a new life and fail. Simultaneously, Ivan Wolffers published books for children in order to discuss health issues. In 1988, he received the Mary Zeldenrust award for his book *Een korte cursus voor beginners in de liefde* (A Short Course for Beginners in Love) in 1988. The book was turned into 13 television programs.

Index